LAST CALL

LAST CALL

A True Story of

Love, Lust, and Murder

in Queer New York

ELON GREEN

CELADON
BOOKS

NEW YORK

LAST CALL. Copyright © 2021 by Elon Green. All rights reserved.
Printed in the United States of America. For information, address Celadon Books,
a Division of Macmillan Publishers, 120 Broadway, New York, NY 10271.

www.celadonbooks.com

Designed by Steven Seighman

Maps © Rhys Davies, rhysspieces.com

Library of Congress Cataloging-in-Publication Data

Names: Green, Elon, author.
Title: Last call : a true story of love, lust, and murder in queer New York /
    Elon Green.
Description: First Edition. | New York : Celadon Books, 2021. | Includes
    bibliographical references.
Identifiers: LCCN 2020040971 | ISBN 9781250224354 (hardcover) |
    ISBN 9781250224347 (ebook)
Subjects: LCSH: Serial murderers—New York (State)—Case studies. |
    Murder—New York (State)—Case studies. | Trials (Murder)—
    New York (State)—Case studies. | Anderson, Peter Stickney.
Classification: LCC HV6534.N5 G74 2021 | DDC 363.152/32092—dc23
LC record available at https://lccn.loc.gov/2020040971

Our books may be purchased in bulk for promotional, educational, or business use.
Please contact your local bookseller or the Macmillan Corporate and Premium Sales
Department at 1-800-221-7945, extension 5442, or by email at
MacmillanSpecialMarkets@macmillan.com.

First Edition: 2021

10 9 8 7 6 5 4 3 2 1

To my grandmother,
who encouraged me to pursue stories that had been forgotten

A NOTE TO READERS

This book, a work of nonfiction, is the result of three years of reporting. I conducted repeated interviews with selected family members, friends, and associates of the victims, as well as dozens of law enforcement officials. In order to flesh out the contours of each homicide investigation, I relied on trial transcripts; hundreds of stories culled from newspapers and magazines; the personal notes of investigators; and assorted files that were generously shared. It is with the aid of such documents and interviews that I could faithfully reproduce dialogue.

Some names have been withheld, and, where noted, some names and locations have been changed to preserve anonymity.

CONTENTS

Queer people don't grow up as ourselves, we grow up playing a version of ourselves that sacrifices authenticity to minimise humiliation & prejudice. The massive task of our adult lives is to unpick which parts of ourselves are truly us & which parts we've created to protect us.

—ALEXANDER LEON

I'll be looking at the moon / But I'll be seeing you.

—IRVING KAHAL

LAST CALL

1

JOHN DOE

May 5, 1991

Ten minutes short of three o'clock on a moderately warm Sunday after-noon, a turnpike maintenance worker was emptying the green barrels at a rest area in Lancaster County on the westbound side of the Pennsylva-nia Turnpike. He was looking for aluminum cans to sort, when he pulled hard on a plastic trash bag that he simply couldn't lift. A strong five foot six, he'd never had a problem emptying the barrels in his six years on the job. *What's in this bag that I can't lift?*

Annoyed, he rooted around for a stick, and opened the bag. "But ev-ery time I opened one bag there was another bag," he recalled years later.

Another poke, another bag. Another poke, another bag. Another poke, another bag.

He assumed it was a deer carcass. Now he realized it was, in all like-lihood, something more sinister.

When he finally got the last bag opened—eight in total—he couldn't make out what it was.

"It looked like a loaf of bread," he says. "But then I saw freckles."

Grabbing a radio, he called his supervisors, who notified the Pennsyl-vania State Police.

The maintenance worker had been an emergency medical technician years before, so he was unfazed by the remains. Later on, though, after he transported the body to the morgue in Lancaster—an unorthodox turn of events, as no one else on scene drove a truck—he shivered with unease when it was suggested he take an AIDS test. He hadn't come into contact with blood.

It was a time of heightened, often irrational caution; only a few years earlier, William Masters and Virginia Johnson warned that AIDS could be transmitted via a toilet seat. Eleven hundred and fifty six Pennsylvanians died of the disease the year before. In February, Jean White, whose teenage son Ryan had died after becoming infected during a blood transfusion, addressed an audience at nearby Elizabethtown College. "People need to be educated about AIDS, to understand the disease and how it is transmitted," wrote the editors of the local paper. "AIDS is a frightening disease. But with education and awareness, people can learn how to take precautions against AIDS and to treat those who are HIV positive as real people, not as monsters."

Queer Pennsylvanians—trans Pennsylvanians, disproportionately—were the targets. It was believed that AIDS dripped off the walls of the Tally-Ho Tavern on Lancaster's West Orange Street. The city's queer bookstore, the Closet, would be bombed twice that summer; the second time—after the proprietor had been shot at—four sticks of dynamite leveled the store, blowing a hole straight through the back wall. The rainbow flag in the window was partially incinerated.

State police are assigned to cases large and small, pressing and inconsequential, in jurisdictions that lack their own police departments. Such was the case in Rapho Township. The criminal investigations unit, considered the elite members of the troop, handled everything from criminal mischief to murder. It was a one-stop shop.

Jay Musser, a tall, fresh-faced officer with bangs cut straight across his forehead, was off-duty that Sunday afternoon. He arrived at the rest area at milepost 265.2 to find his colleagues already at work. He'd been a trooper for ten years and was part-time SWAT, which meant, his boss would say with admiration, he wasn't prone to negotiation. Musser was a member of Troop J, charged with Southeastern Pennsylvania's Lancaster and Chester counties, and this was his territory. It was a lonely, forgettable stretch of road. The last incident that raised an eyebrow occurred thirteen years earlier when the white Lincoln ferrying Governor Milton Shapp—and driven, as it happened, by a trooper—was logged doing nineteen miles an hour over the speed limit.

A dead, naked man with visible chest and back wounds, found in a trash barrel on the turnpike about thirty feet back from the road, was a significant event in these parts.

A few years earlier, Musser was subject to a modicum of press coverage for his involvement in the case of the Amish Hat Bandit. As recounted by the Associated Press: a middle-aged man from Kirkwood, a little farming town, claimed that two assailants, one carrying a gun, broke into his and a nearby relative's home and stole nearly twenty of his family's hats, valued at several hundred dollars. The state police were called in. They suspected he had pilfered the hats himself, in part because he wasn't in church when they'd gone missing. But there was little proof. Musser, however, deployed an interrogation method that exploited the man's religiosity.

"You look me straight in the eye," he told the perpetrator, "and swear to *God* that you didn't take them hats, and I'll believe you."

Unable or unwilling to do it, the hat thief confessed.

But the larger Lancaster County had seen worse. In 1990, there were thirteen homicides. Most of those occurred in the city of Lancaster. Beyond those borders, however, things tended to be more peaceful. "Nothing but forest and farmland," as Musser put it. To murder a man and leave him here, at mile marker 265.2, where there was nothing around but road, trees, and sky, was strange. "This ain't like New Jersey, where the mafia is dumping bodies," noted a trooper.

Musser, in seven years on the criminal investigations unit, had seen only one other dead body—a stillborn baby left by the side of the road in Amish country. He tended to compose himself well, not betray his emotions. In later years, he would fall apart only once on account of the job's horrors, when a young boy who resembled Musser's son hanged himself on Thanksgiving Day.

The rest area was little more than a barren strip on the edge of dense woods. The sight was gruesome: an emaciated man who, in addition to chest and back wounds, had his penis severed and shoved into his mouth. In times of absurdity, we sometimes resort to the ridiculous and banal, and Musser, as he surveyed the wound, was no different. *It was,* the trooper thought, *missing from where it was supposed to be.*

Musser felt intuitively the attack had been personal and deliberate and premeditated. It was not spur-of-the-moment.

The savagery of the corpse was belied by the victim's facial expression. He almost looked calm. Peaceful. In fact, once removed from the bags and laid out on his side on the gravel, in a fetal position with his left hand clenched, he appeared to be sleeping. It looked this way because he had not been there long. Dead bodies tend to smell bad after a while, and this one, which showed no evidence of decomposition, didn't. It was a fresh body.

Harnish, clean-shaven and trim, wearing a suit that drew no attention to itself—a pen nestled in the breast pocket—arrived on the scene a little after 5:00 P.M. He oversaw the troop's criminal investigations unit of ten troopers and two corporals. The longtime local, who raised Christmas trees in his off-hours, was watchful, considerate. He expected his troopers to wear a tie and jacket, and would carefully fold his own and place it in the back seat before getting behind the wheel. This adherence to custom was a holdover from when he got to the academy in 1965. It was a prim and proper time, Harnish would say, when he could not recognize marijuana by either sight or smell.

The precise cause of death was a mystery, as was the man's identity.

Neither Musser nor the other criminal investigators could find any personal possessions.

Who was *this guy?*

At Harnish's behest, the dead man in the green barrel was quickly fingerprinted. But the five-foot-four corpse, barely one hundred pounds, didn't leave much for the troopers to work with. In several areas there was lividity, or postmortem settling of the blood, which suggested the body had been moved more than once. A lack of rigidity, often referred to as rigor mortis, meant death occurred no more than thirty-six hours prior to discovery. There were three bruises on the scalp, all fresh, indicating they were no more than a day old. There were similar, suspicious injuries elsewhere: a particularly large bruise on the forearm, just beyond the bend of the elbow, and one on the shin.

The stab wound in the back, between the inner margin of the right shoulder blade and the spine, was more consequential. But it was the abdomen that suffered the most severe trauma. There was a gaping, oval wound most likely made by something sharp. Just above that was another stab wound, roughly a half inch in length, oriented, a medical examiner observed, "in an eleven to five o'clock line as one looks at a watch." The skin, the muscle, the omentum, and the mesentery—a fatty sheath that holds the intestines to the body wall—were all perforated. These were the wounds that killed.

Another wound showed only a negligible amount of hemorrhaging: the severed penis, blessedly, was a postmortem injury.

The man's diminutive size initially led state police astray, to a racetrack. "We have to think of jockeys," Harnish told a crime-desk reporter. He took the possibility of the dead man being a jockey seriously enough that his squad contacted Penn National, a mile away from where the body was found. Racetrack management reported that none of its forty riders were missing. There were other blind alleys: troopers from the Bowmansville barracks visited turnpike tollbooths and truck stops to inquire about suspicious people who might've passed through.

Meanwhile, the state police's latent fingerprint examiner was given the eight trash bags. Using cyanoacrylate fuming, known colloquially as superglue, he developed twenty-eight fingerprints and three palm prints. The fingerprints were put into the state's database, but there were no matches. The prints were then sent to New York, Virginia, and New Jersey. These searches, too, yielded nothing.

Tips came in, some of which were heartbreaking. A Lancaster woman wondered if the dead man was her son, missing a month. A New Jersey sergeant inquired if the body was, perhaps, a man who hadn't been seen since December. Or the Pennsylvania man who'd gone missing. "Slight build, in 30's but looks 50," Harnish wrote in elegant cursive. "Tattoos on fingers." It wasn't his John Doe. But maybe it was a thirtysomething who had vanished three months ago? No—in that case, the upper teeth were missing. A call to the morgue confirmed that Troop J's body had all his natural teeth and expensive dental work.

Other tips were intriguing dead ends. A woman driving east on the turnpike glanced in her rearview mirror and saw a man walking by the barrel. He appeared to be in his early twenties and had dark hair. Another call came in suggesting that, owing to the placement of the severed penis, their unknown man had been the victim of organized crime. The mob, after all, was known to do something similar to enemies. On any given case, Harnish estimated, more than half of the tips don't go anywhere. Musser, for his part, didn't often find them useful. They frequently came from people who just wanted to be part of the investigation.

State police placed posters with a composite sketch of the John Doe on the side of tollbooths. The payoff was immediate: the image looked familiar to members of First Troop Philadelphia City Cavalry, a National Guard unit.

The group, headed to a gathering at Fort Indiantown Gap, believed that the dead man was one of their own. They were even more certain when, upon arriving at "the Gap," their friend was absent.

Suspicions were soon confirmed.

Five days later, at mile marker 303.1 along the Chester County stretch of the turnpike, a truck driver stumbled on two fifty-five-gallon trash containers. Among the effects were several pairs of socks—argyle, pink, blue—a corduroy hat, two pairs of boxer shorts, Brooks Brothers charcoal slacks, a brown belt, a T-shirt with THE BLACK DOG, MARTHA'S VINEYARD printed on the back, and traveler's checks in fifty-dollar denominations.

There also was a parking ticket issued in Philadelphia, two pieces of paper with names and phone numbers, nineteen Mellon Bank checks with numerous deposit slips, and an identification card that confirmed membership in First Troop. The personal effects would prove useful to piecing together the man's life, but they weren't necessary for identification. National Guard dental records were a match.

John Doe was Peter Stickney Anderson, fifty-four, of Philadelphia, Pennsylvania.

2

THE BANKER

During the initial examination of Peter Anderson's body and personal effects, a trooper found a note in his briefcase with the name of a woman. The woman reported seeing Peter the Tuesday or Thursday before he died, at the Blue Parrot, a piano bar on Philadelphia's Drury Lane. This would prove to be one of many queer establishments visited by Harnish and Musser during their two-week investigation.

Harnish and Musser made the rounds, interviewing patrons and employees of Raffles, Woody's, and 247, all bars clustered near Center City. With each visit, the troopers got a better sense of Peter's social circle and routine. It was apparent that, of all the establishments, his favorite was the Blue Parrot.

Hidden down a back alley, the Blue Parrot didn't look like a typical piano bar. With the dark wood walls and late-nineteenth-century prints of ducks, it looked, recalled one regular, "like a gentlemen's lounge at a hunting lodge." As patrons walked in, the bar was to their left along the wall. The drinks were reasonable—a bourbon manhattan was five dollars. Three quarters of the drinkers on any given night were regulars, many of whom were active in the city's theater scene.

The big Friday and Saturday draw was Michael Ogborn, a composer and lyricist then in his late twenties, who played the piano and sang American standards in a tenor. To the regulars of the Blue Parrot, the experience of singing with Ogborn was akin to church. A beloved, oft-remembered bit from his set was a snarky tribute to dead divas, including Karen Carpenter. It was preceded by chants from the audience: *Dig. Her. Up! Dig. Her. Up!*

Peter Anderson was a regular. Even amid a packed and rowdy house, his vices were clear to see. He drank heavily and had plenty of company. "There were a lot of people around Michael Ogborn who were about to be going to AA, and I was one of them," chuckled a patron years later.

The Blue Parrot's clientele skewed middle-aged, and the vanilla nature of the place was perfect for Peter. This was no den of hustlers and leather men. It was not, recalled a bartender, "a meat market." It was just a place to go for music and company and maybe to meet someone. It was a place where Peter could, if only for a few hours a day, several days a week, be himself.

A second phone number found in Peter's jacket led troopers to an acquaintance from Church of the Holy Trinity, an episcopal house of worship on the northwest corner of Rittenhouse Square. The congregation, starchy and reserved, was largely upper-class and upper-middle-class. Each Sunday, there was glorious singing. It was not a place for fire breathing. The acquaintance didn't know Peter intimately (twice they'd had dinner, and Peter seemed lovely but deeply sad), yet he was knowledgeable enough to inform troopers about the victim's personal life—there was a second wife, from whom he was separated, and he had been a portfolio manager at Mellon Bank. Once they learned this, Harnish and Musser began calling the case Banker in the Barrel.

The authorities continued to build a profile of Peter: he was born on March 14, 1937, in Milwaukee, Wisconsin, to Betsey Brooke and Giles Anderson, a salesman. His mother graduated from Wellesley College, his father from the Massachusetts Institute of Technology. They married four years before Peter's birth and raised their son in Pittsburgh. A sister was born in 1940.

At eighteen, Peter departed for Trinity College, five hundred miles away in Hartford, Connecticut. In his yearbook photo, under which is noted his degree in government, Peter looks serene and kind in a jacket and tie. The yearbook entry also mentions his membership in a number of clubs: Canterbury, Sports Car, Young Republicans, Corinthian Yacht Club. In May 1959, the student newspaper where he was on staff, *The Trinity Tripod*, documented the yachters' fifth-place finish behind Harvard: "Tom Ludlow and Howdy McIlvaine acted as skipper with Peter Anderson and Paul Goodman as crew."

Trinity College during the latter years of the Eisenhower administration was, by reputation, an unruly place. Two days before a football game, students destroyed the goalposts of rival Amherst, whose student paper accused Trinity of theft. The *Tripod,* rather than deny the allegations, groused that "the Trinity gentleman seems to be headed into oblivion." The unsigned editorial continued: "Trinity has been known for some time as one of the worst behaved colleges in the east. It is apparent that the student body, which is ultimately responsible for condoning these actions by silence, does not wish to alter this impression. It is time that both the student body and the administration stopped coddling these offenders."

Peter's fraternity, Psi Upsilon, wasn't felonious, but it wasn't academically minded either. These were smart, unathletic young men whose intelligence rarely translated into hard work or good grades. "Once I got into college, I just slacked off," says Dixon Harris, a contemporary of Peter's who was eventually recruited by the Central Intelligence Agency. Another former member describes his fraternity brothers as "high-living private school boys." W. Croft Jennings, an English major a year behind Peter, likened the fraternity to *Animal House.* The two weren't terribly close, but the Psi Upsilon bond was such that Peter attended Jennings's wedding at the First Presbyterian Church in New Canaan, Connecticut, where he and other brothers served as ushers.

On the weekends, girls from Smith, Mount Holyoke, and Vassar visited. While the rest of the brothers caroused downstairs, Peter was up in his room writing. There were no suspicions he was gay, and for good reason: the possibility would not have crossed anyone's mind. Trinity students didn't admit to such yearnings. What stuck with Jennings, decades after Peter's death, was how much he liked him. And, as with everyone who met Peter, Jennings took note of his size and tendency to dress well, describing him as a "dapper little person."

A girlfriend of a fraternity brother remembered Peter's loneliness: "He just wanted to be a part of the boys. He was more like a mascot." There was a deep sadness about him, and a palpable eagerness to be not only liked, but moneyed. "He wanted to appear to the manner born."

As detectives were investigating Anderson's death, a break in the case came from several tips, which led them to Tony Brooks. Brooks, twenty-six, a partner in a management consulting firm, was now running for a seat on the Philadelphia City Council. He was considered an excellent candidate—if only, wrote the *Philadelphia Daily News*, "a little less grizzled than prime time would require."

In his younger days, Brooks dreamed of politics and the priesthood. But fear of being outed as a gay man had been a deterrent. Brooks's mother once asked why he no longer dated girls, and he told her the truth. This led to a year of broken relations with his mother, and Brooks was devastated. To cope with his desires, and society's presumed demands, he went to the gym and put muscle on his six-foot-two-inch frame, believing that no one would equate a brawny man with homosexuality. He even got engaged to a woman. In that light, it wasn't really a surprise that, as he ran for the open council seat in 1991, he was in the closet to Philadelphia at large.

Brooks told the troopers he and Peter drove to Manhattan together on May 3 to attend a fundraising dinner. They'd left Philadelphia at three o'clock and arrived at five. Peter came along, in part, because Bill Green, a New York representative Peter knew, would be there. Brooks, as far as the troopers could discern, was the last person to see Peter alive.

* * *

On May 11, 1991, a coterie of troopers, including Harnish and Musser, visited Peter's apartment at 2020 Walnut Street, a thirty-two-story condo building better known as Wanamaker House. A few years earlier and with great fanfare, the Wanamaker was converted from a rental building to a condominium. An ad in *The Philadelphia Inquirer* boasted of "discriminating" tenants who enjoyed a twenty-four-hour doorman, a health club, and indoor parking. One-bedrooms went to market for about $100,000. From its roof, residents could enjoy a view of Center City, home to a lot of industry but also the Gayborhood, the nickname for an area with many gay- and lesbian-friendly businesses.

The Wanamaker was two blocks off Rittenhouse Square, a public park that predated the creation of the United States. By the early 1800s, the park had become the domain of the rich. James Harper, a merchant and brick manufacturer, built the first townhouse on the north side of the square in 1840, at 1811 Walnut Street. Over the next ninety years, the barons flocked: Alexander Cassatt, president of the Pennsylvania Railroad and brother of Mary; William Weightman, a chemical manufacturer and one of the largest landowners in the country; and the founder of the city's first department store, John Wanamaker, who also served as postmaster general under President Benjamin Harrison.

Since even before World War II, the square was a locus for gay men and lesbians: a cruisy expanse where folks of all different backgrounds could find each other. Rittenhouse was a formative place—it was where queer Philadelphians first encountered a community. As a Rittenhouse regular put it to Marc Stein, author of the seminal history *City of Sisterly and Brotherly Loves*: "When I met those people, it was equivalent to coming out, to understanding that there was a gay life."

By the 1950s, Rittenhouse Square was a necessary proxy for bars. Elsewhere, it was too risky for men to dance or be seen touching each other. Philadelphia's beefy, grease-haired future police commissioner, Frank

Rizzo, did not hide his disdain. Of his political enemies, he once said, "Just wait after November, you'll have a front row seat because I'm going to make Attila the Hun look like a faggot." Rizzo was famous for raiding establishments that were friendly to queer people. In the late fifties, when Rizzo had achieved the rank of inspector, that meant coffee shops. One of his obsessions was Humoresque Coffee Shop, a few blocks west of Rittenhouse on Sansom Street. Over an eight-month stretch between 1958 and 1959, Rizzo's men busted the place twenty-five times. The shop's owner sued for damages and requested an injunction against the inspector. The judge sided with the cops, declaring there was no doubt that Humoresque was "so operated as to constitute a public nuisance." Furthermore, he said—correctly—the shop was "a gathering place for homosexuals."

And so it was that the queer community was driven outdoors. On any given night, Rittenhouse was a seven-acre open-air club enjoyed by hundreds. Inevitably, such meeting spots, which had been adopted out of necessity, couldn't just be allowed to exist, and there was a tug-of-war over who, precisely, could stake a claim to Rittenhouse. In 1966, a *Philadelphia Inquirer* columnist summed up the dispute in blunt terms: "The just-plain-folks want it to be a quiet, leafy glade of proper people, properly dressed. And the young kids want it as a turned-on meeting place. And the homosexuals want it to drag and swish in."

A member of First Troop accompanied the investigators as they conducted the search of Peter's apartment. The one-bedroom wasn't well kept. Their first impression, recalled a trooper, is that it was obvious the occupant was a bachelor. "It wasn't trashed," he said, "but it could've used a little housekeeping." What stuck out in his memory was the bathtub filled with magazines. *Where,* he wondered, *did Peter bathe?*

The search, which ended after a few hours, provided evidence of a recent male houseguest. A jar of K-Y gel on the nightstand raised an eyebrow among the straitlaced investigators. They identified him and tracked the man to his own apartment, which he shared with a girlfriend. There was blood on the ceiling—residue from shooting heroin—but no indication the couple was involved in the killing.

Two days later, Jay Musser and a partner took a trip to New York, hoping to learn about Peter's final night. The troopers checked in with the local precinct and then headed to the apartment of Robby Browne, who had hosted the fundraiser for Tony Brooks's political campaign. A Manhattan real estate agent, Browne sold high-end residential property, including the sale a year earlier of Geraldo Rivera's penthouse. The troopers reasoned that whoever murdered Peter may have passed through Browne's grand Upper West Side apartment overlooking Central Park.

It was Browne's first fundraiser, but queer-related causes had been near to his heart since 1985, when his brother, a graduate of Andover and Yale and a pilot during the Vietnam War, died of AIDS. Nobody gave a damn about his brother. Browne wondered, *Does he not count?*

Browne had gone to Harvard Business School, where homosexuality was not embraced. He acted accordingly. When he put personal ads in *The Boston Phoenix,* he pretended to be bisexual because "of course you couldn't be gay." Eventually, Browne found a boyfriend. But then AIDS hit. Browne "freaked out and shut down." He later said celibacy kept him alive. The disease had since decimated Browne's social circle; in his later years, he was left with almost no contemporaries.

Spurred by the death of his brother, Browne made an effort to be around queer people and to support them. He went to a party in the Hamptons and began to make friends. Soon, it became impossible to live a lie. He became an activist, serving on the respective boards of the Gay and Lesbian Alliance Against Defamation and the Gay Games, and got involved in politics. Browne first met Tony Brooks at Fire Island Pines, a hamlet that a visitor once astutely analogized to a gay Brigadoon. The Pines, Browne reflected, was the only place he experienced freedom, "or what a straight person feels every day of their life."

When Brooks—charismatic and startlingly handsome—wanted to run for office in Philadelphia, Browne was impressed. He agreed to hold a fundraiser in Manhattan. Forty or so men and women, beautifully dressed and mostly Log Cabin Republicans, milled around Browne's home on May 3, 1991.

Within a decade, half the attendees of the fundraiser were dead from AIDS-related complications.

As the guests talked and drank, Peter Anderson stood by the entrance, nudging new arrivals to donate. In walked a man he hadn't seen in nearly twenty years: Anthony Hoyt.

It's not clear what Peter was thinking, but Hoyt remembers his own reaction: *Oh. My. God.*

On the New York trip, the troopers drilled Browne and Hoyt with questions, trying to piece together Peter's last night alive. Browne was asked to produce his garbage bags, as the investigators believed there was a chance the murderer had attended the fundraiser and left with them.

Of the two men, the focus was on Hoyt. He had left the fundraiser with Peter. He took a polygraph test and passed. As far as troopers knew, Hoyt was an executive in magazine publishing who, decades earlier, had roomed with Peter.

This was the truth. But not the entire truth. It would be a long time before Hoyt told anyone what had happened all those years ago, and how important he and Peter had been to each other.

Around 1961, after graduating from Trinity College, Peter moved to Manhattan. There he met a tall, skinny, clean-cut man named Tony in a bar. There was a room available in his apartment on East Eighty-first Street, Hoyt told him. It was a doorman building, but the apartment, a two-bedroom that already held two men, was not finely appointed. Peter needed a place to live and moved right in.

Peter had already begun his career in finance, at Bank of New York, while Hoyt worked for the advertising agency Fuller & Smith & Ross, on the Air France account. The rent, six hundred dollars a month, was split equally among the three.

Even in his later years, after other memories had gone hazy, Hoyt retained a piercing clarity when he talked about his love for Peter: "Peter and I had sort of a romance. *More* than sort of a romance—we had *quite* a romance." Peter was charming and caring and sensitive. "A good guy," Hoyt would say, with a healthy wistfulness. And who could forget Peter's nattiness? "He always wore a bow tie, and I'll remember that always."

It never came off, he joked, even in the shower.

Tony and Peter went to bars on Third Avenue in the evening, and sometimes entertained at home. Croft Jennings, Peter's fraternity brother, remembered a party at the apartment, mostly because the host didn't serve dinner until midnight. Peter, he marveled, "hadn't a clue as to what he was doing."

Peter and Hoyt were firmly in the closet. Neither had had any same-sex experience. But a physical relationship soon began. Hoyt is certain a lot of alcohol was consumed, as it took courage to stop pretending. Even with a six-inch height disparity, their bodies just fit together.

"The time," Hoyt said, "was so different." Just ten years earlier, the U.S. State Department was purged of gays and lesbians, whom Senator Joseph McCarthy deemed a threat to national security. All told, thousands of federal employees were fired. But the terror wasn't just on a federal level. There was a 1923 state law under which it was a criminal act for a man to even *ask* another man for sex, so New York City police in the 1930s sent their best-looking officers undercover into gay bars. Once a target suggested they leave the bar for a more intimate setting, an arrest was made. Tens of thousands of men were entrapped in this fashion until the late 1960s, when gay activists pressed Mayor John Lindsay to end the practice. "If it had been today—in today's society—we could've been partners," Hoyt reflects. "But in those days, you weren't gay. Gay was not good." He and Peter hid their relationship from everyone they knew, including their own friends.

Hoyt got married to a woman in the mid-1960s and moved out. But he and Peter stayed in touch. One night, Hoyt was in Manhattan. It was late, and not wanting to trek home to Long Island, he needed a place to stay. So he called Peter. *Come on over.* Peter, still unmarried, lived on the Upper East Side. Hoyt stayed over quite a few times after that.

After working for the ad agency, Hoyt was hired by Time Inc. as a salesperson. Five years later, now divorced, he moved to California to run *New York*'s West Coast sales office. Clay Felker, the magazine's editor, asked him to help launch another publication, called *New West*—essentially a California version of *New York*. The first issue, which hit the newsstands in 1976, was promising—Joan Didion, Tom Wolfe, and Joe Eszterhas graced its pages. But it didn't last. "There wasn't an audience for that magazine, at that particular point, without putting a lot of money into it and developing an audience for it. We just didn't have the resources to keep it going," says Milton Glaser, the magazine's famed design director. "Tony seemed to be an adequate but not extraordinary personality. He did as well as one could hope for."

Until Hoyt moved out, he was an avid skier and had a season pass to Stratton. There he met Edith "Edie" Blake, a Martha's Vineyard fixture and a columnist for Edgartown's *Vineyard Gazette*. Edie, who would remain physically vigorous into her nineties, also had a season pass. She had a home on Seventy-second Street, off Madison Avenue in Manhattan, so it made sense that she and Hoyt, who lived fifteen minutes away, should carpool.

One trip, Hoyt brought his roommates along.

Peter, Edie decided, was "sort of funny," and teased him. "He took to me like he thought I was high society, or important," she recalled. She introduced Peter to her daughter, Edith "Sandy" Blake, when she returned home from school.

From then on, they skied as a group. Peter was in her life, Edie felt, for better or worse.

One night in 1969, Edie went to a party at Peter's. A guest asked why he hadn't gotten married. "Oh," Peter replied, "I'm waiting for a woman who can give me a wedding at the St. James and a reception at the Colony Club." As Peter said the words, he eyed the elder Blake, who took an uncharitable read of his thinking: *He's a social climber, and a marriage to Sandy would give him entrée to high society, in both New York and the Vineyard.*

Peter proposed the next day.

In 1970, Peter and Sandy married. *The New York Times* reported on the engagement and then the wedding, which took place in New York at St. James Episcopal Church. A photo of the bride ran in the paper, along with a notice:

> Mrs. Anderson is the daughter of Mrs. Edith G. Blake of Edgartown, Mass., and of Robert H. Blake, who is with the municipal department of the Chemical Bank New York Trust Company. Her husband is the son of Mr. and Mrs. Giles W. Anderson of Greenwich, Conn. His father is vice president of the Union division of Miles Laboratories.
>
> The bride attended Poggio Imperiale and Le Fleuron in Florence, Italy, and graduated from Vernon Court Junior College in Newport, R. I. She is the granddaughter of Mrs. F. Gordon Brown and the late Philip Graham, who was an architect here; and of the late Robert H. Blake, who was general manager of the Cunard line here.
>
> Her husband, who is with the investment company of Drexel Harriman Ripley, Inc., was graduated from Trinity.

Edie says she opposed the marriage, and told her daughter so, repeatedly: "Because honestly, I thought he was what we used to call a pansy."

After the wedding, Peter and Sandy settled in Dedham, Massachu-setts, forty-five minutes outside Boston. He was now an institutional stockbroker for Laird, Bissell and Meeds.

Sandy isn't wistful about the marriage. She remembers Peter going to work, then coming home to cook dinner. They socialized with friends. But it was never a union of equals, and it seemed to Sandy that Edie was right—that Peter was using her to get ahead. "He thought of me as his possession, and that's where it all went wrong. He collected antiques, and I was just one of his antiques."

For as long as she knew him, Sandy recalled, Peter had a complex about being short. He was never tall enough for his satisfaction. His friends were frequently above six feet, so he would add three inches to his height as compensation. When he was buried "in the tiniest little coffin you'd ever seen, that broke my heart more than anything, because he just wanted to be big."

The marriage lasted nearly a decade. Edie was pleased by its disso-lution: "Sandy met someone who was a real man, and that was the end of that."

After the divorce, Sandy found out from an acquaintance that Peter was attracted to men.

"Peter," she said to her ex-husband, "I hear you're gay."

He said nothing, and just stared.

Even after the split and Sandy's remarriage, Peter still visited Edie. He loved the Vineyard. Standing on the wharf, he snapped photos of his former mother-in-law as she sailed.

In 1979, Peter remarried, this time to Cynthia Reid, for whom it was also a second marriage. They had a son together. The couple led an outwardly traditional social life. They went to parties. They belonged to clubs. But they were, to some degree, living separate lives. Peter was presumed to be gay but friends didn't bring it up. "You don't talk about who's cheating on their wives," one said.

Peter had been hired by Philadelphia's Girard Trust Company in

1975, a friend told detectives. (It isn't clear what precipitated the move from Massachusetts to Pennsylvania.)

Founded as Girard Bank on South Third Street in 1811, the bank underwrote most of the War of 1812—to the tune of $8 million—and kept the government solvent for two years. Girard became a trusted establishment. But in 1983, after a long and prosperous run, it was absorbed by Pittsburgh's behemoth Mellon Bank.

Mellon, accustomed to its top position in Pittsburgh, expected Philadelphians to line up outside its doors to have their accounts managed. They did not. In disgust, many bank officers left, as did clients. But Peter, who was personable and charming, stayed and flourished. In 1985, he was elected to the board of the Philadelphia Securities Association.

Peter was notable, or at least notable enough for the *Philadelphia Inquirer*'s society column to report that he and Tony Brooks were seen at "pre-opening night cocktails" for the Friends of Shakespeare in the Park, in advance of the production of *A Midsummer Night's Dream*. He and Brooks had a lot in common: They belonged to the same church. Each was a moderate Republican, squarely in the closet. Not once did they confide in each other about their sexuality, for fear of losing their careers. "He was your classic Main Line gentleman," Brooks told a reporter, referencing the ritzy suburbs of Philadelphia and suggesting that Peter was from old money. "I'm assuming it was very difficult being of his generation and social circle."

Brooks, like Peter, was also a member of First Troop. By 1991, Peter was a staff sergeant and had been a part of the organization for more than a decade. When he first joined up, he was assigned to the mess section. He cooked, and liked to sprinkle alcohol into the mix. "That was probably good for most of the troop, but not all of them," recalled Peter's sergeant.

First Troop, a National Guard unit founded in 1774 as a private militia, met one weekend a month and two weeks in the summer for drills. The troop was still in cold war mode, and sometimes the men trained with weapons and tanks, as there was always a chance they could be sent overseas.

First Troop appealed to Peter primarily because of his love of history. Its members sometimes traced their ancestry back to the Revolutionary War and earlier. Peter traced his own lineage to Asa Stickney, a private in the Continental Army.

One summer, the troop was training at Fort Pickett in Virginia and traveled to Virginia Beach for a weekend. The first night in town, Peter got dressed up in clothes his compatriots deemed inappropriate and "fancy." He was assaulted. Not badly enough to require hospitalization, but he sustained a black eye.

Peter had staunch beliefs about the military. The year before he died, he read a story in *People* magazine about women on the front lines in the United States Army. What annoyed him, aside from the notion of women in combat, was a photo of an enlisted soldier. In a letter to the editor, he wrote:

PEOPLE is entitled to promote the idea of female soldiers in the combat arms. However, E-4 Cheryl Purdie should be relegated to a stateside file room forever for violating the most fundamental lesson in weapons training. What on earth is she doing pointing an M16 toward the Panamanian girl with the ice-cream cone? The whole picture looks like an accident waiting to happen.

First Troop compatriots tended to be awed by Peter's wit and intellect. But they also observed in their friend a capacity to consume liquor late into the evening and still miraculously walk upright the next morning. "He was a little fella, but he could drink like a field soldier," said one. Peter was, said another with slightly more precision, "a functioning alcoholic."

The alcoholism worsened around the time the illusion of Peter's heterosexuality began to deteriorate. After a weekend during which Peter's wife had gone to New York for a horse show, she returned home to evidence of a guest "for sexual purposes, and it was not another woman." On another occasion, when they had been married for a decade, she found in Peter's briefcase a "homosexual magazine."

The toll this hidden life was taking on Peter was clear. In March 1987, *The Philadelphia Inquirer* reported that a car on Route 252 had been moving in an erratic manner, and the driver, "Peter S. Anderson, of Philadelphia, was charged with driving under the influence." He was released, but later that year he was fired by Mellon and moved out of the family's home.

Cynthia and Peter separated but remained friendly. "We were still married with no real intentions of being divorced," she would testify. It was, then, not a surprise when she got a call from Peter, saying he was hospitalized. Peter had wasted away to such a degree—forty pounds lighter than on their wedding day—that Cynthia stated "it was perfectly evident to me that he might be HIV positive."

By 1991, Peter was profoundly unhappy. He had inherited $400,000 from an aunt but squandered all but $75,000; he estimated that, too, would be gone in six months. Despite the health concerns (at least one friend expected he would be dead by the year's end), Peter still took part in First Troop events, attending a get-together to mark the death of George Washington. He didn't eat much, and still drank to excess. Friends were embarrassed on Peter's behalf. He'd come to luncheons bearing a flask that he would tip into tomato juice. Once, at a Christmas party, an unconscious Peter was draped in tree decorations.

Months later, on May 1, Peter showed up at the Blue Parrot for the last piano set of the evening. He caught the eye of the manager, who remembered his plaid jacket and bow tie. He downed the usual, either a martini or scotch.

On the afternoon of May 2, Peter and Cynthia spoke for the last time. Peter was going to New York, and they discussed his plans for the trip. He told her where he would stay, and when he would return. Peter made two promises: one to his wife, that he would return to Philadelphia on Friday night, and one to his son, that they would spend Sunday at a baseball game. The Los Angeles Dodgers would be in town to play the Philadelphia Phillies.

Back in Robby Browne's apartment, troopers began to get a sense of what happened to Peter during the fundraiser on May 3, and what transpired after he left: Peter had been noticeably drunk. Or, as Browne put it, "wasted."

Around nine, Brooks left, and the event began to wind down. Hoyt and Peter, however, didn't want the night to end, and so, an hour later, they decided to keep it going over cocktails.

Peter knew just the place: a bar on East Fifty-eighth called the Townhouse.

As soon as Peter and Tony arrived, around ten o'clock, they headed for the back room, where the piano player was easing into Broadway standards. For Hoyt, the visit stirred up old feelings, but they were tempered by the realization that his friend was in poor shape, mentally and physically. As drunk as Peter was when they left the fundraiser, his condition worsened at the Townhouse, aided by the bar's famous tendency for generous pours.

Late in the evening, the bartender politely but sternly informed Peter he'd had too much to drink; he and his friend were welcome to take their business elsewhere. Peter suggested they retreat to Hoyt's apartment. Sober enough to see where the night might proceed, Hoyt lied. He had guests, he told Peter. Instead, he called the Waldorf Astoria and booked his dear friend a room. Then he lowered Peter into a taxi outside the cozy, elegant piano bar and asked the driver to head nine blocks south and three avenues west.

Upon arrival at the Waldorf, the security supervisor helped Peter out of the cab, took his garment bag, and walked him to the front desk. Peter wore a bow tie, he would recall, and fumbled for his credit cards. Then Peter got frisky, reaching over to squeeze the security supervisor's buttocks. Unused to such behavior, he told Peter that, while he was welcome as a guest, staff members did not "come with the room."

Why didn't Peter just go upstairs and sleep it off? No one knows. But he never checked in. *Penn Station,* he said, and was escorted back outside. The supervisor's pager buzzed, so he left Peter on Lexington Avenue, holding his garment bag.

Hoyt, decades later, is quite sure Peter simply forgot he had been cut off at the Townhouse and returned for another round.

On May 14, the investigation neared an unsatisfying conclusion. First, Peter's wife called. She declined to identify the body in person. The First Troop member who'd been at the search of Peter's apartment went to the morgue in her stead. The next day, the coroner released Peter's remains. Carl Harnish handed the case off to Jay Musser.

A week later, a memorial service was held at a church in Bryn Mawr, a suburb a dozen miles from downtown Philadelphia. "How could such a brilliant and talented man die such an ignominious death?" asked the reverend. "In days such as these, the silence seems to scream."

Once Jay Musser retired in 1992, the investigation into Peter's death was sent to cold-case purgatory. Leads had been exhausted. Hoyt and Brooks had alibis. Speculation aside, no one could account for Peter's movements after he left the Waldorf. In the end, there were no suspects but quite a few questions: Whose fingerprints were on the bags? Why was Peter's body left at a rest area in Lancaster County? What happened after he left the hotel?

All was quiet until the troopers were contacted by the New Jersey State Police later in 1992.

They were investigating a murder. A Violent Criminal Apprehension Program questionnaire, meant to gather details of a crime, had been sent to the FBI in an effort to find possible suspects or a related case. ViCAP, as it was colloquially known, was a bureau unit created less than a decade earlier, tasked with compiling information on cases including sexual assault and homicide. Detectives frequently filed ViCAP questionnaires to discern if there were similar crimes in other jurisdictions.

There had been a match.

The New Jersey detectives were startled by the discovery of Peter's case. They, too, had found a man in a barrel. Their victim had been stuffed in garbage bags. He was seen at the Townhouse in the days before his death. Years later, a New Jersey detective was asked for his reaction to finding such a similar case: "There's somebody out there that's extremely dangerous and we gotta stop him."

3

A GOOD PERSON

July 10, 1992

Wayne Luker and Theodore "Pee Wee" Doyle, employees of the New Jersey Department of Transportation, were on the 7:30 A.M. to 4:00 P.M. shift. They drove a small yellow dump truck through Southampton Township, a heavily wooded, sparsely populated expanse about two hours south of Manhattan.

The sunny and warm day began unremarkably. Starting on Route 70, which cuts west to east through the bottom of the township, Luker and Doyle drove toward the rest area in Burrs Mill. The men found a couple of DOT trash cans—fifty-five-gallon drums with tan plastic liners. The usual haul: mostly the refuse of lunch, empty soda cans and half-eaten sandwiches. They wrapped and tied the bags, and heaved them onto the truck's bed.

Luker drove farther down Route 70 to the next rest stop, in Upton. Everything was normal there, as well. Then a left onto Route 72, home to the Butler Place rest area, nestled in the Lebanon State Forest. It was here that Luker sensed something was not quite right. There were the usual tan bags, but there were bags piled around the barrels, too. One was white and lacked the heft of everyday debris. If you took 72 east and slightly south, breezing past Penn State Forest to the right and Forked River

Mountain wildlife preserve to the left, you soon hit the beach communities of Mud City and Beach Haven West, respectively. This was a popular route for day fishing, so the barrels often contained waste from the trips. The white bag, Luker thought, felt heavy, as if it contained a pumpkin.

The men then noticed a couple of the bags were leaking blood. That wasn't out of the ordinary, but Luker thought it worth mentioning.

"It's probably just dead fish," Doyle replied. "Don't worry about it."

Everything was thrown into the back of the truck.

After Luker and Doyle returned to the maintenance yard, they began unloading the bags and tossing them into a maroon dumpster. That's when Luker noticed that the white bag—the one that seemed inordinately heavy—had a pinkish hue. It felt wrong. It didn't feel, he would testify, "like normal trash." Curiosity got the best of him, and he opened the bag.

"Pee Wee," he said, "I found a man's head."

Luker called the state police.

Hours later, at another rest area—this one on the Garden State Parkway, a road stretching the length of New Jersey—two other maintenance men were doing similar work. The younger man emptied a trash barrel as his boss sat in the truck. They had last been there a couple of days earlier and now found a number of black bags. The barrel was simply too heavy to lift.

"Well," said the older man, "consolidate and put the bags in the other bags."

As he began pulling the first bag out of the fifty-five-gallon barrel, it ripped. There was a leg, and it appeared to be human.

"Oh, shit," the man said to his boss.

It fell to Matthew Kuehn, a detective in New Jersey State Police's major crime unit, to lead the homicide investigation. Kuehn, eight years into his career, was off-duty that Friday when the sergeant paged him, demanding his presence at the barracks. *Proceed to the Red Lion.* Red Lion was part of Troop C, which served a number of jurisdictions across the state, including Ocean County in the south. Kuehn had a reputation as by-the-book, and not a man to chase false leads. He had a sculpted jaw, a rabbity nose, and found happiness amid the quiet, feeding the ducks and gulls of Newton Lake with his two daughters. He was not a gabber. A colleague said, "He didn't say shit just to hear his own voice."

Kuehn's detectives inspected the contents of the garbage bags. The first contained a head—its mop of gray hair falling in all directions—completely severed at the level of the fourth cervical vertebra, through the vocal cords. Detectives could see the spinal cord. The vocal cords had been cut, and the detectives saw the spinal canal, the vertebrae through which the spinal cord passes, as well. The second bag, white with a red drawstring, held a set of arms dismembered at the shoulder joints and a four-by-four-inch piece of skin. In the third bag: eviscerated intestines, but also a bloodstained striped shower curtain, bloodstained surgical gloves, a king-size fitted bedsheet from Liz Claiborne, and four straight black hairs. The fourth bag, brown with a yellow drawstring, held the upper torso—the chest, the upper trunk, and a part of the abdomen—which had been severed just above the navel. The next bag, the fifth, contained the lower abdomen and pelvis. The final and sixth bag: the legs, cut at the femur.

In addition to body parts, detectives found a brown plastic bag on which was written THANK YOU FOR SHOPPING HERE, the previous Sunday's New Jersey section of *The New York Times,* and New York tabloids the *Post* and *Daily News,* placed against the wounds to act as a blotter. Wondered an investigator: *Who reads both of those papers?*

It was all a bit too familiar to Kuehn. Three years earlier, a woman's head was found on the seventh hole of a New Jersey golf course. Her legs turned up in a river fifty miles to the north. She was the first victim of Joel Rifkin, a prolific serial killer from Long Island.

The autopsy for the new victim was performed in Newark, in a slightly cold room, not unlike an industrial kitchen, large and barebones, full of steel cabinets and rows of forceps, scalpels, scissors, stainless-steel rulers, and a colander for washing organs. The medical examiner had been given a plastic body bag inside of which were six smaller bags. The contents, once removed from the bag, formed a person.

Beginning at the head, the medical examiner saw a patch of missing skin on the nape of the neck. The removed skin, which she found in another bag, had on it what appeared to be a bite mark. Farther down, inspecting the torso—carefully arrayed, like the rest of the body, on a gleaming metal table—she observed a series of wounds: One below the left nipple, four inches deep, perforated the heart. A second penetrated the abdominal cavity. There was a third on the left side of the abdomen. All were stab wounds. Based on the bruising in the surrounding soft tissues, all were incurred perimortem, which meant the victim had been alive after the stabbing began.

She noticed that the head of the humerus, which runs from shoulder to elbow, was intact; the arms had been carefully disarticulated, rather than dismembered. Removing an arm in this fashion, she knew, required dexterity. Cutting through numerous ligaments and a fibrous, thick capsule that holds in place the upper arm with the shoulder is considerably more difficult than simply cutting through bone. Whoever did this was strong and determined, and had a sense for anatomy.

There were ligature marks caused by a rope or a string around the wrist, and evidence of fresh hemorrhage under the skin. This suggested the man had been bound. This, too, occurred while he was still alive.

The medical examiner concluded the man's death was caused, in aggregate, by stab wounds to the chest and abdomen, which penetrated the heart, lung, mesentery, and stomach. The wound to the heart caused immediate arrhythmia and bleeding into the pericardial sac, which contains the heart, and resulted in immediate death. Weeks later, the results of a toxicology screen—a test for the presence of alcohol and drugs—recorded the deceased's alcohol level at .230 percent, well above the legal limit of .10.

The name of the man found at the maintenance yard was never in doubt. When detectives opened two white trash bags, they found not only a compass saw but also a briefcase and wallet belonging to Thomas Richard Mulcahy, fifty-seven, of Sudbury, Massachusetts.

Even ahead of the autopsy, detectives could make several critical assumptions about Tom Mulcahy's manner of death and disposal. Kuehn noticed ligature marks around his wrists, ankles, and knees. (The medical examiner, for her part, saw ligature marks on the thighs.) The man, he'd later speculate, had been restrained in "a hog-type fashion." Noting the trauma of disarticulation, detectives were drawn to another preliminary, mildly sexist conclusion: the perpetrator was probably a man—because disarticulation took a fair amount of strength—and he probably had medical experience, because the process required a certain finesse. This view was augmented by the fact that the body parts had been double-bagged and the bags double-knotted.

The disarticulation suggested a further hint, however vague, about the crime scene: separating bones from joints takes several hours, and such an operation demanded seclusion. This was confirmed when a pair of detectives drove to a maximum-security prison in Comstock, New York, and interviewed a man who shot another man for calling his mother a Russian whore. He dragged the corpse into the bathroom and proceeded to dismember it. He told the detectives that, all told, the procedure took about six hours, and he had to stop a few times to rest and eat pizza.

Clearly, the perpetrator, or perpetrators, had been methodical. The parts had been severed, washed, and double-tied. Neat and orderly, thought the detectives. There was, indeed, a perverse care taken with the body, which had been drained to such a degree, said one years later, "you couldn't get a Dixie cup of blood out of the remains." A senior detective was struck by the precision. He'd never seen anything like it. "The cuts were so clean. There were no jagged marks."

Wherever this man had been killed, it wasn't at the rest stop. It was the secondary crime scene—put more crudely, a dump site. The lack of a primary crime scene was, for investigators, an impediment. Such locations often provide touch DNA, hairs, and bodily fluids such as semen and saliva—all of which could be traced back to a suspect. In fact, Kuehn believed that the lack of such evidence gave the murderer a degree of confidence. The perpetrator was so confident, in fact, that he hadn't bothered to dispose of Tom's identification. As Kuehn told an interviewer years later, "we felt that whoever had done this felt that his connection to Thomas Mulcahy would never come back to him."

The perpetrator's fastidiousness prompted another assumption, and it was chilling: whoever had done this had most likely done it before.

Margaret Mulcahy was nervous. It was Thursday, July 9, and her husband of three decades was supposed to be home in time for supper. They last talked to each other two days ago. Despite her nerves, she waited. But by eleven o'clock, concerned and impatient, Margaret called the Barbizon, a neo-Gothic hotel on East Sixty-third Street where Tom stayed when he was in Manhattan. It was conveniently located—a fifteen-minute walk to Radio City Music Hall and the Rainbow Room, which he loved. She asked the staff to check Tom's room, which they did and found only his clothes. He had checked in, they said, but not out. Then she called a colleague, who was surprised Tom hadn't returned to Sudbury. Finally, Margaret called the New York City Police Department, and was told to file a missing person's report in her hometown.

The next day, an increasingly concerned Margaret drove to the Sudbury police station. She explained that her husband had been on a business trip and should have been home already. Rather than take the report immediately, however, Margaret was told to sit tight. "I couldn't understand," she would testify, "why I had to wait."

Minutes earlier, the Sudbury police had gotten a call from New

Jersey. Tom was not, in fact, missing. And that is how Margaret learned that her husband, two weeks short of his fifty-eighth birthday, had been murdered and left on the side of a highway.

In the hours after the Mulcahy family learned of Tom's death, his eighteen-year-old daughter Tracey did something that previously seemed beyond comprehension: She prayed her father had been shot. "Somehow that seemed to be the quickest method with the least pain," she would say. "It seemed more human, as if murder could be human." It wasn't for a couple of days, when Tom was officially identified, that detectives told Margaret that he had been mutilated. Tracey learned the details from the local paper.

As Margaret grieved and the family began planning a funeral, detectives combed Tom's life for clues to what had happened. They obtained his business records and expense accounts. They visited every place he had gone on five years of prior trips to New York. Wherever Tom had been, detectives flashed his photo.

Much of the initial focus was on his work, perhaps because it consumed so much of his life. He had been an employee of Bull HN Information Systems, a computer company in Billerica, Massachusetts, since 1960. Hired by an earlier iteration of the firm, Minneapolis-Honeywell, Tom rose through the ranks. A college newsletter noted his promotion to head of the firm's international division in 1968. For the last fifteen years, he focused on international sales, which demanded a great deal of travel to far-flung locales, including the firm's global headquarters in Paris.

"He had a view of life that everything was great, everything was wonderful. The classic forward-thinking American," said a European colleague, who learned of Tom's death from the detectives who knocked on his door. "He would always say nice things about people. Coming from Europe, where all you do is criticize others—he was the exact opposite."

Detectives learned that Tom and Margaret had been married for three decades and had four children. That Tom was, by any reasonable measure, a professional success. He was a good father, and got along with his neighbors and coworkers. To his kids, he wasn't physically affectionate, but he was warm and loving. Of the two parents, he was less inclined to act as the disciplinarian. He was a typical neighbor, said the man who lived catty-corner from the Mulcahy house. That spring, he told a reporter, "we complimented him on the fact that he planted a lot of annuals in the garden."

Detectives learned something else about the Irish Catholic: Tom liked men, and when he took business trips, he tacked on an extra day to give himself time to visit the gay bars and clubs. As it happened, this was not a surprise to Margaret. She discovered his predilection a year earlier, when, preparing his clothes for the cleaners, she found in his pocket a pamphlet advertising a gay bar. This became a topic of discussion when they went for marital counseling.

Tracey wondered years later if her perspective of Tom was skewed by the circumstances of his death. She believed he was a happy person—an unusual person, too: he was far more cosmopolitan than any of her friends' fathers. He traveled internationally and loved it. She understood that, to some degree, business trips were his other life, where he drank and partied: "He got to live the part of his life that he wasn't able to live publicly."

When Tracey was in grade school, Tom and Margaret drank a few glasses of wine each night. They reached a point, however, where Margaret drew a line in the sand, telling Tom he was an alcoholic. He went to Alcoholics Anonymous while she attended meetings at Al-Anon, which offers support for families and friends of alcoholics. As Tracey got older, she could tell when her father, who favored whiskey but didn't know when to stop, came home drunk.

For Margaret, exercising control over her household became increasingly difficult. Leading up to 1992, Tom's drinking had been an issue, and now she knew about the men, too. The children, for their part, could see that *something* was troubling their parents. They felt Margaret was making Tom feel guilty, but about what they weren't sure. The children, not aware of the bigger picture, were disproportionately critical of their mother. To Tracey, "it seemed like she made him feel like shit, but you didn't know what was the reasoning behind it."

After Tom was found, Margaret asked that New Jersey detectives meet her in person. She flew from Logan to Philadelphia International Airport, where the state police met her at the gate. As Margaret sat in the barracks near the airport, she recounted problems in the marriage. Tom would go on business trips and frequent gay establishments, she said. She gave them names of friends and associates. "Just anything," recalled Kuehn, "that she could do to help us in our investigation."

Tom's mother, Mary, emigrated from Ireland to Boston in 1920, when she was twenty-three. On July 24, 1934, then well into her thirties, her only child, Thomas Richard Mulcahy, was born in Brighton, a working-class neighborhood in northwest Boston. Her husband, also named Thomas, died of pneumonia before their son's third birthday. Mary didn't have much of an education and, like many of her fellow immigrants, found menial work—cleaning the floors of the Boston Post Office. Her petition for naturalization, which she filed in 1937, listed her occupation as "domestic."

While raising Tom alone, they were perpetual guests as they bounced from house to house, family to family, living in Hyde Park, Mattapan, West Roxbury, and Roslindale—all staunchly Irish neighborhoods that were, by virtue of geography and sheer will, cloistered.

Despite a lack of money, Mary prioritized education. For an Irish kid, the best education one could hope for was Boston College High School, an all-male prep school at the end of a long five-cent bus ride from Roslindale to the South End. The school now sits on forty acres, but in 1948, classes were held in an apartment house in a neighborhood beset by violence. Just that January, an old man named Patrick Canty was thrown to his death from a speeding car. In April, seventeen-year-old Arthur Mac-

Gillvary stabbed Dorothy Brennan during an argument at MacGillvary's apartment on Corning Street. He dumped her body into Fort Point Channel. "It was an area of derelicts," said a classmate of Tom's. "Poor souls begging for money, alcoholics."

In 1950, to escape the South End, the school moved to a Dorchester building on an undeveloped plot of land a priest described as "a kind of moonscape." Several years earlier, tuition had been raised to $150, and most parents, Mary included, struggled to pay it. And yet it was considered a worthwhile investment because the students were all but guaranteed a rigorous education. Alumni became part of a brotherhood that survived the Latin, Greek, and British literature taught by priests in black robes looking for an excuse to expel them. In a novel about BC High, a teacher wrote of a "Jesuit education where there was no room for the faint of heart or weak of spirit."

Out of either habit or self-preservation, the work ethic extended beyond the classroom, as kids sat in the stands during football games, doing homework. The result was an unusually accomplished class: bishops, college presidents, judges, even a commander in chief of the United States High Command.

However, in a class of such extremity, the dark clouds were spectacular as well. Members of the class of 1952 would eventually contribute to the most consequential scandal in the history of the Catholic Church. A yearbook entry next to a photo of a bright-eyed boy with a wide smile begins: "Jim, one of our livelier classmates, is noted for his uninhibited witty sayings and good spirits." It continues:

> Minstrel show enthusiast. Has played basketball with his own team in New York and Connecticut. BC next.

"Jim" was James Porter, who would be ordained as a priest in 1959 and hired by St. Mary's Parish in North Attleborough, Massachusetts, the next year. It was here that Porter, as the *Globe* put it, "allegedly fondl[ed], assault[ed], and sodomiz[ed] scores of boys and girls." A decade later, well past the point where it was helpful, he wrote a letter to Pope Paul VI. "I had become homosexually involved with some of the youth of the parish," he confessed, and requested laicization.

Upon Porter's 1993 sentencing to a term in prison, where classmates from BC High would visit him, Bernard Law, Boston's cardinal, called the disgraced priest an "aberrant." Which he was, but not sufficiently so.

John Brendan McCormack, also class of '52, was Secretary for Ministerial Personnel under Cardinal Law. In that capacity, McCormack heard complaints against priests accused of sexual misconduct—one of whom was the notorious John Geoghan. By many accounts, he did not treat such complaints with the required seriousness. In 1994, the Boston archdiocese was, the *Globe* would write, "being deluged with complaints that scores of its priests had sexually molested hundreds of children." McCormack responded by shielding from parishioners the identities of more than one hundred accused priests.

This eventually metastasized into a national scandal, but first it was a local shame. Many Boston-area Catholics were horrified by the Church's inaction, so in a desperate last-ditch effort to pressure the Church into cleaning house, individual parishes banded together to form a group called Voice of the People. The chairman of the Sudbury parish group was a BC High classmate of Tom's who eventually left the Church in disgust. But not before seeing Margaret Mulcahy at a meeting.

Tom is not remembered in great detail by most of his classmates, except to say they liked him. He made an impression on William Michael Bulger, who commuted to Boston College High School each day from a third-floor apartment in South Boston. The seeds of the politician he became are evident in his yearbook entry. Bulger, classmates wrote, "always manages to come out with a quip which never fails to bring a laugh from the class and teachers alike." While sitting for their school photos, most of the boys seemed to look at a spot just over the photographer's shoulder. Bulger, however, cocked his head ever so slightly and looked directly at the camera.

Bulger and his wife, Mary, rented a home near the Mulcahys during the late 1960s in Mashpee, on Cape Cod. He'd been a member of the Massachusetts House of Representatives for nearly a decade, while his brother, James "Whitey" Bulger, was the Boston mob's towering figure.

"I think of Tom very favorably; he was a good person," said Bulger in October 2018, just over a week before his brother was fatally beaten in prison. "You'll never hear anyone say otherwise."

That was the consensus: Tom wasn't aloof or a loner. He was a sweet kid, but indifferent to sports and extracurriculars, which is primarily how friendships were formed. His yearbook entry was tongue-in-cheek: "every morning . . . enjoys baseball, football and swimming . . . lists Latin as favorite subject . . ." It's unlikely that any of this was true. When the day's classes ended, Tom went straight home.

None of his classmates suspected Tom was gay. They wouldn't have understood what that meant, they say, for there simply was no awareness of homosexuality on campus. "Every now and then, somebody would seem to be, I don't know, *sissified*," says Bulger. "You'd be conscious of that. But I don't think you made a further conclusion about it." The subject of homosexuality wasn't engaged with in the classroom, either. To the extent priests broached it at all, they did so just to forestall discussion.

Nor would the children have learned about queer life at home, from either parents or local periodicals. To be gay or lesbian in Mattapan, West Roxbury, and Roslindale was a lonely experience. Bereft of bars and clubs, one had to travel seven or eight miles to Bay Village and Beacon Hill for the Napoleon Club, Playland, Punch Bowl, and Jacques. Out of desperation, even the bathrooms of the city's subway system were a destination. Until the mid-1960s, the public toilets were a hot spot for "Subway Sammies," who, upon entering a restroom, would place a nickel on a shelf by the door to signal their availability as a sex partner.

Such measures were necessary; not even private parties offered protection. In March 1945, police raided a house party in Back Bay. It was fairly raucous. "People were just dancing and mingling and kissing and so forth," an attendee reported. A plainclothes policeman had infiltrated the party, and a couple dozen revelers were escorted to the Charles Street Jail. There was a trial, during which the accused were found guilty on morals charges and outed. As a result, the city's gay men curtailed house parties.

No place was truly safe. Instead of being a refuge, Boston's gay bars and clubs were raided by the police with regularity.[1] There was no expectation of privacy. The *Mid-Town Journal*, a South End tabloid published by a straight man named Frederick Shibley, recorded the arrests ("Butch Ball Baffles Bulls" went one headline) for transgressions as minimal as kissing. Shibley, it should be noted, was an equal opportunity antagonist; the Boston Catholic Church tried, unsuccessfully, to shut the paper down.

Mid-Town Journal's habit of printing the names of arrested queer people was pernicious. In 1953, nineteen-year-old George Mansour went to a party in Bay Village. At the moment it was raided by the police, he was administering oral sex to a sailor. Mansour, who became an influential film programmer, had known he was gay since his early teens, when he began having sex with men, including his sister's husband. A fat child, he decided he'd "rather eat dick than mashed potatoes" and lost weight. An error-riddled account of the party ran in Shibley's scandal sheet. Mansour, a high school valedictorian, was accepted at Boston University. Upon realizing the incoming student had been convicted on a morals charge, the university revoked his acceptance.

* * *

1 There are persistent rumors that the Boston mob held a financial interest in the city's gay bars. However, in an email, *Black Mass* coauthor Dick Lehr wrote, "Sorry, but never came across any hard evidence you're looking for."

Unlike George Mansour, Tom did not shine academically. His final year, Tom earned an occasional 80 or 90 in his English and Latin composition courses, but otherwise his grades declined; overall, he ranked in the bottom quartile of the class. Even so, Tom was accepted to Boston College, a school favored by students set on continuing their Jesuit Catholic education.

During his four years on the leafy Chestnut Hill campus, Tom majored in psychology. He was more open to extracurriculars, it seemed, participating in the Spanish Academy, the Psychology Club, and the Debating Society.

The moderator of the Psychology Club was Dr. Joseph Cautela. He practiced medicine during what, in retrospect, was a dark period from the perspective of how homosexuality was perceived and addressed in the medical field. The year Tom graduated from high school, the American Psychological Association published the first *Diagnostic and Statistical Manual of Mental Disorders*, which classified homosexuality as a "sociopathic personality disturbance." The second edition of the *DSM*, published in 1968, reclassified homosexuality as a "sexual deviation." Once homosexuality was deemed a disorder, psychologists naturally wanted to treat it, often by reparative therapies. Cautela was a proponent of such therapy. In 1967, he published "Covert Sensitization," a paper that promised a "new treatment for maladaptive approach behavior." These behaviors included drinking, stealing, and homosexuality. Cautela recommended that therapists treating gay men adopt a script inviting patients to imagine they were in a room with a foul-smelling naked man, covered in "sores and scabs . . . with some kind of fluid oozing from them." Patients were conditioned to associate homosexuality with the stench and the sores; implicitly, "nice clean air" and a shower were akin to heterosexuality.[2]

Tom, if he had any notions about his own sexuality, told no one. Homosexuality, said a classmate, "was a terrible stigma in those days." (Indeed, a decade later, the city's gay men were targeted without cause, as

---

2 It's not clear if Cautela's beliefs about gay men made their way into the classroom.

a response to an infamous rash of strangulations later pinned on Albert DeSalvo.) Any gay life at Boston College would have been deeply underground. No one really knows how Tom dealt with this. But a classmate who knew Tom for most of his life offered a possible hint: "We all drank at Boston College. Drinking was a national sport. Mulcahy would drink with the best of us."

Tom and Margaret Mary Casey met at the Boston Public Library in the mid-1950s. Margaret was a teacher with a Radcliffe degree, while Tom, who'd worked at the library since he was a teenager, was a lowly extra assistant. But it was a steady job, paying seventy cents an hour, and he kept it well into college. They started dating soon after they met.

After graduation, Tom continued his psychology studies at Fordham University in the Bronx. He lived a couple of blocks from campus and worked in his off-hours at the Stork Club, a glamorous nightspot known for its clientele of movie stars and showgirls. It was a tumultuous time in the life of the club, owned by Sherman Billingsley, an anti-Semitic mobbed-up former bootlegger. In 1957, when the club had been in business for nearly thirty years, unions attempted to organize Billingsley's staff. An effort a decade prior had failed, but the new push was different: as a nonunionized shop, the Stork Club was now an outlier among its competitors. The owner was obstinate, however, so many employees walked out.

What was potentially ruinous for the club was fortuitous for Tom. Billingsley sent his men to Fordham to scrounge up replacement workers, and the graduate student was hired as a waiter. He worked six nights a week in the Cub Room, the Stork Club's inner sanctum for the famous and powerful, wearing a white jacket and a black bow tie, and waited on Roy Cohn and the Gabors. He came home with a pocketful of money. "One of the nicest guys you'd ever want to meet," says a Stork Club colleague. Tom wasn't aggressively outgoing, but people were drawn to him. He was sociable and a gentleman, and had a particular ease with women. Girls "just went gaga for Mulcahy."

All the while, Tom ferried back and forth to Boston to see Margaret. On October 11, 1958, after several years of dating, they married. The *Boston Globe* society column wrote up the union, reporting that the couple was to be married that morning and depart for a honeymoon in the Virgin Islands. Upon their return, the newlyweds planned to settle in Concord, Massachusetts, a fifteen-minute drive from Route 128.

By the late 1950s, the area along and around Boston's Route 128, a seventy-mile highway, was a hot spot for burgeoning computer companies. There was so much rapid growth along the Magic Semicircle, as *Businessweek* called it, that the road was eventually widened from four to six lanes. By 1957, there were ninety-nine companies employing thousands along 128. One such firm was Honeywell, which, after a recent partnership with Raytheon, specialized in mainframe computers. Fond of Boston College graduates, Honeywell hired Tom in 1960.[3]

The detectives would have been somewhat aware of Tom's work history, thanks in part to William O'Brien. O'Brien had recently left the company, which, thirty-two years later, was called Bull HN Information Systems. He helped Detective Matthew Kuehn get a sense of Tom's last days.

On Wednesday morning, July 8, 1992, Tom and O'Brien gave a sales presentation to an audience of twenty staffers from Deloitte & Touche, at their office on the ninety-second floor of the World Trade Center's Tower 1. O'Brien's presence was a favor to Tom, with whom he had been friends for more than a decade. One of O'Brien's major accounts at Bull had been the behemoth accounting firm, whose bankers were coming in from Tuscany to explore new technology. They were making the rounds,

---

3 News reports were split on whether Tom was hired in 1960 or 1961. None of them shed any light on the specifics of his job.

meeting with local businesses and reps, including Tom. "Do me a favor," Tom said to O'Brien. "Just come into New York City and make the presentation for me." O'Brien agreed to come in from his home in New Jersey.

The presentation took most of the morning, but it went well, so Tom and O'Brien walked a block to Edward Moran Bar & Grill for a three-hour lunch. "He was in normal spirits," O'Brien would testify. This was in keeping with his friend's general demeanor as a lighthearted, happy-go-lucky guy. They split a platter of shrimp and each drank more than a half-dozen beers. As O'Brien told a detective, they got "shit-faced."

At 3:00, Tom thanked his friend for his assistance and resolved to keep in touch. O'Brien went home, while Tom moved on to another bar.

The Townhouse was already on the radar of detectives, thanks to the investigation into Peter Anderson's murder. When they visited the bar to conduct interviews, regulars were guarded, reluctant to talk. "The homosexual community wasn't very open about what they were doing in their private lives," said Kuehn.

Nevertheless, detectives found Douglas Gibson. A blond-haired, blue-eyed twentysomething adorned in Brooks Brothers, Gibson made commercials for Pennzoil. He'd been a Townhouse regular since the night it opened in 1989. Not because he liked it all that much—it was snooty, he thought, with its dress code and plush couches and oil paintings—but because he owned an apartment on the same block. Oh, and the Townhouse fed his lifelong affection for older men. He liked them over sixty, generic-looking, Midwestern, and white-haired. Best-case scenario, that meant Johnny Carson. In practice, however, the staunch liberal Democrat was attracted to a lot of Republicans he "absolutely despised."

Tom and Gibson were introduced that night by a mutual friend, around 10:30. The three talked for a bit. Then, in deference to Gibson's affection for men precisely like Tom, the friend excused himself. As the melodies drifted up from the piano, surrounding the patrons who stood in a crush, they talked and talked, about Boston and New York, the Red Sox and the Yankees. Gibson, who preferred men who were married, divorced, or widowed, was deeply attracted to Tom, who was married and, although he didn't live in New York, could theoretically be available whenever he visited on business. No relationship, no commitment: perfect. Gibson thought the probability that he would take Tom home that night was high.

They were a study in contrasts: Gibson, out since he was three years old, had been sleeping with men since he was a kid on an Air Force base, whereas Tom had spent his life in the closet. As they stood by the bar, it seemed to Gibson that, despite their differences, the attraction was reciprocal. But as the conversation progressed, Gibson noticed Tom glancing over his shoulder. A man standing by the piano had caught his eye. Gibson had known him by sight for five years, but they'd never spoken to each other. Average looking and nearly five ten, he guessed, with medium-brown hair.

Disappointing, of course, but not unreasonable.

"This is my only night in New York," Tom said.

It had happened before and it would happen again, Gibson reasoned. It was a gentle kiss-off, with the understanding that, should nothing better come along, he'd circle back. As Gibson liked to say, he was frequently accused of being "president of the Better Offer Club."

"You're not going to find anything better than me," he told Tom, "so go right ahead."

Gibson walked to the bar downstairs, where contemporary music rippled from the speakers. He stayed for the length of a drink—perhaps twenty minutes. When he came back upstairs, he saw Tom and the man talking. Giving a harder look, Gibson made a note that Tom liked dumpy, pudgy types.

He went back downstairs for another drink. When he returned, they were gone.

Two days later, at six in the morning, detectives from the Seventeenth Precinct knocked on Gibson's door. As the last person known to be with Tom, he was the prime suspect. They took him down to the station and "put me in the box." Gibson was numbed by the news of Tom's death. But at first he wasn't even sure who the detectives were talking about, because he was a social guy. *Which man are you referring to?* What saved him, he assumes, is that Townhouse bartenders could attest to Gibson's presence long after Tom left, until closing time. It helped, too, that Gibson had no car and could not have easily driven to New Jersey.

After the murder, Gibson recalled that initial connection he felt with Tom. It wasn't survivor's guilt, exactly, but he wondered: *Why didn't I fight a little harder?*

When police began investigating Tom's murder, Margaret realized that, sooner or later, the kids would find out about their father. She took them to the therapist who, not so long ago, had seen Margaret and Tom. The kids learned of their dad's attraction to men.

Tracey's reaction was, *Okay, is this why he was killed?* It made more sense than some of the stories she'd read in the papers. The gambling angle, for instance. Tom may have traveled to Atlantic City, investigators told a reporter. They theorized he had been killed over a gambling debt. There wasn't much to the idea, however, save for Tom's body being found thirty miles away. In any case, detectives quickly ruled that out, they told the *Globe,* because there was no record of Tom gambling in Atlantic City, "and his financial standing was excellent."

Tracey began to think about her dad, about the little things that were unusual about him. Suddenly he began to make more sense. He loved old Hollywood and *La Cage aux Folles.* He adored show tunes, particularly *A Chorus Line.* (A colleague remembered his attending a Boston production of *Shear Madness,* a long-running musical about gay hairdressers and murder.) Tracey remembered how stylish he was, how Tom was more attentive to his appearance than the average dad. "He was what you would consider nowadays as a metrosexual."

On July 16, with the investigation in full swing, the Mulcahys held the funeral. Four hundred friends, family members, and colleagues filled the pews at Our Lady of Fatima Church in Sudbury. Tracey addressed the mourners. "It is ironic that someone filled with so much love was taken from us in a crime by someone filled with so much hate," she said, and read from a letter she wrote just hours after learning of her father's murder. Her siblings also spoke. Her brother asked mourners to pray for "victims of urban violence." A friend of Tom's read telegrams of condolences and remembrances from all over the world. The crowd sang hymns, including "All I Ask of You."

Persons come into the fiber of our lives,
and then their shadow fades and disappears.
All I ask of you is forever to remember me as loving you.
All I ask of you is forever to remember me as loving you.

A procession brought Tom's remains to a cemetery, where he was buried under the boughs of a dogwood.

Detectives could not establish either a crime scene or a viable suspect. There was no conceivable motive, either. "We had no idea," recalled Matthew Kuehn. "I mean, due to the way that the body was dismembered, we felt that he really pissed somebody off."

What they had were garbage bags, which they presumed would yield fingerprints. The cyanoacrylate fuming, the process by which prints were to be lifted, was not done under ideal circumstances. Instead of being performed at the state crime lab, the processing was done in a mobile unit. The chamber, which should have been airtight, wasn't, and the attempt to lift prints failed. (It's unclear, even now, why the bags weren't simply reprocessed by the state police.) As a result, no fingerprints from the maintenance-yard trash bags were recovered. Investigators did, however, extract DNA from a latex glove, and searched for a match in the FBI's Combined DNA Index System, a database of samples left by convicted offenders. This, too, yielded nothing.

Kuehn and his colleagues looked into the provenance of the bedsheet and shower curtain. The bedsheet, king-size and beige, was sold during an eight-month window in 1984 and 1985, mostly at stores such as J. C. Penney and Macy's. The shower curtain, a Saturday Knight Ltd. manufactured in January 1992, sold for $14.99. It could be found at Kmart, among other retailers. Neither item could be traced to a home, a hotel, or a motel.

Detectives were surprised and disappointed. But they learned something important: the origins of the keyhole saw and latex gloves. The bag containing the gloves had an SKU number traced to the only CVS branch on Staten Island. The sticker on the saw was traced to Pergament, a chain of home improvement stores. There were thirty-two Pergaments in New York and New Jersey, two on Staten Island. One was across the street from CVS.

Detectives thought there was a distinct possibility the perpetrator lived or worked on Staten Island.

Not long after Tom's body was found, detectives completed a ViCAP form, searching for similar crimes. They learned of a homicide from the year before that struck them as usefully similar: Peter Anderson had been mutilated and left in a fifty-five-gallon trash barrel. Like Tom, he spent a part of his last night on earth in New York's Townhouse Bar.

"At that point," said Kuehn, "you're looking at a potential serial killer."

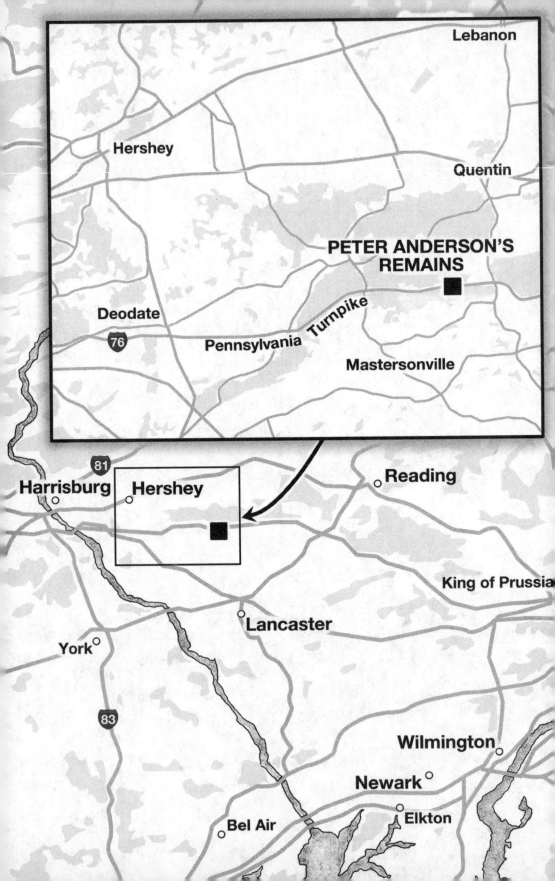

Haverstraw

Suffern

287

Easton

New York

Edison

Princeton

95

Trenton

Brick Township

295

THOMAS MULCAHY'S
REMAINS (1)

Toms River

Philadelphia

Cherry Hill

THOMAS MULCAHY'S
REMAINS (2)

Vineland

4

RICK

Years before Rick Unterberg played piano for Peter Anderson and Thomas Mulcahy's killer at the Townhouse, he played for small crowds on Saint Martin. Unterberg had been living on the Caribbean island, and given its remoteness, he always felt out of the loop. His connections to current U.S. news and culture were limited to the Sunday *New York Times,* Casey Kasem's Top 40, and a tourist shop that sold books like Herman Wouk's *Don't Stop the Carnival* and Robert Ludlum thrillers.

Rick was twenty-one years old and had been on Saint Martin for a few months, playing in a local resort and an ice cream parlor. He had a house with a private beach. Life was wonderful. There'd been an affair, too. Walking along Cupecoy Beach, on the Dutch side, he saw a middle-aged man on the cliffs above. Not great looking, but Rick was intrigued. They talked. His name was Jasper. They went back to the older man's house.

Another day Jasper and Rick stood in the ocean, and Jasper shyly took hold of his hand. It was a tender moment.

Jasper invited Rick and some musicians to his home. He served a dish with morel mushrooms, which were new to Rick. The musicians, who had taken a modern art course and were familiar with Jasper Johns's abstract expressionist work, were in a state of awe. A few months later, the Whitney Museum paid a million dollars for one of his paintings, a record for a living artist.

They slept together; Jasper's bed was surrounded by mosquito netting and nearby was an original Magritte and some Janis Joplin records. According to Rick, the sex wasn't memorable, and Jasper tended to be reserved. One day, Rick and Jasper were in the car. "You know, when I met you, I had no idea who you were," Rick said. "Now that you've told me, I still don't know who you are."

Without a word, Jasper kept driving.

Another day, Rick was supposed to go to Jasper's for lunch. But the artist showed up early and announced, "We're having lunch with Louise Nevelson. You know who that is?"

"Well, yeah," Rick responded, mistaking the dour sculptor for the actress Lois Nettleton.

Two hours later, Jasper arrived, and Rick slid into the back seat. Nevelson was wearing fake eyelashes and a fur coat in ninety-five-degree weather. They went to Oyster Pond for lunch, and while they ate, Nevelson's assistant snapped photos. "I can see it now," remarked Rick. "In a number of years, it'll be 'Jasper Johns, Louise Nevelson, and unknown urchin.'"

In August, Rick returned home to New York to attend his brother's wedding. He paid rent on the Saint Martin house for an extra month so the newlyweds could have a honeymoon.[1]

Rick didn't know it, but when he returned to New York, he was coming back to a maelstrom.

On January 15, 1981, a man watched his lover sleep in a hospital bed.

---

1 In December 2019, Jasper Johns wrote to the author: "I do remember that Louise Nevelson was on the island, but no memory of the date or of the lunch with Rick Unterberg."

He'd been sick for months and had suffered heart attacks, and now foam was coming out of his nostrils and ears. It was time to let him die. The feeding tube was removed. Nearly five months later, *Morbidity and Mortality Weekly Report,* a weekly digest published by the Centers for Disease Control and Prevention, reported five cases—two fatal—of *Pneumocystis carinii* pneumonia. This was the first published scientific account of what would eventually be called HIV and AIDS. But it would be years until Rick took it seriously. He says, "It wasn't like, all of a sudden, we were all wearing condoms."

Back in Manhattan full-time, Rick, a skinny guy with the physical grace of a marionette, got a job at a straight bar on Greenwich Avenue. Just a placeholder, really, but for a couple of years it fed his tendency toward stagnation. That's not uncommon among the gifted—to assume the fire will always be at one's fingertips. And why would he think otherwise? Rick had played piano since first grade in Dolton, Illinois. Contemporary music was anathema to his family, so Rick played numbers from *Gypsy* and *The Sound of Music* that he heard on the record player. He effortlessly excelled; even at the New England Conservatory of Music, he barely practiced. Rick's older brother resented all the attention he received. More or less annual appearances in the local paper: the Yule concert in '74; the fall production of *Arsenic and Old Lace* in '75; and vocal awards in '76, even though Rick's voice was rather thin.

One day in 1983, a bar colleague who had been working the cruise-ship circuit passed on word about a job. Rick had no romantic notions about the sea; his concern, as ever, was whether it was worth the risk of giving up steady employment. After a six-week trial, Rick was hired by Premier Cruise Lines, which he came to think of as "the Staten Island Ferry of the Bahamas."

Clad in a tux and cummerbund, he played three- and four-day excursions for five years, mostly for Middle Americans looking for a quick vacation. Rick was a hit, often seen trailed around the room by a group of women wearing sequined butterfly tops.

In January 1988, the staff was taken on a private tour of the *StarShip Atlantic* when the ship was docked in Port Canaveral. They were shown the Blue Riband Pub, a cozy lounge on the pool deck bookended by the Junkanoo Bar and the Big Dipper Ice Cream Parlor. There was a white piano built specially for Rick. It should have been something to celebrate—how regal! However, Rick suspected the *StarShip Atlantic* would be his last vessel. The cruise line had recently instituted mandatory testing for HIV. Rick wondered if that was even legal.

He had never been tested before, but the results, he knew, would be grim. "Oh, *you're* not. You're not," the ship's nurse told him. When Rick returned from shore with the test results, she wept. Rick was positive for HIV.

During the next cruise, a representative for the cruise line came aboard. "We don't want to lose you, but we've got to let you go," he told Rick. In nearly every corner of the United States, insurance companies could require that applicants be tested for AIDS and then, depending on the results, deny coverage. Rick fell into this group. The cruise line was reasonably merciful, given the times, and hired him as "shoreside entertainment coordinator." For the next six months, Rick was paid a weekly salary, which made him eligible for eighteen months of COBRA, and he didn't work a day.

Another man from the ship tested positive, too. "The awful thing is," Rick said thirty years later, "I don't know whether this guy gave it to me, or I gave it to him."

Regent East was a bar on East Fifty-eighth in Manhattan that catered to professionals, often fashion designers. It wasn't fancy: an entrance under the stairs, one room, no food. Years after the bar closed, a regular remembered "hunting prints, club chairs" and lights "supplied with the pink bulbs that were typically used in funeral parlors to make the corpses look natural."

At the outset of 1988, the bar was in need of a pianist. Rick, now back in New York, had never played in a gay bar before, but auditioned and got the job. That first night, sitting at the piano in the back, he was out of sorts. After so many years playing for straight audiences, he feared he lacked a repertoire to suit his new audience. Barry Manilow, he knew, thanks to his time on the ship, but he hadn't played show tunes since childhood. He remembered the records he used to play. "I could probably play songs from *Mame*," he thought. As soon as he sat down, a customer came over. "I hope," he said, "you're not going to play something from *Mame*."

A good piano player will amass a following. Just as the Blue Parrot's Michael Ogborn had his devotees, so too did Rick cultivate a band of regulars (or, as he thought of them, groupies) who came to Regent East, not for the drinks, but to sing along with "Willkommen." Among the devoutly enthused were Ted, Phil, and a nurse named Richard. To the detriment of Regent East, the group was also loyal. When a new bar opened on East Fifty-eighth and its management poached Rick, the groupies followed him out the door.

The Townhouse Bar, situated in that vast midtown paunch of the city, was equidistant from Central Park and the East River. It was founded after a doorman at Regent East made the mistake of snubbing Paul Galluccio, a musician cum boutique-clothing-store owner. Galluccio, purely out of spite, opened a piano bar down the block.

Quiet and respectable, with red wallpaper, leather chairs, and oil paintings, the Townhouse was invariably described as *well-appointed*. It became known as a place where older gentlemen pursued younger men and vice versa. A businessman in from out of town, perhaps closeted, would be comfortable in a bar cloaked by an ostensibly heterosexual neighborhood.

In the early days, the bar took pains to keep out the riffraff, thanks to a barrier to entry in the form of mandatory blazers. Yet despite the elegant trappings, this was a prime location to pick up a hustler, albeit quietly.[2] These boys were hot and high-end; the older, less chiseled hustlers who walked in off the street were unwelcome.

In an airy room in the back of the Townhouse, perched in the corner, Rick played Thursdays through Sundays and sang with high-baritoned joy. He would eventually learn a thousand songs by heart, most of them Broadway compositions, and perform more than a hundred over a six-hour stretch.

Rick played the late shift on Sundays. It wasn't terribly crowded, but only because it was technically a work night. As far as he could tell, the murders of Anderson and Mulcahy hadn't hurt business. Primarily, he believed, it was because the dead men weren't regulars. That was cold-blooded, perhaps, but it was true: tourists were easier to miss. It helped, of course, that the murders weren't getting much coverage in the New York papers. Crime rates were near their historic peak, with more than two thousand homicides by the year's end. Duncan Osborne, an investigative journalist who wrote for many of the era's queer periodicals, noted, "If you were a crime victim and you wanted to get written about, you had to be a white person and you had to get killed in Central Park."

There were plenty of regulars dying of AIDS to mourn, and Rick was often asked to mark the passing of men who wasted away. In the span of a few years, he lost two piano players and a bartender. Death was a constant hum. The year 1992 saw 10,828 diagnoses of AIDS in New York City. St. Vincent's Hospital, the venerable institution that once treated survivors of the *Titanic*, had stretchers crammed wall to wall. Patients weren't there long. They might be admitted with pneumonia or toxoplasmosis, and they died fast. Rick considered himself the grim reaper.

By the middle of Rick's set, the patrons who had been drinking for hours were primed. One evening, a regular from the Regent East days

---

2 The Townhouse had a lot of company in this regard, with Second Avenue around Fifty-second Street known as a spot where muscled diversions could be found filtering in and out of half the area's establishments.

walked in and approached the piano. Rick knew him well enough. As always, the rather unremarkable man of medium height and medium build was pleasant. As was his wont, he ordered a cold scotch, hung back, and listened to the music play.

The day it opened in 1989, the Townhouse was already a throwback. This was by design, and it was, frankly, what made it alluring. Whereas Regent East really *was* a piano bar that had been around for years—part of the wave of "proper attire" bars that sprang up after the Stonewall uprising—the Townhouse was a perfect replica. It was antithetical to the trajectory of New York's early-1990s gay nightlife. Geographically, the Townhouse wasn't so far away from the noise and the grime and the cut-rate sex workers—walking distance, even, for the ambitious. But milling around that warm, inviting back room, nursing a cocktail a few feet away from the piano and elegantly attired men, you could almost pretend it was another country.

In a city that was host to a vibrant, thumping smorgasbord of subcultures, fetishes, and scenes, piano bars were a tiny bulwark against change. Most, unlike the Townhouse, tended to be downtown, many clustered in the West Village—what Michael Musto, the cheeky *Village Voice* columnist, called a "Bermuda Triangle of showbiz aspirants." Not far from the famed Stonewall Inn were Arthur's, the Duplex, Five Oaks, and Marie's Crisis, which a local bar owner pronounced "the gayest" of the bunch. Marie's had a remarkable lineage, with antebellum roots. It stood, in fact, on the spot where Thomas Paine died in 1809. The building was razed, rebuilt, and by the 1850s had become a house of prostitution. By the 1890s, wrote a historian, "the basement club was literally an underground bar for gay men." In 1970, it opened as a piano bar, named for Romany Marie, an early-twentieth-century Greenwich Village restaurateur, and Paine's famous pamphlet.

The bars were a refuge. A proprietor observed, as his establishment was folding, how necessary they had been. "We were," he said, "the safe, sane choice." The alternatives were the scuzzy piers, Central Park—its Ramble, where gay men had once been thrashed—and the disease-ridden baths, most of which were already shuttered by health officials. In their day, the baths were popular, having attracted ordinary men as well as Truman Capote and Rudolf Nureyev, both of whom went to an establishment on West Fifty-eighth. AIDS put an end to that. Even before they were closed, the baths had a history of a lethal lack of maintenance; in 1977, nine men were incinerated in a fire at the Everard Baths because most of the windows on the upper floors were sealed and the sprinklers didn't work.

The Five Oaks, at 49 Grove Street, was about a hundred feet from Marie's. Half piano bar, half restaurant, the Oaks, as regulars called it, had been around since the 1950s. It was rumored to have once been a speakeasy, with a secret door in the kitchen opening up onto Bleecker Street. There were thirteen steps between the sidewalk and the street, which was quiet and mostly residential. As you walked in, adjusting to the low ceiling and the darkness, you'd see off to the right a thirteen-seat horseshoe bar. To the left was a dining room of a dozen tables. And in between, near the entrance to the ladies' room, was a Black woman playing piano.

Marie Blake was the anchor of the Five Oaks, and its most sustained draw. Classically trained, throaty, and scat singing, she bobbed her head gently as she played, while beautifully dressed men crooned into the microphone to her right. Why she played at a tiny bar on Grove and not at Carnegie Hall was a mystery. Patrons brought her music, which she sight-read without hesitation. "When you sing a song, you have to sort of act it, too, to put it over to the people," she once said. "You have to feel the song within you."

For Broadway folks, the Five Oaks had long been a destination: Liza Minnelli and Shirley MacLaine dropped in, and Tharon Musser, a lighting designer who worked to acclaim on *A Chorus Line,* was a regular. Hal

Prince, too, came in for early dinners with his wife each Sunday. Stephen Sondheim recalled the Five Oaks as "a fixture in the Village." It was Judy Garland's favorite bar; when she passed out, the owner would carry her upstairs to a cab.

The Five Oaks was a refuge from violence, but not from the raging AIDS epidemic. "I stopped counting at two hundred fifty people I knew," says Lisa Hall, who tended bar. "I mean, they would come to my bar and sit there, and their alarms would go off for AZT. Or you'd watch the Kaposi's go on their faces, or them getting thin, you know? Telling me, *How am I going to tell my parents?*" Hall's therapist told her if she mothered one more gay man she would have to find a new therapist. "When I look through my photo albums, most every other person is dead. I lost six piano players."

The Greenwich Village bars, of which Five Oaks was just one, were the city's most famous. Few were more mainstream—loosely defined as a big, brightly lit bar in which one could hear contemporary popular music—than Uncle Charlie's, which had a preppy vibe that attracted a white collegiate crowd of gay Alex Keatons. The writer Augusten Burroughs visited a few times and reported it was "just exactly as loathsome as the name implies."

The West Village attracted a large contingent of tourists, dipping into the bookstores and card shops. Many of the tourists were closeted men who yearned for a taste of the gay life. Around Sheridan Square—Grove Street, West Fourth, and both sides of Seventh Avenue—had been the locus of gay establishments since the 1920s and '30s. Christopher Street, a minute walk from Sheridan Square, had something for all tastes: for Western, there was Boots and Saddle; for the older, touristy crowd, there was Julius', which had been around for so long, the Mattachine Society once staged a "sip-in" there. Keller's, at the tip of Christopher, catered to a specific clientele—Black men who were into leather.

But walk uptown for fifteen minutes and head west, and you were in another world: Chelsea. The colonization of the neighborhood—swaths of which had once been the estate of author Clement Clarke Moore, whose 1823 poem "A Visit from Saint Nicholas" became one of the most famous in the English language—began in the mid-1970s. The gay pioneers, as they were sometimes called, had worked with a blank slate: a few diners and greeting card shops, intermittent streetlights, and very few sidewalks, according to one resident. Conveniently near the Village, but it was far more affordable. And violent.

Residents followed unwritten rules, a Chelsean recalled: "We did not walk on the west side of Eighth Avenue between sunset and sunrise and avoided Ninth Avenue altogether if possible because of a gang of teenaged bashers who roamed the neighborhood. Walking to the Eagle or Spike, we either walked north up West Street or west along Twenty-third Street until Twelfth Avenue and then south again."

There was a sense among the pioneers that the Village had gone irreparably upscale. Bleecker had turned into a boulevard, and one developer in particular, William Gottlieb, tore up the street and evicted commercial tenants. Gottlieb is remembered, and resented, as a distinctly unpleasant landlord. As Sarah Jessica Parker put it, "He slept on a mattress made of my checks!"

For the price of an apartment in the Village, one could buy a townhouse in Chelsea and fix it up. Young people moved in first, and the businesses soon followed. It was something of a clean break. "The older guys stayed in the Village for a variety of reasons, one of which was they *couldn't* move," said a man who moved to Chelsea in 1983. Many of the "older guys" had been rendered invalids by AIDS and were on Medicaid, so lacked the money to leave the neighborhood.

The young men who migrated began converting or restoring brownstones. By the mid-1980s, one could rent a studio for $900 a month or, for $125,000, buy a new condominium on Twenty-third between Eighth and Ninth. Eighth Avenue, which previously was mostly dotted with bulletproof liquor stores and thrift shops, was now home to the neighborhood's first gay restaurant, Rogers & Barbero, founded by its eponymous couple. Despite the influx of new residents, and the buildings being torn down and raised up, the older residents of Chelsea stayed put, hanging on to their rent-controlled apartments with admirable single-mindedness. Applicants might wait more than a decade to get into a co-op.

A cornerstone of Chelsea were the heavy-duty leather bars. Along the river were the most prominent: the Eagle, on West Twenty-first, and the Spike, one block south. The Eagle had been in business since 1970, and was already considered a fixture. (The Meatpacking District, which encompassed five or six square blocks south, boasted Badlands, the Ramrod, and the Mineshaft.) Farther east, along Eighth Avenue, were small, almost neighborhoody bars, including Chelsea Transfer on Sixteenth Street, which attracted an older crowd of chubby chasers, and the Break, near Twenty-third Street, which attracted preppies to its backyard barbecues.

It was Splash, which opened in 1991, that was the landmark: "the first true nineties gay bar," said Matthew Bank, cofounder and editor of *HX*, the influential bar rag. It would immediately be the bar of the moment, even at two in the morning. Sculpted bartenders, mirrors at every turn, and lube and condoms on offer. On a stage, in a clever approximation of a shower, water fell over muscular pretty boys, nicknamed Splash Dancers, who became celebrities among the neighborhood's gym rats. A patron recalled a spacious place, eclectic videos, and "the stable of buff bartenders to stare at as they strutted around bare chested in their skimpy, and very flattering, briefs." You'd walk in and everything outside would fade away. When Splash closed, *The New York Times*—which had, for years, largely avoided coverage of gay life and then AIDS itself—memorialized its innovations: "Translucent shower stalls where muscular, nearly naked men would dance," and noted with admiration that such a format had spread from New York to Paris to Mykonos.

The Upper West Side of Manhattan was the periphery. The neighborhood's gay population went back to at least the 1950s, and James Baldwin, on the cusp of publishing his novel *Another Country,* bought a row house on West Seventy-first. But nothing gay "opened up above the 80s," remembered Bank. Particularly popular were the Cork Club, on Seventy-second, and the 415 Bar on Amsterdam Avenue. Of the latter, wrote one patron, "you walked in, saw a few locals talking with the bartender, & figured you'd made a mistake. But through an unmarked door in the back & down a flight of stairs, you entered a cavernous basement teeming with hundreds of gay men who were dancing & laughing & cruising & kissing & drinking & passing out in the johns."

If you were an older gentleman, the Works, on Columbus and Eighty-first, was fairly inoffensive, even preppy. The area's draw, though, was Candle Bar, near West Seventy-fifth. Upon entering, there was a bar off to the left, and on the right a jukebox and shuffleboard, which was considered "obnoxiously loud and intrusive in such a small space." Red cloth-covered tables rounded out the room. The bar had been in the neighborhood for decades. In the early years, it had been known as the Candlelight Lounge. In 1959, the New York State Liquor Authority temporarily shuttered the bar on account of "homosexual activities."

All things considered, these bars were anodyne. One could, however, indulge in some grit farther down the West Side. Hell's Kitchen had a cluster of bars that were spectacularly sleazy. Cleo's Ninth Avenue Saloon, which attracted theatergoers, was a decent place to purchase cocaine. Nearby were the drag bars, such as Sally's and Edelweiss, the latter of which, wrote Musto, "was a fascinating hangout for trans women, cross-dressers, and every type of gender outlaw that makes New York sparkle."

The roughest bars sat in the Theater District, just to the east of Hell's Kitchen. It was here, according to one chronicler, that "obvious 'fairies,' (many of them heavily made-up) created their own flamboyant culture," and had done so since World War II. There was Tricks, with its charmingly on-the-nose name, and Hombres—depending on the year, also called the Savoy—a bar on Forty-first Street behind Port Authority Bus Terminal frequented by cut-rate hustlers.

The science fiction writer Samuel Delany was one of the regulars. A *New York Times* reporter found him there in the midnineties, red loose-leaf notebook in hand, scribbling away. He loved the place, visiting whenever he happened to be in Times Square for a movie or the bus to his university job in Massachusetts. In 2017, Delany recalled a visit from the old days during which a sex worker, on the job and penis exposed under the bar, advertised his wares. "That's the kind of thing that would go on from time to time," he said. "It was an attempt to get your attention." Twenty dollars was a relative pittance, and an acceptable price point for Delany.

The bar could also be dangerous. "Dear sweet Jesus, was that hellhole something else," wrote a patron. "You were more likely to get mugged than hook up." Another, a young man who'd stopped by during a New Year's Eve bar crawl in 1992, found Hombres to be "really, really, *really* gross."

No one considered the Townhouse to be dangerous. But no one knew that one of its most mild-mannered and inconspicuous patrons was a murderer.

5

THE TRYOUT OF EDDIE MARRERO

May 10, 1993

At 7:30 in the morning, Donald Giberson was waiting on Wranglebrook Road in Whiting, New Jersey, for a friend. Giberson, sixty-five, had lived in the area long enough to remember when the street was unpaved. He looked at his watch; his friend, who lived a short drive away, wasn't due for a half hour. So he drove a mile and a half to Crow Hill, a single-lane dirt road that traversed a forest and had once been a wagon route. There was a blimp flying in the area, Giberson had heard, and he hoped for a glimpse.

As he made his way up the road, Giberson passed what appeared to be a deer carcass. It would not have been strange; the site, he testified years later, was a known dumping ground for leaves, garbage bags, and assorted matter. Anyway, when Giberson reached the top of the hill, he looked around but couldn't spot the blimp. On the way back, as he passed the carcass, Giberson rolled down the window. That's when he saw human fingers, and got nauseated. Giberson drove the mile home, then called the Manchester police.

The police ordered Giberson back to Crow Hill.

"Upon arrival, Mr. Giberson approached me & said body part was just up the road," recorded the patrolman in an incident report.

I asked him to show me exactly where part was. Mr. Giberson began to walk down the dirt road, with me following in patrol car. He changed his mind, saying it was too far & got in patrol car. After traveling approx. 500' Mr. Giberson pointed to what appeared to be an arm.

Within thirty minutes, detectives from the Ocean County Prosecutor's Office arrived on scene: Michael Mohel, Thomas Hayes, and the ranking investigator, Mark Woodfield.

Mohel was a big man with a big mustache—a grizzly with a badge who'd investigated seventy-five homicide cases and had a talent for eliciting confessions. Growing up in Lakewood, New Jersey, in an Orthodox Jewish family, he didn't see his first dead body until he became a cop. Hayes, the youngest of the three, had been in the homicide unit only since 1989. Despite his relative lack of experience, he was unaffected by gore. It was the job. Only years later, during retirement, would death affect him. Woodfield, clean-shaven but for a mustache, grew up in Ocean County. He had been in the homicide unit since 1980—and a cop since the early seventies, in Broward County, Florida. After a year of undercover work in Miami, he moved back home and took a job with the prosecutor's office. The trio worked about a dozen homicide cases a year.

There was a left arm, bloodied and dirty, in the road. The hand appeared to have a plastic bag in its grip. An animal, perhaps a raccoon, probably pulled the arm out of the bag, noted a detective. Under the bag was a clothesline, and several feet away was another arm.

As before, there were garbage bags: thirty-gallon, dark green. Six, all told, each containing human remains. As before, the body was divided into seven parts: two legs, two arms, a torso bisected horizontally across the abdomen, and the head—severed at the back of the spine.

All that remained of the victim's face was pulp. Little was left of his eyes. Dark brows were askew, and the mouth, topped by a thick mustache, was agape, as if he had been violently interrupted while answering a question. There were multiple small stab wounds in his back, and obvious ligature marks around his ankles. This dismembered, discarded man had no driver's license, no business card, no passport. Nothing by which to immediately identify him.

Intact bags were taken to a funeral home in Toms River, as the Ocean County medical examiner lacked a freezer. The head was contained in an Acme bag, from the supermarket chain, emblazoned with the words PRESIDENT'S CHOICE and MADE WITH PRIDE BY BOB H. AND JERRY H. The upper torso was found in a white trash bag inside three dark green trash bags. The lower torso and the legs were similarly encased.

An Ocean County Sheriff's Department crime scene investigator examined the arms and took fingerprint impressions. The body seemed to have been washed, he noted, and there was very little blood in the bags. He snapped photos of a few tattoos. On the right hand between the index finger and thumb was inked LINDA. On the left foot, written in fine cursive, was FAST EDDIE.

Fingerprints in hand, the crime scene investigator went to the State Police Identification Bureau in West Trenton. He input the prints into the Automated Fingerprint Identification System (AFIS). No hits. He sent the fingerprints to Philadelphia and New York, too, as well as the FBI. That evening, a reply: a match to a man named Eddie Ramos.

Within hours, the detectives heard back from the Philadelphia Police Department, the New York Police Department, and the FBI. The victim had an arrest record. In a mugshot taken in 1990, the stone-faced man has thick, dark hair just beginning to recede and a dense mustache. Life had taken its toll, but he was intensely handsome. The man New York knew as Eddie Ramos was known in Philadelphia by another name: Anthony Edward Marrero.

There was some initial confusion about where Anthony lived. In a press conference on May 11, the day after the body was discovered, the Ocean County prosecutor identified him as a resident of Philadelphia. But, said the prosecutor vaguely, "There may be some connection to Monmouth

County." He was proud that his office had identified the victim, whom he referred to as Eddie Ramos, so quickly. It wasn't clear what had been used to dismember the body, but the prosecutor believed it "wasn't any ritualistic kind of thing."

A spokesman for the prosecutor's office took pains to emphasize that knowledge of Anthony's life was limited. "We know practically zilch," he told the Associated Press. That wasn't likely to change, wrote a local reporter: "No one notified police Marrero was missing . . . and no one has come forward since the discovery of his body to say they knew him."

The claim that detectives knew very little about Anthony wasn't a ruse to deceive a potential suspect. They really had scant information. At the outset of the investigation, they knew he was born on May 2, 1949, in Puerto Rico. They also quickly pieced together that he had lived in several locations around Philadelphia from 1969 through 1983, before moving to Manhattan. But that was it. As the *Asbury Park Press* suggested, friends and family were not eager to assist the police. There was no equivalent of Margaret Mulcahy, willing to board a plane to help investigators.

As a consequence, information about Anthony's life that would ordinarily be easily gathered—his circle of friends, where he'd grown up and gone to school, past employment—was hard to come by. Indeed, decades later, it would be difficult to substantiate any of his family ties, and his arrest records from the late 1980s and early 1990s were sealed. His name would appear once in a publicly available official document: New Jersey's death index. His name was misspelled, and the Social Security number is for a woman born a year later.

For Mohel and Hayes, given the absence of immediate help from friends and family, the starting point, then, was the arrest records. A Port Authority detective pointed his New Jersey colleagues toward a grimy six-block colossus just west of Times Square. Anthony, they learned, was a sex worker who, over a decade, had accumulated a record of pandering, loitering, and solicitation, which included arrests in and around New York's Port Authority Bus Terminal.

Mohel and Hayes walked around the terminal, badges and guns prominently displayed. Still, Mohel was propositioned. A young, unkempt woman asked if he wanted a blow job. "Yeah," he chuckled, "but not from you."

This didn't startle Hayes, who remembered passing through the bus terminal when, as a teenager, he visited from New Jersey. Going back to at least the 1960s, the place had been a hub for all forms of sex work; in 2004, *The New York Times* would indecorously call it a "hooker magnet." Indeed, the terminal and the ten blocks to the north was known as the Minnesota Strip, a dark reference to Midwestern girls who, failing to make it on Broadway, hooked along Eighth Avenue.

Among those ensnared by the area was David Wojnarowicz, who began turning tricks at sixteen. In his journals, Wojnarowicz, a prominent painter and performance artist, recounted the first time he watched a man and woman have sex, in a hotel on Forty-fifth Street:

> This prostitute I remember from in front of Port Authority walked in with this Spanish guy and they threw off their clothes and the guy hops on the bed and this girl jumped on top of him and the two of them went at it, changin [*sic*] positions every couple of seconds until he shot.

This was, rather than an anomaly, another wrinkle in the area's rich history of sex work. Starting in 1880, the west side of Midtown Manhattan had a thirty-year run as the city's tenderloin district. By the early 1900s, male prostitution was commonplace. George Chauncey, in his book *Gay New York*, recounts the owner of a newsstand in 1927 grousing that "whenever the fleet comes into town, every sailor who wants his d— licked comes to the Times Square Building." The prostitution ebbed and flowed but never went away. By the late 1980s, public attention turned largely to the child runaways. The *Daily News* wrote of boys selling themselves for "as little as a fast-food meal, a warm bed or a pea-sized fragment of crack worth $3." The rapes, which newspapers queasily called "liaisons," could occur at the homes of pedophiles, but just as often happened amid the urine and dirt beneath the terminal stairwells. At the outset of the 1990s, Port Authority detectives were focusing on what was termed "illicit homosexual activity."

The existence of widespread sex work wasn't news to the Port Authority higher-ups. Not only were they aware of it—they may even have used that knowledge for personal gain. A retired senior Port Authority official would recall stories of detectives nabbing powerful men and using transgressions as leverage. "In those days, sometimes being able to hold that over somebody was more effective to [Port Authority officials] than to actually arrest them and charge them," he said. "I don't want to say blackmail, but it's sort of like that."

On the second floor of the bus terminal was a restroom. It was here, Mohel and Hayes were told, that Anthony had been working for as little as ten dollars a trick. The tip came in from Carlos Santiago, a pal of Anthony's who lived on West Fortieth, between Eighth and Ninth Avenues. Looking up from the sidewalk in front of his building, Santiago could see Port Authority across the street. He told detectives that Anthony's territory was "basic bars," including a Chelsea leather establishment called Rawhide, which, he said, attracted "blue-collar, business types" interested in being picked up. That was his friend's bread and butter. Santiago said Anthony also worked out of Tricks, a bar on West Forty-eighth in Hell's Kitchen.

Santiago could not place Anthony inside or outside the Townhouse, where Peter Anderson and Tom Mulcahy had been. However, he would later testify that Anthony hustled on Fifty-third Street and Lexington Avenue, a nine-minute walk away. This may be wrong, however, as there was no gay bar on that corner. But two blocks to the east, at 303 East Fifty-third, was Rounds—a bar famously, and overtly, catering to older men looking for young, or at least younger, hustlers. As *HX* described it: "Young entrepreneurs meet older investors." The piano player would look out at the throng of wealthy New Yorkers and over-seas visitors and ask, "How are things going out on the sales floor?" Handsome Anthony, had he cleaned up, could have fit in among the Rounds crowd.

The sex workers at Rounds could be useful. A "kept boy" named Dale, who often sought a third party in his relationship with a renowned Manhattan interior decorator, would pick from among its patrons. There was an unspoken code of conduct for transactions, Dale recalled: "The guys who were for sale were on one side of the bar, while the guys who were buying were at the bar. It was a marketplace." The sidewalk outside Rounds also hosted an agora. The street trade, as it was called, was invariably older and more socioeconomically downscale than the men inside. This bar was a seven-minute walk from the Townhouse.

On May 5, 1993, Anthony was Santiago's houseguest. They had been friends for six years, having met in front of Santiago's building. Anthony had no fixed address and frequently stayed over. He had been up late drinking and smoking marijuana. When he smoked, said Santiago, "his eyes turned real small." At seven o'clock, Santiago briefly awoke. At noon, he got up for good and ran into his friend, still in a haze, at Port Authority. Anthony said he was going to the Village for work.

Three days later, Santiago celebrated his twenty-sixth birthday. Anthony was invited but didn't show up. Santiago never saw him again.

Mohel and Hayes hadn't set out to find the johns, but they couldn't be avoided—these are the men who knew Anthony best. On a tip from Santiago, they visited a husband and wife in Manhattan who acted on Broadway. They weren't stars. The man, who had stark-white spiked hair—not unlike an albino, thought Mohel—had been paying Anthony for sex. The detectives tried to do the john a favor by interviewing him outside, beyond his wife's earshot. "Oh," he said, "she already knows." The actors, who had a bag of Anthony's belongings, told Mohel and Hayes about a man in Hamden, Connecticut, who saw Anthony quite often. He had a Cadillac and whisked Anthony away for a week at a time.

That seemed promising, but the Connecticut man turned out to be in his midsixties and frail; even if he murdered Anthony, he surely lacked the strength to dismember him. He was neither cooperative nor friendly, but more than anything, the john seemed pathetic. He lived with his brother, who was infirm. Hayes opened a closet, and what smelled like a dead body was, in fact, soiled rags.

Once the New York leads were exhausted, which took about a week, Mohel and Hayes visited Philadelphia to follow up on the police reports. They checked in at headquarters, known as the Roundhouse—a mile and a half from where Peter Anderson lived on Walnut Street—and were taken around to Anthony's old stomping grounds. They flashed his photo and moved on. They learned nothing of value and left before the day was out.

Mark Woodfield and a Manchester detective went to Philadelphia, too. It was a multipurpose trip: First, to discern if Anthony had been living in the city, because they still hadn't found an address for him in New York. But, second, to make a notification. They visited Anthony's brother, Louis, at his small, single-family home. They informed him that his brother had been murdered.

Failure to prepare, prepare to fail, Woodfield told his detectives. Whether it's a suspect, a witness, or a family member, know as much as possible before the conversation starts. Find points of commonality. Empathize. Anything to get them talking. Some people, observed Woodfield, won't even tell you what day it is. Louis, however, didn't have to be pushed. Hearing the news about his brother, he was despondent, embarrassed. Oftentimes, families would fall apart or embrace the comfort of denial. But not Louis. As Woodfield took notes, Louis told the detectives what little he knew. Once in a while, he said, Anthony wandered home to Philadelphia, but then he'd leave. The family wasn't blind to how he earned his living. Woodfield got the impression they had come to grips with his life, that eventually, they knew, it would end with a knock on the door.

A few days after Anthony's body was found, New Jersey's assistant medical examiner, Geetha Natarajan—whom detectives affectionately called Doctor Nat—performed the autopsy. Natarajan, efficient and fast-walking, believed a corpse could communicate. As she once told a reporter, "Dead bodies can talk a lot."

In the cold of the decomp room, with Thomas Hayes observing the proceeding, she estimated Anthony had been killed three to five days prior to his discovery. His head was severed at the level of the cervical vertebra. The arms were cut through mid-humerus, and the legs were cut through mid-femur. The torso was cut five inches above the belly button. The dismemberment occurred postmortem, with clean cuts through the skin made with a sharp knife. Natarajan believed the cuts through the bones could have been made with a saw, with the cause of death being multiple stab wounds to the back and front. She further noted ligature marks on both ankles, which appeared to be postmortem. A toxicology screen subsequently came back positive for marijuana. No signs of sexual assault or activity.

When Hayes returned home that night, he stripped off his suit in the garage, to spare his wife the smell.

Mohel, Hayes, and Woodfield were sure whoever killed Anthony wasn't a novice, in part because of the case's resemblance to the murder of Thomas Mulcahy. A few weeks into the Marrero investigation, Woodfield went out to Red Lion and sat down with the New Jersey State Police. The parties traded information. "We gotta be dealing with the same guy," he said. The similarities to Mulcahy, whose body was found eighteen miles from Anthony's, were unavoidable: the trash bags had been either double- or triple-bagged and double-knotted; the bodies had each been sliced into seven parts; each man had connections to Midtown gay bars, Tom as a patron and Anthony as a hustler. (In fact, early in the investigation, detectives briefly wondered if the men were acquainted, but they couldn't find a direct link.) There were differences, too, but they were slight. Anthony had been dismembered, rather than disarticulated, which suggested the perpetrator, in cutting directly through the bone, had prioritized speed over precision. Also, the victimology was inconsistent; one man was white-collar, the other a sex worker.

The state police assigned to Tom's case suspected his killer was based on Staten Island. Anthony's investigators quickly reached the same conclusion, after tracing the origins of the Acme bag containing his head. Detectives contacted Acme security, which determined where and when the bags with MADE WITH PRIDE BY JERRY H. AND BOB H. written on them had been used. Security told them that, as a promotional tool, people who made each bag branded them with their initials. Thus, Acme could say definitively where Jerry and Bob's bags were distributed. The list was long: Westtown, Pennsylvania; Oxford, Pennsylvania; Bath, New York; Mantua, New Jersey; Lansford, Pennsylvania; Collegeville, Pennsylvania; Union City, New Jersey; Wrightstown, New Jersey; and Tuckerton, New Jersey.

One location stuck out: Staten Island, New York.

Detectives fanned out in New York City's southernmost borough. They were running down a rumor passed along by one of Anthony's friends.

Anthony, it seemed, may have been "recruiting" Hispanic sex workers on behalf of a manager of Colony Records, the legendary record store in Manhattan's Brill Building. The man, who had an Italian surname, lived on Staten Island. The lead proved mostly false. Two fingerprints and a palm print were recovered from the Acme bag containing Anthony's head, but were not a match to the Colony Records employee—who had, in fact, been pimping men out of his Staten Island home. But Anthony was not among them.

The fingerprints didn't match anything in AFIS or elsewhere. This enraged Woodfield. "Here I've got a serial killer, and he's never been arrested? This is nuts."

In August 1993, *The New York Times* published a story about the murders, and a significant portion of it was about Anthony. In retrospect, that's a surprise. After Peter and Tom were killed, their hometown publications, including the powerful *Philadelphia Inquirer* and *The Boston Globe,* respectively, wrote about them in detail. Anthony's death, however, was largely ignored at first by the New York media, and had been the subject of only a few short articles in the *Inquirer,* the *Asbury Park Press,* and the *Courier-Post.*

Most of what is publicly known about Anthony's life is from the *New York Times* story. His brother, Louis, told a tale of drug addiction, a failed marriage, and general turbulence:

Roughly handsome and powerfully built, Mr. Morrero [*sic*] was a mystery to his family, reappearing after long absences, sometimes filled with stories of good fortune, other times asking for money. His brother traces the biggest problems to [the] break-up of Mr. Morrero's marriage in 1980, a union that was apparently strained by his desires for men.

"He started to travel around," said his brother, adding that Mr. Morrero also continued to see women. "He never stayed in one place. He went to Washington, to California to see our mother. He went to New York and came back. Sometimes we didn't know where he was."

Louis recounted a high point in the life of his brother, who dreamed of pitching for the Philadelphia Phillies. During an unspecified year, Anthony was invited to a daylong tryout. He was not asked back. "But he showed me the invitation to the tryout," Louis told the reporter. "He was very proud of that invitation."[1]

Around 1985, when he was in his midthirties, Anthony moved to New York City. For eight months in 1990, he worked as a custodian. It's not clear when he began hustling.

A few weeks after Anthony's body was found, detectives stopped actively working the case. Mohel and Hayes were assigned to other homicides and solved a few cases that summer. "We were constantly out on dead bodies," says Mohel. Teletypes trickled into the Ocean County Prosecutor's Office from various agencies with similar cases. They did not advance the investigation.

Meanwhile, in a little office in Chelsea, the small staff of the New York City Anti-Violence Project—an organization created more than a decade earlier in response to police indifference—was angry. The city was an increasingly violent place for the queer community. One of its key members, Bea Hanson, had contacted the New York Police Department nearly a year before, to inquire about the murder of Thomas Mulcahy, shortly after his body was found. After Anthony Marrero's body was found, she called again.

"Their response was nothing," she told the *Advocate*.

---

1 According to a representative of the Phillies, the organization has no record of Anthony's tryout.

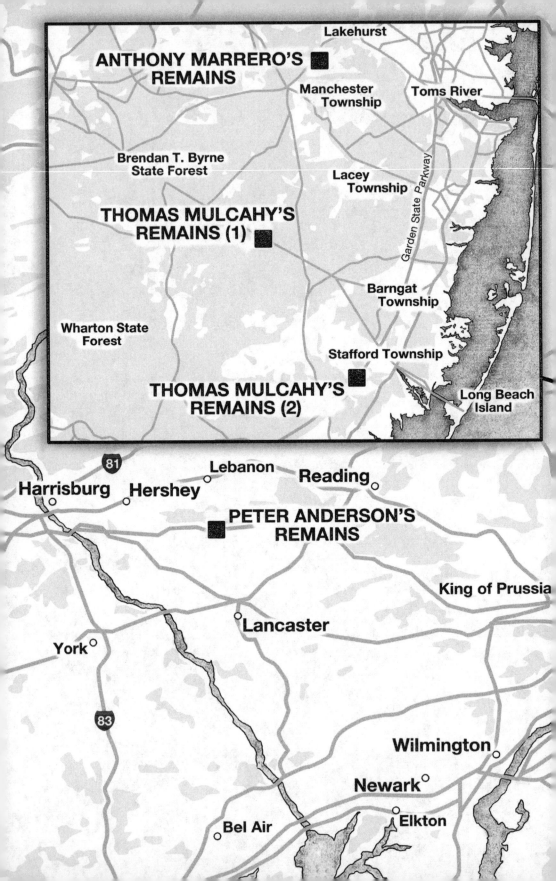

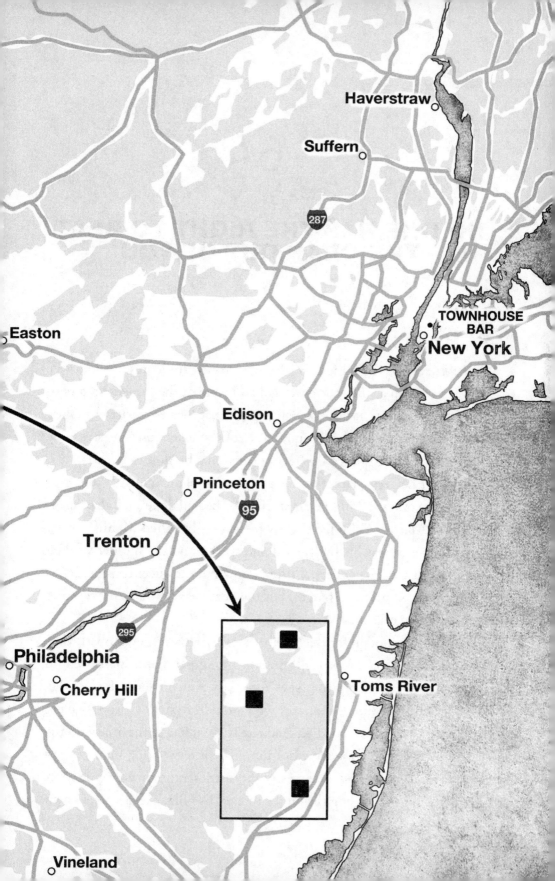

6

NO ONE HAS THE RIGHT TO BEAT THE CRAP OUT OF YOU

On February 23, 1985, Eigil Dag Vesti, a fashion student, was shot twice in the head with a rifle. The evening had begun at the Limelight, a popular Chelsea club that on its opening night had hosted a party by Andy Warhol. It ended in a Stony Point, New York, smokehouse—Vesti's body charred and bullet-riddled, his face encased in a black leather mask.

Bernard LeGeros, twenty-three and the son of a United Nations official, admitted to shooting Vesti but claimed he had done so under the influence of Andrew Crispo, a slightly pudgy, curly-haired Manhattan art dealer. LeGeros was his bodyguard and driver, and the murder weapon was found at Crispo's gallery. Crispo, known in the queer community as a sadist, evaded murder charges, but the next year he was sent to prison for income tax evasion.

This wasn't enough for the Manhattan district attorney, Robert Morgenthau, who wanted Crispo off the street for good. For help, he went to a fledgling organization, the New York City Anti-Violence Project. He asked, Could they find witnesses who would attest to Crispo's violent streak? Yes, indeed: a Canadian graduate student had spent time with the gallery owner and was terrified of him. The jittery young man was introduced to Linda Fairstein, an assistant district attorney now chiefly remembered for supervising the prosecution of five Black teenagers, known as the Central Park Five, for a rape they did not commit. She had run the sex crime unit for a decade. The student told her that, four years earlier, at Crispo's behest, four men—including LeGeros—beat him and demanded he provide the name of someone they could kill for a snuff film. When he refused, the men shoved his head in a toilet and made him sing "Happy Birthday." Crispo, already serving time for tax evasion, was charged with kidnapping. Despite the student's testimony at the trial, Crispo was, again, acquitted.

For the Anti-Violence Project, known colloquially as AVP, the Crispo case was a success, despite the acquittal. That it was considered a success reflected the low expectations queer New Yorkers had of the judicial system's handling of bias crimes. As an early AVP staffer put it, "We thought success was if somebody took any of this seriously." Indeed, that the trial happened at all was a result of AVP's fieldwork, some of which was beyond the scope of law enforcement.

The Anti-Violence Project was, at heart, a reaction to systemic apathy to queer life, and it began on the cusp of the AIDS epidemic.

In March 1980, three men in Chelsea were attacked by white kids wielding bats. One man lost two teeth; another sustained thirty-six stitches to his forehead, a damaged eye, and a broken nose. This did not make the local papers. Assaults of gay men were commonplace, and this one, at first, was no different. For months, men had driven in from New Jersey, Long Island, and the outer boroughs of New York City to throw bottles at Village and Chelsea residents who were presumed to be queer. Sometimes attackers would get out of the car, chase them down, and beat them. Reporting such violence to the police was considered not worth the trouble, for there rarely was any recourse. As an activist told the *Daily News* that December, "If you go to court and it's brought out that you're gay, the defense will make a bum out of you."

It is, therefore, difficult to accurately quantify the anti-queer violence in New York City during those years. In 1980, the NYPD claimed not to collect such figures. *Daily News* columnist Pete Hamill, writing the year before about protests of the movie *Cruising*, succinctly described the situation:

> Such violence has been common for a long time now; much of it does not get reported to the newspapers, or even to police (because many homosexuals remain firmly in the closet). Some of this violence is merely part of the texture of city life, a risk faced by all citizens. But some of it is clearly directed at homosexuals.

Official statistics aside, however, there's an evident trajectory. Between 1985 and 1989, the number of anti-queer incidents reported by local groups increased from 2,042 to 7,031. These figures are almost certainly on the low side. As for the nature of anti-queer violence: a paper, published at the beginning of the decade, argued that murders of gay men were characterized by an uncontrollable anger, present in nearly every case. "A striking feature of most murders," wrote the authors, "is their gruesome, often vicious nature.

"Seldom is a homosexual victim simply shot," they continued. "He is more apt to be stabbed a dozen or more times, mutilated, and strangled. In a number of instances, the victim was stabbed or mutilated even after being fatally shot."

The March 1980 incident is remembered, and would be repeatedly cited, only because of the fallout. The victims were escorted to the neighborhood's Tenth Precinct, accompanied by members of the Chelsea Gay Association. Formed in 1977, CGA was conceived not strictly as an activist organization but as a means for new, queer residents of Chelsea to meet each other and build a community. In practice, its membership was limited to hundreds of gay men and a few bisexual women.

Eventually, circumstances required radicalization. In Chelsea, law and order seemed not to exist, as exemplified by the beatings. CGA representatives demanded the Tenth Precinct place additional patrols on the streets, particularly before summer, when violence would surely increase. The precinct commanding officer refused, on the grounds that there was no need. In other words: *You're on your own.*

Six weeks later, sponsored by more than a dozen community groups, CGA held an emergency forum on the second floor of the Church of the Holy Apostles' parish house. "YOUR NEIGHBORS ARE ORGA-NIZING TO FIND SOLUTIONS TO VIOLENCE AND CRIME IN CHELSEA," read a flyer.

Among the attendees were city council members and neighborhood activists, including Thomas Duane, who would soon be elected state sen-ator but was, for the time being, selling advertising for the *New York Native.* Precisely what was said during the forum was never recorded, but the gathering had its desired effect—it demonstrated the consider-able strength of the attendees, who represented a burgeoning political constituency. As recounted in Arthur Kahn's *The Many Faces of Gay,* within days or weeks, activists secured meetings with the offices of the Manhattan district attorney, the chief of police, and the City Housing Authority. Within months, a spinoff of CGA was formed: the Chelsea Gay Association Anti-Violence Project.

The spinoff began in the apartment of Russell Nutter and Jay Wat-kins, who were described by a friend as "devoted to each other; a couple in every sense of the word." Within weeks, they were receiving tips from a hotline about anti-queer attacks, providing informal counseling, and helping victims grapple with the Victim Services Agency and other bu-reaucracies. "As time went on," a CGA board member wrote years later, "several of the volunteers learned quite a bit about the ins and outs of the various state and city organizations, and some became quite well known to police, district attorneys, and agency staff."

As news of the hotline spread, calls came in from throughout the city with reports of all manner of violence. It was a painful success. To meet the growing need, Nutter and Watkins scaled up, amassing a crew of forty volunteers to work out of a room subleased from a gay-owned real estate company. The pair continued to coordinate the volunteers, raise funds, and monitor the hotline. It was exhausting, and Nutter and Watkins were noticeably drained.

In September 1982, the *Native* reported the hotline was overtaxed and needed fresh volunteers. There were recent reports of entrapment by police patrolling the Jacob Riis Park bathhouse. Nutter estimated that 1,200 arrests had been made that summer alone. Hotline volunteers must be willing to talk to survivors for several hours a week, wrote the *Native*, and "[e]ssential characteristics for volunteers would include patience, understanding . . ."

That year, with the help of Duane, AVP received a grant of $6,000 from the New York State Crime Victim Compensation Board. A press release announced a new name and expanded ambitions: the New York City Gay and Lesbian Anti-Violence Project. In its short life, the release noted, the organization had documented cases of anti-queer violence in all five boroughs, dispatched volunteers to accompany victims of violence to the police, and worked with district attorneys' offices in Manhattan, Brooklyn, and Queens. Volunteers soon received reports of more than a dozen anti-queer crimes a week.

With its new funding and independence, AVP needed an inaugural executive director and found one in Rebecca Porper, a recent graduate of Manhattan's Union Theological Seminary. She was brought in to fundraise, make a name for the organization, shine a light on anti-queer crime, and act as a liaison with governmental entities—including the district attorney's office, the police, and the mayor's office—to whom, according to Porper, most of AVP's board was hostile: "They didn't know how to go about it except to scream at them."

Outreach to the police began at the precinct level, and had been one of CGA's initiatives since the beginning. Back then, when such sessions were called "sensitivity trainings," Lance Bradley, known primarily as a self-defense instructor, provided guidance to cops about anti-queer violence. AVP would eventually expand those services to neighborhoods in less affluent queer communities, such as Jackson Heights, Queens, and Park Slope, Brooklyn. But the initial focus was on so-called gay ghettos: Chelsea's Tenth Precinct and the West Village's Sixth Precinct.

Following the morning roll call, Bradley led discussions about crimes committed against his community. He told the officers why the city's queer citizens were afraid of them and what they could do to alleviate such fears. Trainings were not welcomed; Bradley and his successors were often ridiculed. Once, during a discussion of anti-queer violence, an officer sitting in the front row produced a pair of women's panties and began fingering them.

Decades later, when Porper reflected on her own training sessions, her view of their efficacy was measured. The chasm between the police and AVP was unbridgeable, she felt, and success was on the margins: "They didn't want to know from gay guys, at that time. They weren't so afraid of AIDS, but they *really* didn't like gay people. So my strategy was to simply say, *Look, guys. You come into my city. I pay you very generously. I give you training. I give you a uniform to wear. I give you health benefits that are the most extraordinary health benefits in the United States. In exchange for that, what I want you to do is take every thought you have about gays and throw them out, and treat the gay men and the lesbians that you meet as people. When you take off the uniform and go back to wherever you live, you can do whatever you want. But when you're in New York City: no.* Then they relaxed, kind of, because I wasn't challenging their preconceptions."

For years, the cops referred to Greenwich Village's Sixth Precinct as Fort Bruce. "It was a tongue-in-cheek reference to the gay community, in the fact that *Bruce* had gay connotations to it," says a retired policeman. More serious, and dehumanizing, was the police's insistence on calling AIDS "the gay disease" and donning gloves when handling anyone suspected of being afflicted. This reflected a fear of AIDS, but also a department-wide unease with queer New Yorkers.

The Tenth Precinct in Chelsea, which covered the west side of

Manhattan between Fourteenth and Forty-third Streets, was equally problematic. General corruption was an issue, of course, with many of its officers accused of taking payoffs from bars, clubs, and brothels. Where queer-related crime was concerned, the Tenth's response tended to be, *What did you do to deserve this?* The officers deployed a tactic from domestic disputes: mediation. As the *Native* reported, as an alternative to an arrest, a victim of an anti-queer crime who desired prosecution had to "serve a summons on his or her attacker to report to an Institute for Mediation and Conflict Resolution Dispute Center."

Despite such indignities, AVP calculated it was more productive to create a partnership with the Sixth and the Tenth precincts and appeal to their sense of decency, rather than act as a thorn in their side. *We're New Yorkers who need your services,* they told police. *We are being victimized because of who we are.*

In July 1985, ostensibly as an attempt to improve community relations, Mayor Edward Koch's office founded the Police Council on Lesbian and Gay Concerns, headed by Chief Robert Johnston. A big Irishman, Johnston was considered tolerant, to a point. He said all the right things and seemed personally empathetic, but he allowed his officers to arrest seventeen members of ACT UP during its first protest—of pharmaceutical-company profiteering—in front of Wall Street's Trinity Church. What ACT UP wanted was to protest long enough for media outlets to snap photos before police either dispersed the crowds or arrested those who refused to leave. As perhaps the only queer organization with a positive working relationship with the NYPD, the Anti-Violence Project served as an intermediary between the two parties. Johnston was asked if, from now on, the police would give the protesters more time. Sometimes they did.

The council, whose members included AVP, the transit cops, the DA's office, and Koch's gay and lesbian liaison, met every six weeks at NYPD headquarters, Manhattan's One Police Plaza. Individual cases weren't discussed, but Johnston brought in commanders to talk about precinct-level trainings, the AIDS crisis, and bias crime. In practice, it was as much for the benefit of the police as it was for the civilians, because it was in Johnston's interest to placate the queer community—particularly if he wanted to stay in Koch's good graces. As a colleague put it, "The last thing he wants is for people to call up the Mayor's office and say to Ed Koch, 'Hey, you know that guy, Johnston? He's a real pain in the neck.'"

Koch's representative was among a number of liaisons positioned as conduits between the city and the queer community. The district attorney's office had its counterpart, which grew out of Morgenthau's reelection campaign. The young woman, Jacqueline Schafer, was tasked with outreach to such organizations as Gay Men's Health Crisis and AVP, training ADAs on how to improve treatment of gay victims, communication on issues related to law enforcement, and, at least in the early days, accompanying victims to precincts to report crimes. Schafer was hired by ADA Fairstein, whose office's sex crimes unit oversaw more than five hundred cases a year. "There had been so many times when witnesses had come to the criminal justice system, and had not been met fairly," Fairstein recalled. From the DA's perspective, the liaison was a chance to say to the queer community, *You're going to be well met here. You're going to be listened to.*

A less charitable view of the councils and liaisons holds that they were, by design, incapable of serving the needs of the constituents. While queer New Yorkers believed liaisons existed to represent them to the mayor's office or the district attorney, observed an activist, "The truth is, in fact, exactly the opposite. These liaisons exist to represent the Mayor's office, the DA, and whomever else, to the community, and to essentially be apologists for those offices. Their job is to suppress community dissent, placate the community when the community is making demands of the powers that be."

During Porper's tenure, Morgenthau's office asked AVP to work with his attorneys on anti-queer-violence prosecutions. Such crime presented a challenge because the judicial system was only beginning to take these cases seriously. This was, in essence, a new kind of crime and required a new strategy for effective prosecution.

The prevailing defense in those years was "gay panic"—a defense against charges of murder and assault that enabled perpetrators of anti-queer murders to receive diminished sentences or even avoid punishment entirely by, in effect, blaming the victim. This defense had been commonplace for decades, going back to at least the 1960s. It tended to come in one of three variants of defense theory: provocation, in which the defendant argued that discovery of the victim's sexual orientation was sufficient to drive him to murder; self-defense, in which the defendant claimed that the discovery of the victim's homosexuality caused him to reasonably believe he was in grievous and immediate physical danger; and, finally, diminished capacity or insanity, in which the defendant argued that being made aware of the victim's sexual orientation induced a short-term mental collapse or mental breakdown, which spurred the killing.

A few months before he died at the age of ninety-nine, Morgenthau pungently described the gay panic defense as "that bullshit excuse."

To law enforcement, activists, and prosecutors, the arrival of AIDS appeared to intensify the use of the panic defense: queer people were being blamed for the virus. When a Los Angeles man was arrested for killing five men during the 1980s, he told investigators, "You don't understand, I want to get these men before they get me. They're spreading AIDS." Fairstein, for her part, isn't sure when she first encountered the gay panic defense, "but certainly in the 80s and certainly, to my mind, connecting to the timing of the AIDS epidemic."

A commonplace and, quite frankly, sensible fear of being outed made such cases difficult to prosecute and the defenses difficult to pierce. Victims, already mistrustful of the judicial system, were not always forthcoming with prosecutors about the circumstances of an assault. They could be reluctant to admit even to being gay, or simply denied that a sexual overture turned violent. When they did disclose their sexuality, it might not be until a second or third interview with an ADA. It was an awful quandary: victims who told the truth would be outed, potentially have their lives ruined, and possibly not see justice done; but if they kept quiet, the perpetrator would remain free. Some cases, says Fairstein, "you couldn't even take to court, because the opening story wasn't credible. It was heartbreaking. Unless you could explore the truth in a courtroom, you knew they were going to lose."

AVP's goals for the district attorney's office were, in retrospect, modest. "We had to make the ADAs understand that, just because you're leaving a gay bar late at night, no one has the right to beat the crap out of you," says an early AVP staffer. There was neither moral nor legal justification for harassment and violence. In training sessions with the attorneys, AVP drew a comparison between sexism and heterosexism: *When you approach a female survivor, do you blame her for what she was wearing?* they would ask. *Do you blame her for where she was late at night?*

Ermanno Stingo, who often ran the training sessions, also headed up AVP's court monitoring program. David France, the journalist and filmmaker, wrote about him in his landmark history, *How to Survive a Plague*:

> A courtly figure in his mid-sixties, with a square head and one crooked front tooth, he took up "court monitoring," as he called it, on his own initiative after retiring as a personnel director. Several mornings a week, he fixed a pink triangle to his suit and planted himself on courthouse benches around the city in silent vigil, hoping to influence judges and jurors.

AVP helped prosecutors prepare victims for hostile, often pernicious and accusatory cross-examinations. The preparation itself was frequently an uncomfortable experience for the victim, so AVP served as a support system and suggested to the lawyers less offensive lines of questioning. Some were more eager than others to embrace the guidance. John F. Kennedy Jr., for one, was immediately receptive to suggestions about cross-examination prep. Plaintiffs respected him, though they were occasionally too enthralled. In one instance, an older man was beaten, and Kennedy conducted his interview. During the debrief, Stingo asked how it had gone, and the man reported the interview had gone well, but for the distraction of the ADA's hair.

Kennedy obtained a conviction.

In October 1985, Rebecca Porper was burnt out and left AVP. She was replaced as executive director by David Wertheimer, an alum of the city's Victim Services Agency and a lecturer in pastoral theology at Yale. Wertheimer was compassionate and charming, and as adept with the press as with the municipal bureaucrats. He took the relationships forged by Porper, strengthened them, and expanded the organization's programming: a same-sex domestic violence program, one of the first in the country, was added in August 1986, and a program for male sexual assault the next year.

As ever, the workload continued to expand: 247 victims in 1985, a 41 percent year-over-year increase. The cases included seven homicides, fifty-six robberies, and twenty-two sexual assaults. In the first seven months of 1986, AVP tabulated 263 crime victims—fourteen homicides and seventeen sexual assaults. AIDS, it seemed, had indeed turbocharged anti-queer violence, with a third of it explicitly related to the disease.

In June 1986, the United States Supreme Court ruled in *Bowers v. Hardwick* that Georgia's criminalization of oral and anal sex—in practice and intent, homosexuality—was constitutional. At a protest in New York a week later, a young AVP staff member told the Associated Press, "Young people growing up gay all over America must now feel that they are also growing up criminal."

A few months later, however, there was significant movement in another branch of government: the House of Representatives. After a push from Barney Frank, the representative from Massachusetts, John Conyers, representative of Michigan and chair of the House Subcommittee on Criminal Justice, convened a hearing on anti-queer violence. It was the first of its kind. "I don't think [Conyers] was an activist on behalf of the gay community, but he wouldn't have needed powerful persuasion," says Kevin Berrill, then the director of the National Gay and Lesbian Task Force. Berrill, who organized the hearing, helped choose the slate of men and women who testified, which included Wertheimer, the NYPD's Robert Johnston (chosen to give the hearing credibility with law enforcement), Diana Christensen of Community United Against Violence, University of California, Davis's Greg Herek, on behalf of the American Psychological Association, and three survivors of anti-queer attacks.

Among them was Robert, who lived in Maine. "I am here to tell you about my ordeal as a gay man," his testimony began. For eight months, Robert had been followed by a group of men who persistently threatened him, verbally and physically. He'd gone to the police fifteen times to report the incidents and to court for a restraining order. Rather than back down, the men promised to "kill the faggot." Robert borrowed a gun. Two days later, the men surrounded his house and began to kick the door in. Again, he called the police. "Apparently they were busy," he told the lawmakers.

Robert told the police he would "take care of it myself," which, he assumed, would induce a response. It did not. As the men continued to kick the door, Robert grabbed his gun and again called the police. He looked out his third-story apartment window and saw men out front. *There is no way I can get out of this apartment except to jump,* he thought. It would be better, he decided, to face the men. After all, they might light the building on fire. So he went downstairs and opened the door. "He's out here!" yelled a man. As the group advanced on Robert, he fired the gun into the air. This did not have its desired effect. He brought the gun down and, having no firearms training, accidentally shot one of the men, who crumpled to the ground. While attempting to push back the crowd, Robert then unintentionally shot and killed the injured man.

The state police picked Robert up and took him to the station. They saw the complaints he'd filed. They saw that nothing had been done in response. They let him go. "Three weeks after the shooting, I went to the man's grave who had decided he wanted to kill me," Robert told Congress. "I knelt in prayer, put my hand over his grave, and I told him I forgave him for his hatred and wanting to kill me."

The hearings led to H.R. 3193, a bill sponsored by Conyers to "provide for the acquisition and publication of data about crimes that manifest prejudice based on race, religion, sexual orientation, or ethnicity." It is almost certainly the first time queer Americans were officially represented in a piece of federal legislation.

Despite Wertheimer's efforts, the Crispo case, and the congressional hearings, AVP struggled to attract mainstream media coverage for anti-queer violence. There had been fine reporting in the *New York Native* and the *Advocate*—small but influential queer newspapers—but little beyond that. In November 1986, however, Wertheimer got a phone call from William Greer, a young reporter at *The New York Times*. Greer said he had been talking to a colleague who wondered if there was a story in violence against gay Americans.

"I have been waiting for your call," said Wertheimer.

The story, headlined "Violence Against Homosexuals Rising, Groups Seeking Wider Protection Say," ran on page 36 of the Sunday paper. It began:

> Attacks on homosexuals appear to have increased sharply around the nation in the last three years as homosexuals have become more vocal in their pursuit of civil rights and more visible because of publicity surrounding the spread of AIDS.

Wertheimer believes that story marked the first time anti-queer violence was taken seriously by a mainstream publication. That was progress, of course, but, as with the American Bar Association's official condemnation of anti-queer violence in September, it was incremental.

The situation in New York, both city and state, was dispiriting. In May 1987, factions of the New York Police Department publicly opposed gays and lesbians populating their ranks. "We're against homosexuals in the Police Department and in the community," said the president of the Jewish Shomrim Society. "It's a shame we can't get moral people on the job," said an officer from the Irish Emerald Society. "Cops do mind working with homosexual officers," said an officer from the Catholic Holy Name Society. In a letter to Johnston, Wertheimer criticized the "outrageous verbal acts of bias violence."

The refusal of police societies to embrace gay and lesbian colleagues—or even to see them as upstanding, moral people—coincided with further evidence that gay men in particular were being scapegoated for the existence and spread of AIDS. A young man on his way to a Gay Pride Day parade had his jaw broken by five men who called him a "filthy AIDS carrier" and a "faggot." In New York City alone, incidents of beatings, knifings, rapes, and threats against gay people grew by 83 percent between 1985 and 1986. The virus, a sergeant from the NYPD's bias unit said, "has undoubtedly had an effect on the number of attacks." Visibility, too, could be a factor; several years earlier, a lurid CBS News documentary, "Gay Power, Gay Politics," was credited with a dramatic spike in violence.

Worsening matters, lawmakers in Albany were disinclined to treat anti-queer violence as equal to other forms of violence. A Black man named Michael Griffith, twenty-three, died after a dozen white men in Howard Beach chased him onto the Belt Parkway, where he was struck by a car. In response, Mario Cuomo, New York's Democratic governor, and the assembly speaker attempted to pass a measure that would strengthen sentences for bias-related crimes. Republicans opposed the bill because of its inclusion of gays and lesbians. Without such a provision, Wertheimer told the *Daily News*, the bill would be "a potent anti-gay statement and a tacit condoning of anti-gay violence."

This was soul-crushing work. Wertheimer hung in for two more years.

AVP staff amassed a record of effectively, if gently, prodding the NYPD, both the precincts and the police chief himself. In 1990, they got involved in the investigation of the killing of James Zappalorti, a Vietnam War veteran stabbed in the chest and throat by two men. "They killed Jimmy because he was gay," his father told a reporter. "But he was a good gay, not a pervert. He would never harm anyone."

It was, perhaps, thanks to Zappalorti's status as a "good" victim that local lawmakers felt compelled to respond. Mayor David Dinkins, Manhattan Borough President Ruth Messinger, and Council President Andrew Stein demanded the state legislature approve a bill that would, reported the *Daily News*, "create a special class in the penal code for racial, ethnic, religious and sexual orientation bias crime." The Zappalorti murder was the first in New York prosecuted as an anti-queer crime.

That summer, Matt Foreman, AVP's new executive director, and Bea Hanson, another recent hire, were at loggerheads with the 115th Precinct in Queens. Foreman, hired in January 1990, had been counsel to the Corrections Commissioner of New York, and had considerable criminal justice connections. Hanson, who joined AVP the same year, had worked in the Bronx doing tenant organizing. Their AVP was barely recognizable compared to the early days of Rebecca Porper; there was now a staff of ten and funding was provided, in part, by private dollars.

That July, Julio Rivera, a twenty-nine-year-old gay Puerto Rican man, had been set upon by three men, who bludgeoned him with a claw hammer and stabbed him, fatally, with a knife. A month later, the NYPD still hadn't declared the Rivera murder a bias crime. The police believed the killing was the result of a drug deal gone bad and stuck with the theory even after they learned the suspect had been telling people he'd killed a "cocksucking fag."

"You could not have had a more classic gay-bashing case," Foreman told a reporter. "I think they branded Julio as a Latino, drug user, hustler and therefore not worthy of anything." Eventually, the Queens district attorney took over the case; two of the men were charged and convicted of second-degree murder, while the third took a plea and was convicted of manslaughter.[1]

The Zappalorti and Rivera murders taught AVP that drafting family members to speak to the press generated publicity and empathy for the victims. Rivera's brother and sister-in-law became the public faces of the crime. In the Zappalorti case, his brother, a staunch Catholic, talked to reporters. "It was incredibly helpful to us," says Foreman.

In July 1992, the AVP was working around the clock, nights and weekends. On any given day, the staff was taking part in a demonstration or planning one. "We felt we had a responsibility to the community to try to improve safety, and to let them know when there was risk out there," Hanson says.

After the murder of Thomas Mulcahy, Foreman and Hanson contacted the NYPD. Whereas New Jersey detectives took calls about, and evinced interest in, anti-queer crimes, their New York counterparts did not. The NYPD, Hanson told the *Advocate,* was unresponsive and did not convey a sense of urgency about solving these crimes. After Anthony Marrero's body was found in New Jersey, AVP did its own legwork on the investigation, visiting Port Authority bars to scrounge up information. They again contacted the NYPD. The absence of response, Hanson told the reporter, was "indicative of their response to gay-related pickup crimes—too little, too late."

---

1 The murder convictions were overturned four years later, on account of procedural errors.

NYPD detectives argued their lack of involvement in the initial investigations was simply a matter of jurisdiction. There was something to this: Peter Anderson's body was found in Pennsylvania; Tom's and Anthony's remains, in New Jersey. Absent a primary crime scene, jurisdiction— despite the initial encounters being in Manhattan—was dictated by where the bodies were left. But a veteran detective who worked with the NYPD on the investigations doesn't believe it. "Let me tell you something," he says. "If you had a pie, and it had eight slices, and a third of one slice had something to do with the NYPD—and it was politically expeditious to be involved—they'd be involved a hundred percent."

In addition to keeping tabs on the murders, AVP was dealing with a curly-haired, thick-necked predator known to pick up gay men in bars, only to rob and beat them. AVP, to the man's chagrin, flyered Chelsea with WANTED posters, and coined a term to describe such incidents in which queer New Yorkers were assaulted by men and women they took home from bars and clubs: "pickup crimes." AVP saw the respective murders of Peter and Tom as both bias crimes *and* pickup crimes. "They were an easy target because they're intoxicated. It was a hideous, grisly, preplanned murder that targeted gay men," says Foreman. AVP hadn't a clue who had done it, but there was discussion about what sort of person would be capable. As a pickup crime, it was most likely someone who was conflicted about being gay. "There was an internalized hatred of gay people," Hanson adds. "A need to show, *I'm a man. I'm not gay myself.* It's got to be personal."

After Anthony Marrero was murdered in May, AVP—fully aware that three gay men had been victims of a single murderer since 1991—could have been forgiven for assuming that whoever ended Anthony's life would not strike again soon. After all, it was more than a year between Peter's and Tom's deaths, and just under a year between the killings of Tom and Anthony.

But the next one, in fact, would occur in just a matter of months.

7

I'LL BE SEEING YOU

July 29, 1993

It had been a slow Thursday night at the Five Oaks, the little bar at 49 Grove Street in Greenwich Village. Lisa Hall, a short, mouthy blonde who acted and sang, was behind the bar. An off-duty bartender, Barbara Ross, sat in front. At 10:30, regulars filed in for a birthday party. Among them were Dominick, a bisexual man who split time between Manhattan and Allentown, Pennsylvania; Richard, an ex-dancer who owned a furniture store; and Sal, who owned a travel agency. Greg sat at the bar, too. He was friends with Hall, and was there to see her. There was little room even to stand. Marie Blake was on the piano and the patrons were singing. "It was boisterous and loud," Greg recalled.

The Oaks, founded by Bill Normand in the late forties, had long been known for its menu (a "true gustatory delight," reported the *Brooklyn Daily Eagle*), its music (Nina Simone, it was rumored, accompanied customers on the piano), and as a sanctuary. Since the bar's inception, Normand's wife, Mae, cultivated a loyal crowd of queer regulars, mostly couples. At the century's midpoint and for many years thereafter, it was dangerous for gays and lesbians even to hold hands in public, so the basement establishment without so much as a window—virtually invisible from the outside—provided a measure of protection.

In 1976, Normand sold the Five Oaks to a trio of semiregulars. Tom Regan, a professor of chemical engineering, and his wife, Ginger, not only lacked bar and restaurant experience—they didn't even live in New York. But they were young and loved the city. So they uprooted, refinanced the house, and went into business with Jeremy Burrell, who'd worked for the restaurant Serendipity 3. Burrell ran the front of the house, and Tom, whose professional life had been one of exactitude, kept a ruthless eye on the books. Tom and Burrell convinced waiters and bartenders in the Theater District to send crowds downtown to the Five Oaks when their bars closed, at midnight or so. In the early years, great business was done between 1 and 4 A.M.

The new owners didn't tamper with their customer base. Although the bar attracted straight people, typically devoted to Marie, the business's bread and butter was middle-aged and older gay men, grateful for a safe, warm, noncruisy place to enjoy dinner and a drink.[1] Tom, in fact, soon realized he was among their number. After several years, he came out of the closet, sold his share of the bar, and left Ginger.

At 11:30 P.M., Hall belted out a few songs, including Peter Allen's ode to ending a relationship before it withers, "I'd Rather Leave While I'm in Love." Ross, the off-duty bartender, became upset about something and went home.

By 1:00, the birthday guests were gone. Then Ross called. She'd left her apartment keys at the Duplex, a couple of blocks away, but before retrieving them planned to stop by the Oaks again. She was greeted by an old friend: a big, bearded regular, well over six feet and two hundred pounds, named Michael Sakara.

Michael, it was often said, was to the Five Oaks what Norm was to

---

1 Even so, recalled Michael Musto, "there was a sexual energy in the air, even if you were just there to sing show tunes."

Cheers. Every night except Mondays, when he didn't come to the bar, Michael ordered round upon round of Cutty Sark and water. The last stool at the end of the horseshoe bar was his. From that vantage, facing the street, he could see everyone coming down the entrance steps. He sang the same song at the end of the evening and acted as the social director, making introductions. "I spent more time with him than anybody else in the world at that point in my life," Hall would testify. Having worked at the Five Oaks on and off for more than a decade, she had known Michael since 1976, and across the years they'd become close.

From 2:00 to 2:30 A.M., the only people seated at the bar were Michael and Ross, who read his horoscope, as was her custom. They bickered like siblings. She was worried about him, that he drank too much. Which was true; he could down three scotches in an hour. Michael thanked Ross for her concern and offered to retrieve her keys. This was unusual; it was not his practice to leave the bar before closing. Michael was gone no more than ten minutes, and when he returned with the keys, Ross left.

It was the early hours of July 30, and the Five Oaks was mostly empty. Marie Blake, half an eye on the entrance, was still playing. Last call was soon, at 3:45. Around this time, Michael would usually walk over to the piano and ask Blake to play a number about romantic nostalgia. The song, by Sammy Fain and Irving Kahal, had been popular during World War II, but more recently was embraced by Liberace. It began:

I'll be seeing you in all the old familiar places
That this heart of mine embraces all day through

The bar officially closed for the night in fifteen minutes, but patrons could stay to finish their drinks. This was later than most restaurants in the area, so bartenders, too, would stop by for a round after their own shifts ended.

Shortly before last call, a man descended the thirteen steps and entered the bar. He sat down to Michael's immediate left and requested the house scotch and water. Hall sized him up: white guy, maybe five foot nine. Average build. Wore a blue button-down shirt and had his sleeves rolled up. She guessed he was in his early thirties, and would, when questioned by detectives, remember his thick, wavy hair and "brown glassy eyes."

Other patrons had seen the man around the bar, and had even gone home with him. Hall, though, didn't recognize him. But she assumed he and Michael knew each other; why, after all, would you sit next to a stranger in a near-empty bar? Hall, in fact, would later speculate that perhaps they'd run into each other at the Duplex.

"This is Mark the nurse," Michael said, ordering a scotch and water. "He works at St. Vincent's."

The men talked, but Hall couldn't hear the conversation. The nurse seemed drunk. Hall was wary of the man, as she was of any new customer who came in just before closing time. There was an increased chance of being robbed by a late arrival. Still, she was grateful Michael had company. She loved him, but he required a lot of attention. *Thank God,* she thought, *he has someone to talk to now.*

Sitting nearby was an editor from *The New York Times.* He came to the Five Oaks twice a month, venturing downtown after work. Preparing to move out of the city, he had come to say his goodbyes. The newsman knew Michael and could see he was lost in conversation. "Engrossed in their own little world," is how he described it years later. He also knew the man talking to Michael, having gone to college with him in the 1970s. They'd run into each other in September at the Townhouse and had crossed paths a few times since.

But he let the two men be and said nothing.

Hall had a lot of work to do and turned her back to the bar so she could wash glasses, count money, and take inventory. She carefully wrote down the bottles she'd used that night.

Peripherally, she could see Michael and the nurse still in deep conversation.

It was finally time for last call. A dozen new customers had arrived, maybe more. If you bought a drink between two and four in the morning, you got a second one free, so Hall was busy.

"This is it," Hall announced.

"I want everything," replied Michael, which is what he always said. He'd downed twelve scotches already and had eaten nothing. Sometimes he and Hall shared a dinner, but not tonight.

As for the nurse: he professed to be done for the evening, on account of having to drive home. But then he changed his mind and ordered another scotch and water. Hall noticed he hadn't finished the first drink, so she watered down the second with ice.

Just after 4:00, Hall collected her tips and took the candles off the bar. She grabbed Michael's leather briefcase from the cubbyhole, where he always stowed it. As Hall placed it on the bar, she noticed condoms inside. That was strange. Michael wasn't the type for one-night stands and had been, until recently, in a long-term monogamous relationship.

Fifteen minutes later, Hall and Marie Blake left the Five Oaks, got into a cab together, and flew up the west side of Manhattan.

Barely a day later, at 7:00 A.M. on July 31, a man collecting bottles and cans at a Haverstraw Bay overlook found a briefcase and a bag holding shoes, pants, a shirt, and a wallet identifying the belongings' owner as Michael J. Sakara of Manhattan. The man considered keeping the bounty, but looking at the personal papers gave him an eerie feeling. He deposited his discoveries at the police station in Haverstraw, a sparsely populated village an hour north of Manhattan.

A few hours later, Ronald Colandrea, forty-eight, arrived at the overlook, at the lunch truck he owned and operated on Route 9W, a highway running north to south through New York's Rockland County. The parked truck hugged the guardrail just before a bend in the road and was emblazoned with the words RON'S BEST. That morning, he stopped for coffee and then shopped for supplies. He got to work at 10:30, just as a light purple van was pulling out. Colandrea's family had sold hot dogs on that very spot since 1943, going back to his father, Anthony, an immigrant from Naples. Colandrea knew precisely how much garbage ought to be in the four fifty-five-gallon trash barrels near his truck on any given day.

The barrels were emptied the prior morning. But that Saturday, when Colandrea returned to the overlook, he found the barrel nearest to his truck almost full; it should have been one-third full, which was how he left it on Friday. Colandrea inspected the contents, hoping to find the address of whoever left the garbage. This wasn't out of mere intellectual curiosity; he was inclined to dump garbage on the lawn of those who used his barrels without permission.

Resting near the lip was a green plastic trash bag tied in a knot. Colandrea partially opened it, and wooziness overtook him.

Staring up at him was a face.

The head, double-bagged, had been sliced off but not cleanly, about an inch below the closely trimmed beard. Colandrea looked further. He found a set of arms, cut off well below the shoulder, fingers clenched in a loose fist. They, too, were double-bagged. The arms, Colandrea would remark, "were cut nice and even, like butchering a cow."

At 11:15 A.M., he enlisted a customer to drive to the Haverstraw Police Department.

The first patrolman on scene was skeptical. "You think there's a head in the barrel?" he asked Colandrea. But when he donned gloves and opened the bag, he, too, felt ill. The patrolman called his command, which, in turn, contacted the Rockland County Medical Examiner. The Rockland County District Attorney's Office also was notified. It wasn't their case by statute, per se, but the Haverstraw police lacked the capacity to investigate a murder.

Detective Stephen Colantonio, a decade into his career with the DA's office, arrived within a half hour. He lived eight miles away, in Nanuet.

Dark-haired with a dimpled chin, Colantonio exhibited a tendency toward self-improvement. Now in his early thirties, he'd earned a bachelor's degree in criminal justice and a master's in public administration. He'd been studying karate for years and was a student instructor at the local dojo. The martial art, he told a reporter, "teaches you self-control—maintaining your composure."

Colandrea's truck was familiar to the detectives, who picked up hot dogs when they went to a nearby shooting range. It was clear the body parts hadn't been there long. Even the hot dog vendor could see that. "He had to be dumped overnight," he told a reporter. "It was still fresh and there were no flies." This was soon confirmed by the medical examiner, who, peering into the garbage bags, pronounced the body parts "very fresh." The crime scene was elsewhere, the detectives realized, because there were no signs of a struggle, and no blood on or outside the trash barrel.

The police presence was not good for Colandrea's business. Once customers found out why the truck was swarming with lawmen, their appetites waned. "I couldn't eat hot dogs now," said an elderly woman. Locals pulled up to the crime scene tape, asked police why they couldn't get to the food truck, and left. As police worked, a mile-long stretch of 9W was closed off so police dogs could search for additional body parts.

It didn't take long for a desk sergeant to tentatively match the photo on the ID found earlier at the overlook to the face in the bag. With that identification, detectives put together a teletype announcing the prosecutor's office's recovery of body parts. It was sent out late that night to surrounding areas in the hopes of finding similar cases. In the meantime, however, detectives continued to search for the man's torso and legs, and began the investigation in earnest.

Hours later, Colantonio and his colleagues were in Manhattan. They checked in at the local precinct and went to Michael's apartment at 771 West End Avenue. The studio, which he'd lived in since 1964, was cluttered. They ventured into the bedroom and found on the dresser a tray of matchbooks and business cards. There was a *TV Guide* on an end table, opened to the day detectives believed Michael had last been home. They didn't know yet what they were looking for and didn't really have a plan. But the detectives determined the apartment was not a crime scene, so they split up to collect evidence and interview the doorman and neighbors. The doorman hadn't worked in the building long, but he was knowledgeable. Until seven months ago, he told them, Michael lived with another man. It was common knowledge they were a couple. "His lover would sometimes be dressed like a woman when he walked out of the building with Mr. Sakara," he told a reporter.

The detectives continued to gather information. Absent lab results, fingerprint analysis, and an autopsy, all they could really do was learn about the victim's life. "You work backwards," Colantonio said years later. "Who was he? Where did he work? Where did he live? Who was he associated with? Did he have family? Where are they? When was the last time they saw him?"

Michael's parents, unfortunately, were in no condition to be helpful. Mary Jane was hysterical, Michael Sr., known in the family as Big Mike, was outwardly unemotional, but inwardly devastated. It fell to his sister, Marilyn Sakara, who was twelve years his junior and lived in Santa Fe, New Mexico, with her partner, to answer some of the more rudimentary questions.

Michael was born in Youngstown, Ohio, on September 19, 1937. He was a lively ten-pound baby, and a precocious infant. The Sakaras lived in a home with a big backyard and a three-car garage on the South Side, bought a few years after Michael was born. The house was large enough that, originally, it had been divided into four apartments—two on the ground floor, two upstairs. They converted the downstairs into a living space and rented out the upstairs.

Neither parent graduated from high school. Big Mike made it as far as third grade, Mary Jane to eighth. He was a machinist for the steel company McKay-Wean, while she worked as a waitress and a cashier at discount stores around town. Both had difficult upbringings. He had been incarcerated at the Ohio State Reformatory in his early twenties on a robbery conviction. He claimed innocence and, years later, when he and Marilyn went to the grocery store, he stole little things like bologna. In his view, this righted the scales of justice. As for Mary Jane, her father wasn't around and her mother was poor. The family didn't have much more than chickens and a cow, and as a child Mary Jane sold eggs and worked as a house cleaner. She quit school, in part because not having decent clothes to wear was embarrassing.

Big Mike and Mary Jane "participated in domestic violence," as Marilyn carefully put it. The effects of such violence rippled, and Michael, too, was a victim. The father-son relationship was particularly corrosive, as Big Mike could barely stand to be in the same room with his son. But Mary Jane could be antagonistic as well. Once, when Michael was a teenager, she went after him with a cast-iron frying pan. As they ran through the house—lightly decorated with photos of the family members Mary Jane actually liked—he had an epiphany: at six feet, he was far taller than his mother. He no longer had a reason to fear her. Michael stopped, pivoted, and said, "Don't you ever do that again." She relinquished the frying pan and walked away.

Mary Jane is generally remembered fondly. Big Mike, however, is recalled—at best—as a "grumpy, tightwad son of a bitch," but mostly as an equal-opportunity bigot who openly despised anyone who wasn't heterosexual and white. When he and Mary Jane bought their home in 1940, Youngstown's South Side was nearly all white. But then, beginning in the fifties, cities across the country enacted urban renewal programs. In Youngstown, Black neighborhoods were bulldozed, and residents were driven into historically white neighborhoods. This trend angered Big Mike, who openly referred to his new neighbors as "niggers." Michael's disenchantment with his father was so complete that, as an adult, he called himself Michael Sakara II, rather than punctuate his name with Jr.

In 1949, a sister was born. In Marilyn's earliest memory of her brother, she is three, chasing Michael around the house. "He had these huge, long legs. He'd climb over the back of the couch, and I couldn't do that so I'd have to go all the way around." She adored him, and he was protective of her. He was doting but didn't lavish her with gifts, save for the occasional candy bar. A Christmas in the mid-1960s, when Michael put three joints in his jacket and smuggled them back to Youngstown, is a fondly remembered exception. Marilyn relied on her brother's stability because "he was saner than my parents."

Looking back, it's clear that Michael was an unusual child and adolescent. He took an obsessively broad, fickle approach to interests. Marilyn remembers him cycling through hobbies: African violets one month, tropical fish the next, then calligraphy. He sketched and painted, too, just like his father, who tried to tutor him. But it didn't take, as the mutual aversion was unrelenting. When he was drawn to a subject or activity, whatever it was, Michael wanted to know everything about it and would read whatever he could get his hands on. He was, his sister says lovingly, a nerd. Eventually, citing the cost, Big Mike and Mary Jane declined to fund their son's hobbies, so he took a paper route.

From the start, Michael was inclined toward music and theater. Which made sense. He was, said his mother, a "handsome cuss." He played the piano and accordion. Marilyn would crawl into the accordion case because she liked the soft, pink, furry liner. He was in South High's a cappella choir and stagecraft club. Senior year, with dreams of Broadway, he played David Kingsley in a production of *Stage Door* and appeared in shows at the local playhouse. "He carried himself well," said a classmate. "He had a lot of poise."

Big Mike and Mary Jane were aware Michael was studious and smart, and believed his success was inevitable. He was a member of South High's Honors Society and even skipped a grade. The Sakaras wanted their son to have the education they lacked. *Go to college,* they told him. *Become a doctor; make money.*

They wanted him to marry, too, although surely they knew that was a pipe dream—even when Michael dated Daryll, a tall, blond, buxom girl. They adored each other, but members of the family assumed the relationship had an expiration date. When Michael left for the army, Daryll was heartbroken, and was likely unaware that he was attracted to men. There were family members who sensed he was *different,* even if they couldn't explain exactly why. "From the earliest years, I knew Michael wasn't a regular guy," said his cousin, "but I didn't know what that meant."

Neither, in all likelihood, did most of Youngstown.

The Youngstown of the late 1950s was raucous—a city that was no stranger to the mob, gambling, and murder. Indeed, *The Saturday Evening Post* famously dubbed it "Crimetown U.S.A.," and reported that officials "hobnob" openly with criminals and that arrests were infrequent.

The mob was originally attracted to Youngstown at the beginning of the twentieth century because of its growing economy. The nation had a near-ravenous demand for steel, and Youngstown was considered the capital of "Steel Valley," where mills clotted the edge of the Mahoning River. They employed burly men like Big Mike Sakara, men who over the years had been shot at by Pinkertons and put their lives on the line for a paycheck. They were pro-union and pro–New Deal but culturally conservative. Many believed women should stay home and feared the city's growing African American community would result in a "Black Youngstown."

Naturally, there was no room for any population other than heterosexuals. And yet, as in any sizable town or city of the time, gay life established a vibrant, quasi-underground presence. According to Dharl Chintan, this was the case among Youngstown's "thriving little metropolis" of 160,000 residents.

Dharl, born in 1942, is the keeper of Youngstown's gay history, which so far resides only in his memory. In his teens, when he was a strapping, handsome redhead, Dharl began visiting, moving there for good in 1962.

At first, he worked in a steel mill. In the mid-1960s, when the mills began to fade, he landed at General Motors Corporation's assembly complex in Lordstown as a union official. He handled the dues and finances for the twelve thousand members. He kept the job for nearly three decades.

In his off-hours, Dharl frequented Youngstown's gay hot spots. To be queer during this period was to keep a secret from the world at large. For good reason: in Ohio, as elsewhere, queer people were treated as either a curiosity or a menace. "Dayton Population of Homosexuals Reported Rising," read a *Journal Herald* headline in 1965. The story quoted the director of Dayton State Hospital, who worried that gay men weren't clearly identifiable, and seemed to blame them for being assaulted. "Homosexuals do migrate to a city, where there is less chance of detection, and where easy contact can be made with others with abnormal tendencies," he said. "And such migrations naturally result in an increasing crime rate in those cities."

It was, then, a gamble to be out of the closet beyond the comfort of the bar. In 1962, two men grabbed Dharl outside a bar in Warren, about fifteen miles northwest of Youngstown, and beat him. They knocked out four bottom teeth and cut his lip so severely it had to be sewn back on. Rather than take his complaint, police advised Dharl to keep quiet, as one of his assailants was the son of a police sergeant. No arrests were made.

The closeted life was prudent, and most queer Youngstowners reluctantly adopted it. Neither friends nor family would know their secret. There was a pervasive fear of one's parents finding out. The forced discretion imbued the bars and clubs with great importance. Within those walls, gay men tended to be left alone. They held hands, they kissed, they danced. It was the sort of ordinary life that couldn't be practiced elsewhere. This was a freedom afforded largely because bar and club proprietors paid police, rather than Youngstown's famous mafia, for the privilege. Unlike their New York counterparts, who controlled the Stonewall Inn, the Youngstown mob didn't invest in "finocchio bars," and their interest in straight bars was limited to establishments trafficking in prostitution or gambling.

Dharl tended bar on West Federal Street at the American Bar. Founded in the late 1950s, it was probably the city's first licensed gay bar. The American, as it was called, was in a saltbox with clapboard siding, close enough to the street and traffic that using the front door was a health hazard. In one room were booths and a wraparound bar running the length of the space. In another room were a kitchen and dance floor. A jukebox played constantly as patrons drank beer and wine. "It wasn't fancy," says a patron. "It was a typical, low-grade bar." After a few years, the bar caught fire but did not burn down. It resumed business for a while—Dharl, in 1964, met the man who would be his husband as he served drinks—until the state bought the property. The American was leveled to make way for an expansion of Route 422 from two lanes to four.

On the south side of the city, on the corner of Hillman Street and Falls Avenue, was a Sokol club. The second floor was ostensibly a branch of an old Eastern European gymnastics organization. But the ground floor was a private gay club. It was run by two brothers, a fireman and a policeman, who were straight but saw a business opportunity. It was a divey place, with drag shows every Saturday night. Patrons, as they entered through a door in the back, gave the bouncer a secret phrase. The secrecy was warranted: one Saturday night, a cinder block was thrown through the front window. Farther down Hillman was a gay social club called the Veterans of the Second War. The association with the military was pure convenience, as it was easier to open a social club than a bar. It was nicknamed the Parachute Club because sewn-together parachutes hung from the ceiling to mask the pipes.

After the murder of Martin Luther King Jr. in 1968, Black residents reportedly threw Molotov cocktails at police and set cars aflame throughout Youngstown's South Side. Two patrolmen were shot. There were riots the next year, too, when a white store owner was accused of hitting a pregnant Black woman. Days after the National Association for the Advancement of Colored People picketed the store, a shop on the East Side was firebombed. "The violence spread across the city," reported a local journal. "When fire trucks came to put out fires at businesses, they were attacked as well." In the wake of the violence, Hillman residents fled and businesses closed, including Veterans of the Second War.

These bars in Youngstown, like those in the rest of the state, had what were called short licenses and closed at one in the morning. But fifteen miles west was Lake Milton, a dam completed in 1917, several years after a four-day rain engulfed the Mahoning Valley. On its shores were gay bars with long licenses, and they didn't close for another hour and a half: the Party Bar, the Shore Inn, and Tommy Dalton's, which was run by an agreeable older lesbian named Dorothy. Men would visit on summer Sundays. One night, Dharl swam across the lake, naked and drunk.

To the queer communities of San Francisco and New York, Youngstown must've seemed like the sticks—not anyone's first choice. Indeed, many of Dharl's friends left for the West Coast, for what they called the Emerald City. They wanted freedom without distress. But the desire to leave wasn't universally shared. In fact, aspects of queer life in coastal cities seemed downright unappealing. The Stonewall riots in the summer of 1969 shocked Dharl and his friends. They were used to watching the local cops bounce in and out of the bars, cradling envelopes and bottles of liquor, and rarely bothering the patrons. They didn't understand the level of police harassment that went on in New York. That Manhattan's queer population couldn't drink without hassle was bizarre. From afar, it appeared "they were rioting for the right to be left alone."

In hindsight, says Dharl, that was "sort of a protective naivety."

Michael Sakara was not deterred by any of this. He wanted the New York life, and he wanted it yesterday.

* * *

"He was too big for Youngstown," said a cousin. When Michael was sixteen, just before graduation, Big Mike and Mary Jane returned home to find their son and his friends partially dressed, drunk and laughing. Their suspicions of his homosexuality hadn't exactly been confirmed—they were ignorant of their son's affection for the older man across the street—but the evidence was mounting.

Michael graduated from South High in 1954. Rather than go to college, he enlisted in the army, where he served as a medic. All that survives of his records is the certification of service, which shows that on April 4, 1958, after three years in the ranks, Michael was terminated by "undesirable discharge." Exactly what that meant isn't certain. However, in the 1950s, gay men were considered susceptible to blackmail and, consequently, a national security threat. In the army and other branches of the military, "undesirable" was often code for queer.

For Michael, the discharge was a personal humiliation. Moreover, it was an outing. He told his family, and later his friends, that he'd been caught messing around with a man. Confronted with Michael's homosexuality, Big Mike wasn't supportive. Mary Jane made peace with it. Still, rather than return to Youngstown, Michael moved to Arizona, where he took premed courses. The stay was brief, just long enough for Michael to send his mother a throw rug.

By April 1961, Michael was living in the West Seventies in Manhattan. That month, he was arrested for an unspecified "lewd act" and acquitted, though it's not clear on what grounds. After a few years, he moved to a rental on West End Avenue. When the building was converted to co-op in 1980, Mary Jane gave him money to buy the apartment. She loved Michael, despite a profound disappointment that he would never give her grandchildren.

Not much is known about Michael's first fifteen years in New York. More than a decade after his murder, though, an essay provided a window into that period. A friend who lived a few blocks away, Ann Murray, wrote about their relationship and circle of friends.

They met in 1969, when Ann's mother was dying. "The circumstances of our meeting were awkward and highly charged," she wrote. By Ann's account, they cared for each other and talked frequently. ("We were only a sneeze apart.") She paints a portrait of a man comfortable in his own skin, unfamiliar with half measures, and eager to introduce her to the finer things. Ann and Michael would play chess together. She never won. ("He never criticized me for playing poorly.") They shared meals. He introduced her to escargots, frog legs, bananas flambé, high-end alcohol, good wine. ("There were so many sophisticated adventures between us. I felt as though I were being groomed in a sense.") Michael taught her to lie on the floor wearing headphones to hear music, so she could feel the vibrations. Years later, when Ann bought the best equipment she could afford, that's what she did.

They smoked marijuana. Michael introduced her to mescaline:

And he pulled me across the divide toward recognition that I was in fact, safe and sane in his arms in spite of my terror of the moment. He held me until I got back to the world uninhabited by nightmare visions.

Friends assembled for drinks and conversation at Michael's apartment, with its red walls and abundant liquor and a poster of Theda Bara, in the kitchen. Many were in the arts: music, theater, writing. Ann recalled an evening when an opera singer serenaded the crowd, accompanied by a man on the piano. "Michael's shiny black grand piano sat at the end of the living room in front of large windows," she wrote. "It was a beautiful scene, with her singing against a backdrop of New York lights and big potted plants." A photo from the mid-1960s shows Michael embracing Eva Pryor, his best friend, who is smiling in a big red dress as they stand at the intersection of the bookshelf and the baby grand.

As Ann tells it, hers was an "ugly-duckling, un-dated, un-courted existence," but Michael wouldn't let her stay blue. He raised her spirits as she mourned her mother, taking her to dinner and treating the outing like a date. They talked into the night and fell asleep on his couch.

After Ann left New York, she called Michael. She'd been married, but that was done, and she was moving again. Michael said he was sorry about the marriage but pleased for her new home. Then they lost touch. In 2006, more than a decade after the murder, Ann found a news report about Michael. "I discovered it just a couple of hours ago, and I am going mad from it," she wrote, and began recording her memories for posterity.

I will also always remember the sun rising across the water as we rode the Staten Island Ferry back home to the City during my first trip, as the drug's effect wore off. I will always remember the flowers I bought at a sidewalk stand, and carried with me, just to look at the color of them all through the night. I will always remember the early breakfast at The Brasserie on 53rd St. as we made our way back to so-called real life. I can taste the coffee, I can hear our laughter at the night we'd passed as strange wanderers, and I can see his smile.

In 2016, Ann died in hospice.

While living in New York, Michael returned to his parents' Youngstown home only for short visits, usually during the holidays. Roger Danchise, his cousin, lived on the top floor and was a quasi brother to Marilyn. Michael, he thought, was cosmopolitan and exciting. He took Roger and Marilyn around town in Mary Jane's push-button Plymouth Valiant. "Whenever Michael showed up, the party began," recalled Roger. "He was full of life. He never sat still."

In New York Michael had come into his own, and his happiness made an impression on people back home. Richard Jonesco, a friend of the family, met him in the late 1960s. He had heard a lot about Michael but didn't often see him in Youngstown. They met up at the Five Oaks when Jonesco moved to Long Island. "I didn't know I was gay at the time, but I knew *he* was and that's where I was leaning," he says.[2]

Jonesco considered Michael to be distinguished, suave, talented—a quintessential New Yorker. Gay, yes, but not "a flaming queen." Michael was everything a gay man should be, he felt: "I could see being gay is not that bad." In the late 1970s, Jonesco took friends from Youngstown to the Five Oaks. Michael was at the bar, so he went over to say hello. They reminisced. Then Michael got up, lumbered over to the microphone, and acted as the evening's emcee. He played the piano and sang in a tenor. The Youngstown crowd was impressed. "I was awestruck," says Jonesco, "because I didn't know he sang."

By the early 1980s, AIDS had hit the Mahoning Valley. Officially, anyway, it took a while for the disease to spread. Midway through 1984, the state's Department of Health would cite only one fatality, a man from Trumbull County. But the hospitals quickly learned to convey that AIDS patients weren't welcome. The staff of St. Elizabeth's wouldn't touch them and was reluctant to even breathe the same air. One of the first Youngstowners to perish was a professor at the local college. He died at home, surrounded by friends. There were heroes, too, including a primary care physician who developed standards and protocols at Warren General Hospital.

It was around this time that Michael, who was generally reluctant to introduce friends and lovers to his family—including his first real boyfriend, about whom little is remembered except that he hailed from Lancaster, Pennsylvania—brought Jim Baffin to Youngstown.[3]

Baffin, skinny and shy, was in theater, and had for years been a production stage manager for an off-Broadway revue. He, like Michael, had a beard, though his was light and blond. He looked like a cowboy. They

---

2 Jonesco briefly dated Marilyn during high school, and they joke they "made each other gay."

3 This name has been changed.

were together for nine years, breaking up only seven months before Michael died.

Given his closeness to Michael, it wasn't a surprise that Baffin was, for a short time, a suspect. Detectives talked to him the night they found the body. He told them his ex wasn't the type to pick up men. Michael never had money, Baffin said, living paycheck to paycheck. He was a pack rat. He disliked sex toys and preferred anal or oral sex. He was risk-averse. A week later, apparently rattled, Baffin talked to the *Daily News* and professed his innocence. In the photo accompanying the story, he looked dazed. "They asked me what time I'd last seen and spoken with him and where I was Thursday through Saturday night," he told the reporter. "They asked me if I knew anyone Michael knew with a blue car and, maybe, a blond wig. They asked if we knew anyone with a deformity or any transvestites frequenting the Five Oaks."

Baffin believed Michael had likely known the killer. Michael was very cautious, he said. "He wouldn't have gone with him if he had just met him."

"I'm hoping I'm not a suspect any longer," he said. "I didn't do it."

The detectives assembled the basics of Michael's life in the first days after Colandrea's discovery. From Baffin they learned that, six nights a week, Michael would go to the Five Oaks. This prompted a labor-intensive process of determining which patrons had been in that bar on the night of July 29 and the morning of July 30, and interviewing them all. The result was a detailed four-page account of the night's events.

Statements continued to be taken from those, like Baffin, who were closest to Michael. Eva Pryor told them about her best friend's love of Scrabble, how dishonesty offended him, his capacity to type 120 words a minute, how he realized he was gay during his tour in the army, that he never followed through on anything, that he considered himself an intellectual.

They examined Michael's work life, too. He was a member of the powerful International Typographical Union since 1973, and for the last year he had been a typesetter for the *New York Law Journal*.

In the days of hot type, you couldn't hear much over the machines, but now the composing room was pretty quiet. The men didn't talk much—their relationships rarely transcended the workplace—but they were fond of complaining about the paper's publisher, who was, all agreed, "a pain in the ass." While they kvetched, Michael sang and talked, says a composing-room colleague. "He was gregarious. He'd talk to anybody."

By the 1980s, most of the industry had converted to photographic typesetting, including the *Law Journal*. Michael worked in the composing room, where copy was sent to him by editorial. As a keyboarder, he worked at a device that resembled a typewriter but produced a coded paper tape. Instead of *clack clack clack* like a traditional typewriter, it emitted a *zoop zoop zoop*. Michael would tear off the paper tape, which had holes in it representing letters, numbers, and punctuation, and walk it over to the photographic typesetting machine. He put the tape into a reader, which automatically selected the letters, exposed them onto photo paper, and justified the lines. The exposed photo paper came out into a light-type cassette, which Michael placed into a chemical processor that developed the image. Once dried, it was put onto boards by paste-up artists. The boards had to be sent to the printer in Westchester by the 8 P.M. deadline. Then the *Law Journal* was shipped, first to the post office and then to subscribers—lawyers on whose desks it appeared first thing in the morning.

Five days a week, except on court holidays, Michael and the rest of the typesetters worked for a couple of hours past deadline, inputting the court calendars for the next day's paper, before leaving for home or a bar. The composing-room guys knew Michael went to the Five Oaks after work each day. They knew what that meant—that he was gay—and he didn't try to hide it. Most weren't accepting of Michael's sexuality and would talk behind his back. It was, in general, an intolerant and somewhat retrograde group. When an editor became pregnant, her condition was a source of chatter in the composing room. "It's like they had never seen a pregnant woman before," says a staffer. "And God knows they had never seen one *work*."

It was clear from what Michael's colleagues told detectives that, in his short time at the *Law Journal,* he had made an impression. "A thinker, discussed philosophy," said one. "Held very strong opinions and would quickly engage in debates and discussions," said another. "Very meticulous and organized," said a third.

The detectives continued to interview Marilyn, Michael's sister. She, too, had left Youngstown. In 1971, she went to graduate school and married a man two years later. The union was short, and she eventually moved back home. In July 1977, she visited Michael in New York when the city, still reeling from Son of Sam, lost power for twenty-five hours. Marilyn watched the garbage pile up. Later that year she moved to New Mexico. The year before Michael died, she met Karen Gaylord. They began to date.

In 1993, Karen journeyed to Manhattan to visit a friend. But she had a further purpose. She had heard all about Marilyn's tall, handsome brother, and intended to make his acquaintance. They met at the Five Oaks, of course. Michael greeted her with a massive embrace. Karen, slight at five foot two, immediately took to calling him Huggy Bear. She watched him play the piano and sing. His voice was beautiful. They talked for a bit and drank scotch, which was Karen's favorite, too. He was, she decided, a sweetheart. "Our encounter was probably no longer than two hours."

Michael was dead within ten days.

Marilyn and Karen cleaned out his West End Avenue apartment. Michael had many papers and books. One was *Course in Miracles*, the New Age curriculum by Helen Schucman. Lisa Hall got Michael hooked on the book in 1990. Being surrounded by drunks for so many years had taken its toll on the bartender, and she'd been doing some soul-searching.

She couldn't stick with it, though, because it was so intense. Michael, however, was devout. "My brother just loved it," says Marilyn. "It was a positive view on life."

In November 1990, Michael inscribed two copies of *Course in Miracles*. In gorgeous cursive, he wrote:

> *Dear Marilyn,*
>
> *Have a Very Happy Birthday, Baby Sister. It sure is good to see you again.*
>
> *I've been racking my heart and mind since I stopped working in April '87 and decided to take my midlife crisis off. This curriculum—one of the most important books I've ever come across—is helping me restore, repair, remember, and wake up.*
>
> *I'm learning to "live the Course" more and more thoroughly as I go along—started it in March 17 this year—but still have a way to go.*
>
> *Thought you might be interested in what your big brother is up to.*
>
> *All my Love,*
> *Michael*

The next day, he inscribed another copy:

> *Dear Mom and Dad,*
>
> *A Very Happy Thanksgiving Day to you.*
>
> *In case you've been wondering what your prodigal son has been up to since I was fortunate enough to be able to "drop out" in April '87 and thoroughly enjoy my midlife crisis, this Course is the latest— and the best.*
>
> *I've made a lot of reparations so far and done a lot of forgiving, and I still have a way to go. This book—one of the most important*

I've ever come across—has helped me to understand the mistakes
I've made and to remember who I am and what my purpose is. I've
worked hard to learn this curriculum, and I still have more to do to
live up to principles and wake up all the way, but I'm willing.
     I hope you will find this as interesting as I have.

All my Love,
Michael

The family was surprised Michael latched on to the course. The Sakaras weren't notably religious. Mary Jane had been baptized Catholic, but she was a restless believer and skittered from faith to faith without settling. By the time Marilyn was born, religion had been jettisoned, more or less, and she wasn't baptized. But the course made Michael happy, so she was pleased for him.

When Hall found out Michael had been murdered, she wondered if the course provided her friend with some solace at the end. "Nothing real can be threatened. Nothing unreal exists," according to the text. Hall hoped that, to Michael, death hadn't seemed real.

Dr. Frederick Zugibe began a truncated autopsy on Michael on July 31, the day the body was discovered. He inspected the severed head and arms, which is all he had so far. A local boy, graduating from Haverstraw High School in 1946, Zugibe had been chief medical examiner of Rockland County since 1969.

The parts were in good condition, with little decomposition. He x-rayed the head and noted a comminuted fracture of the skull, which can only be caused by high-impact trauma. He often saw this type of injury in cases of car accidents. Years later in his testimony, Zugibe likened this to cracks on an egg, because the skull was fractured into multiple pieces. His external examination of the head revealed what appeared to be wounds caused by a heavy object, because there was blunt force tearing of the soft tissue. His findings on the internal examination of the skull showed crevices that would have been made by a heavy and sharp object, such as a hatchet or machete, and caused brain bleeding and swelling.

Zugibe proceeded to the face. There was a star-shaped cut on the left forehead and other lacerations on the back of the head.

Last, he examined the arms, which were cut through the humerus just beyond the respective ball joints. The soft-tissue cutting was a little choppy, and there wasn't much bruising, which suggested that Michael's heart had stopped beating when the arms were removed. The bone surfaces were smooth, which to Zugibe meant the weapon of choice had been a smooth-bladed saw.

A few days after Michael's body parts were found, the medical examiner talked to the *Journal News,* which reported the victim had "likely died from numerous blows to his head with a blunt instrument" and the body had been disassembled just a few hours before the initial discovery.

Then the investigations collided. On August 2, after two days of work on Michael's case, the Rockland County Prosecutor's Office had visitors. A half dozen New Jersey state troopers, in response to the July 31 teletype, filed into the squad room. They wanted to talk about the fresh case, but also one of their own.

8

THE LAST CALL KILLER

August 2, 1993

When Stephen Colantonio walked into the Rockland County district attorney's squad room on Monday, three days had passed since the investigation of Michael Sakara's murder began. An admirable amount of work had been done since the victim's head and arms were discovered on Saturday, but basic questions surrounding the killing were still unanswered. Even the scene of the crime was elusive, in part because the rest of Michael's body was still missing. He could have been killed anywhere, the Haverstraw police chief told reporters, so his men were searching "every can and Dumpster from the George Washington Bridge to Bear Mountain."

The squad room, in a three-story redbrick building behind the courthouse, was packed with law enforcement in suits. New Jersey staties, mostly, including a trio of major crime detectives—veterans of the Thomas Mulcahy and Anthony Marrero investigations. They came bearing a message: *Let's join forces.*

Nicholas Theodos, a formidable detective, was their leader. Since being anointed as 1981's Trooper of the Year at the age of twenty-eight, he'd worked drug busts, kidnappings, and homicides. *High Times* named him among the top ten troopers by whom readers would not want to be stopped. Theodos was experienced in homicide investigations in general and task forces in particular, having worked on the Green River and Jeffrey Dahmer cases and, more recently, the apprehension of a serial rapist in East Orange. He'd come to Rockland County to convince the district attorney to authorize a joint investigation. He had visuals: a slideshow, assembled over the weekend, demonstrating the similarities of the Sakara case to the Mulcahy and Marrero cases: the dismemberment, the garbage bags, even the manner in which the bags were knotted.

This was persuasive to Kenneth Gribetz, Rockland County's handsome, flashy, headline-generating district attorney, who enjoyed the publicity of big cases. Each year, he picked a noteworthy or spectacular case to prosecute himself. This, it seemed, would do nicely; a task force of such profile and magnitude was, for a county that rarely saw more than a dozen homicides in a single year, monumental.

Headquartered on the third floor of the DA's office, the task force was made up of more than two dozen investigators from Rockland County, New Jersey State Police, Ocean County Prosecutor's Office, and the Haverstraw and Manchester Police Departments. This was a sought-after assignment, with media attention, cars, overtime, and the expected satisfaction of solving a serial murder being powerful incentives.

Investigators were overseen by self-described "house mouses" Theodos and Colantonio. The rest had varying degrees of experience—Haverstraw's detective, for example, held the rank for only a year. But nearly all involved had some connection to at least one of the cases in question. The men (almost all were men) were assigned partnerships that were intentionally disruptive: a New York cop with a New Jersey cop, or a detective who worked the Mulcahy case with one who hadn't. The hope was to minimize groupthink, and the probability that detectives would "hot dog it"—try to break the case on their own.

There was immediate, albeit minor, disagreement over which cases to include. One faction saw Mulcahy and Sakara as the connective thread: two men from white-collar professions, disposed of in the same manner.

This faction was skeptical about Marrero. He was, owing to his status as a sex worker, and a low-end sex worker at that, an outlier among the victims. The physical evidence also differed; the bags containing his body parts were not left in a trash barrel, a deviation from the prior cases.

Mark Woodfield, the ranking Ocean County detective on Marrero's case, was adamant that it was connected to the others. "In my mind, there was no doubt about it," he recalled. "Just because he wasn't a married, hidden homosexual with a great job—he was murdered, dismembered, and discarded almost identical to the others." Woodfield argued years later that, because Marrero turned tricks in Port Authority, he was intensely vulnerable to a predator, and that made it *more* likely his case was linked. Whereas Mulcahy and Sakara had been plied with alcohol, all that would have been necessary to lure Marrero into a car was fifty dollars.

A second, larger bloc of investigators asked to exclude the 1991 murder of Peter Anderson. There had been a report that, upon leaving the Waldorf Astoria, he hailed a cab and returned to Philadelphia, where he had been spotted. The rumor was not substantiated, but it sowed just enough doubt. After all, no one could definitively say where Peter had gone, so who's to say this didn't happen? There was also the matter of modus operandi: although his penis had been severed, Peter, unlike the rest, suffered no further dismemberment. The counterargument was that he was small, so dismemberment—which seemed to be motivated by convenience rather than sadism—had been unnecessary. Ultimately, the phantom sighting in Philadelphia relegated Peter's case to the periphery.

The task force was up and running on August 4. Optimism pervaded the command post, a room filled with push-button phones, half-eaten food, and a bulletin board on which were pinned photos of the dead men. "We thought we would have this guy in custody within a couple of weeks—we were *that* confident," recalls Theodos. Confidence seemed warranted: they had witnesses, physical evidence, and a nearly minute-by-minute timeline of Michael's day before he went missing. The perpetrator seemed to have slipped up, too. Picking up a beloved patron from a small bar and allowing himself to be introduced to the bartender—and, in the process, cementing in her mind that he was a nurse—was an unnecessary risk. Maybe he was getting careless. The consequences of identifying his killer would be enormous, as it was assumed solving Michael's case meant solving *all* the cases.

Almost immediately, investigators found a witness: Eugene Williams, a skinny homeless man with long dark hair and a white beard who slept at Bellevue men's shelter. He had seen Michael, clad in a black T-shirt and black pants, carrying a briefcase under his arm, in the company of a man leaving the Five Oaks. This was, it was assumed, the very man whom Lisa Hall, the Five Oaks bartender, described to investigators a few days earlier. He was, Hall said, a nurse named Mark, or possibly John, and he worked at St. Vincent's.

As Williams sat in the drab interview room in Rockland County, he told Detective Jack Repsha of the New Jersey State Police that he and a pal had been standing outside the bar, panhandling. Around 4 A.M., out walked Michael and a companion. Thirty to forty years old, between five ten and six foot tall, clean-shaven with blond hair, and wearing a white shirt or jacket with white pants. "A medium-sized guy who's in good shape. He wore glasses, aviator glasses," Williams said. He told Repsha he wasn't sure about the shoes.

Williams had asked Michael, who appeared to be "high," for a couple of dollars. Michael claimed he didn't have any money. As they talked, the blond man went to his car, which was white. As he started the ignition, they kept talking. The man got out of the car.

"Come on, Mike. Let's go," he said.

"Okay," said Michael, turning to Williams. "I'm going upstate."

Then he got in the car, and the pair drove away.

An interesting and credible statement, thought Repsha, *but you always want a corroborating source.*

Two days later, Robert Smith, a second panhandler, gave the investigators another account of the events. Early that morning, Smith said, he and a few acquaintances, including Williams, were in front of the Five Oaks. They were waiting for Marie Blake, who often gave homeless people money. When Blake came out of the bar, she got into a cab and left. After five to ten minutes, Michael and a man exited the bar. Smith recalled him as slim, in his forties, six foot tall, and with blond or light brown hair. He wore a button-down printed shirt, light-colored pants, and glasses. A panhandler asked the man for money. Just as he was reaching into his pocket, Michael rebuked him.

"I will not contribute to their lifestyle," he said.

It seemed to Smith the man wasn't much of a talker, and was markedly less inebriated than Michael. The pair got into a sky-blue compact with New York license plates parked in front of the bar, and were gone.

Smith was questioned by Donna Malkentzos, one of the half-dozen detectives sent by the NYPD, which joined the task force two days in. Raymond Kelly, the police commissioner, had little choice but to lend his detectives to the investigation.

"I felt like I served two purposes," Malkentzos recalled. As a lesbian, with short dark hair, prominent eyebrows, and a wide smile, she was considered useful for interviews—witnesses were more likely to trust a lesbian detective who'd been on the bias crime unit—and an olive branch to activists, who harbored doubts about the NYPD's commitment to solving the murders. It was a suggestion Malkentzos resented: "When you work homicide, you don't give a shit who's dead. It's your *ego*. You want to get the son of a bitch."

Smith's testimony was trustworthy, Malkentzos believed. Sex workers made the best witnesses, because being watchful was part of the job. But the homeless, if they weren't mentally ill, were useful, too. Anyway, Smith had no reason to lie because Malkentzos had nothing to offer. He simply wanted to help.

The next evening, August 8, a volunteer fireman was riding a motorcycle on Route 9W in Stony Point, nine miles north of where Michael's face and arms had been found. He stopped at a pull-off and smelled something "foul." An aspiring cop, the fireman decided to investigate. He found a bag containing deer bones. Something, however, was not quite right about the smell, so he continued to look around. Peering over a cable guardrail, he saw four green plastic trash bags. Lifting one bag, he saw the outline of a human leg straining the plastic.

He had found the rest of Michael Sakara.

Until now, stories about the murders had largely been relegated to home-town newspapers. Tom's death garnered coverage in Boston, while Peter's had gotten press in Philadelphia. Despite the nature of the crimes, traditional New York media, which typically delighted in writing about gore, evinced little interest.

The day Michael's last remains were found, the most high-profile story on the case yet was published on the front page of the *New York Times'* Metro section. Written in a few hours, the feature effectively introduced the city to the four murdered men, as well as a fifth, unrelated victim. The lede was sweeping, lyrical, and accurate: "They spanned the broad experience of gay life, a life led with a current of tension and secrecy under even the most tolerant of circumstances." The young reporter, who decades later remembered the story only because it was written the very day he met his future wife, portrayed Peter, Tom, Anthony, and Michael with great empathy. The reporting, much of it done by old newsroom hands, brought the victims to life, through their aspirations, professional associations, and families. It was a small masterpiece of crime journalism.

The interest in the murders was, for the Anti-Violence Project, an opportunity to publicize the case and pressure the NYPD. "Gay men and lesbians have been killed for a long time, and it is just a low priority with the police," Bea Hanson told a Philadelphia reporter. It seemed to be a low priority with the New York mayor's office, too. AVP felt it had not treated the murders, or similar crimes, with sufficient urgency.

Gay men were routinely being preyed on in bars. Often the incidents were the work of men conflicted about their own sexual orientation, Hanson believed. It was a manifestation of self-hatred—which, in an era when gay men were being blamed for a plague, was not uncommon. AVP began pasting up flyers in bars around the city as a preventative measure. *"LOOKING FOR A GOOD TIME?"* they asked.

♂♂ *Get the boy's name.*

♂♂ *Chat him up.* You don't need to interrogate him, just find out a little bit about the man you're bringing home: where he works or goes to school, where he lives, what he likes and doesn't like . . .

♂♂ *Be proud of your catch.* Introduce him to your old and new friends, and to the bartender.

♂♂ *Do you believe in moderation? Like to drink when you go out?* Remember, alcohol and drugs cloud your judgment. Think about alternating drinks with water and soda. Think.

♂♂ *Last dance? Last chance. Don't let desperation rule your night.* But, if you leave with someone, make sure he knows that you told a friend that you left with him.

♂♂ *My place? Your place?* Where does he live? If you go to his place, make sure you know how to get home, and have money to get there. Go where you feel safer.

♂♂ *Trust your instincts.* If something feels even a little off with this guy, move on, make an excuse with a smile. It will happen again—tonight or another night.

Hanson and her boss, Matt Foreman, began planning a press conference. AVP had already taken aggressively visible action, hanging effigies
dipped in red paint from light poles in the Village and around City Hall.

As it happened, the press conference was set for the very day the
fireman found Michael's legs, upper torso, and lower torso. On August
8, Foreman, Commissioner Kelly, and Mayor Dinkins stood at Manhattan's Gracie Mansion. They announced the expedited launch of Safe Bar,
a campaign to educate gay men on the virtues of caution; New Yorkers
were advised to watch their drinks, introduce anyone with whom they
were going home to a friend or bartender, and announce where, precisely,
they were headed.

Foreman looked on as Dinkins, who had once described his city as
"a gorgeous mosaic" of race, faith, and sexual orientation, addressed the
crowd: "We do not know if a gay serial killer is stalking our city, but we
do know that over a two-year period the dismembered bodies of five gay
or bisexual men have been found, and that four of them were last seen
in New York City gay establishments." As Joseph Borrelli, the chief of
detectives who sixteen years earlier handled the Son of Sam investigation, stood behind him, Dinkins continued: "While this is not a time for
panic, it is a time for mutual concern."

The next day, Mike McAlary, the *Daily News'* swaggering police-beat
columnist, gave the murderer a pungent moniker. "Your name is the Last
Call Killer, and you fear no man," he wrote. "You are to gay men what
Son of Sam once was to young brunette women—a stalking hunter to
be feared." The body count would rise, McAlary warned, and he identified why the string of murders had been ignored in his hometown: the
quality of the victims. Had they instead been young brunette women, he
wrote, hundreds of reporters would have questioned an incensed mayor.
Instead, it was open season.

You are not going to frighten the city the way Sam did unless you
make a mistake, and kill someone you *think* is gay. . . . Chop up

one boozy Nebraska yahoo on his way out of a Greenwich Village piano bar and the city will belong to you.

Lisa Hall was on the subway when she saw someone reading that day's *Daily News*. She broke down in tears.

Between the press conference, the flyers, and the newspaper stories, the city's queer community was now paying attention. For one young, closeted regular of Village bars, the murders forever altered his dating life. "It was a vague and ominous threat to the gay community of the West Village, and the piano bars specifically," he said years later. "It definitely affected my likelihood of going home with somebody. That persists to this day."

"Everyone's frightened," a bar owner told the *San Francisco Examiner*. A reporter who wandered into the Five Oaks, which was beginning to lose customers, found patrons unsettled. "Nothing like this has ever happened in our little corner of the world," said a manager.

Now that he had Michael Sakara's entire body, Frederick Zugibe performed a complete postmortem examination on August 9. He was intrigued by the double bags and double knots. These measures were familiar; they indicated experience with handling large quantities of blood. One bag would be too thin and could tear, but a double knot was a precaution against leakage. When he and his investigators went to a crime scene, Zugibe would tell a courtroom, "we usually use double bags for the same reason."

Extracting the legs and lower and upper torso from the bags, Zugibe found them severely decomposed. Maggots and flies were present, and he noticed skin slippage. Factoring in the condition of the body parts, as well as the temperature both outside and inside the bags, he estimated the time of the killing: seven to seventeen hours before Michael's head and arms were found near the hot dog vendor in Haverstraw.

There was another odd element to the autopsy: Zugibe chose to keep this information from detectives.

Nicholas Theodos was not amused by this decision. His next morning's daily update captured his exasperation:

DR. ZUGIBE WOULD NOT ALLOW INVESTIGATORS FROM THE TASK FORCE TO WITNESS THIS POSTMORTEM EXAMINATION. DR. ZUGIBE <u>ALLEGED</u> THAT THERE WAS A POTENTIAL HEALTH PROBLEM.

Theodos's troopers from the major crime unit were dismissive of the doctor's excuse. The task force needed answers. *Had the body been dismembered, or had it been, in the manner of Thomas Mulcahy, disarticulated? Were the cuts made by someone left-handed or right-handed?* Attending the autopsy wasn't a mere formality for the New Jersey State Police—it was protocol. Each detective in the unit was a trained morgue assistant who had spent a month working at the medical examiner's office in Newark and was capable of assisting the doctor, if necessary. They were used to the open door of Doctor Nat, and had not anticipated that attendance at Michael's autopsy would be restricted. As they saw it, the secrecy wasn't good for anyone; a detective in the autopsy room could explain aspects of the body's condition using knowledge from the ongoing investigation. In a forensics case, this exchange of information was particularly critical.

Zugibe was in possession of not only Michael's body but also the garbage bags. Ordinarily, within a couple days after an autopsy's conclusion, he turned over evidence to the Rockland County Sheriff's Department's Bureau of Criminal Identification. This was the expectation here, too—that he would give BCI the bags to be dried, photographed, and examined for fingerprints. Instead, he told the troopers he wanted to dry them out first. That was, to be fair, understood as his right. As medical examiner, Zugibe was in charge of a crime scene, and thus the physical evidence. He relished this responsibility. "You have that evidence because

I *let* you have that evidence," he would say. Zugibe's territorial nature wasn't news to the Rockland County detectives, who knew better than to request admittance to the autopsy. But it enraged Theodos, who confronted the doctor. "Why should I share the information?" Zugibe told him. "I don't have to share the information with you!"

Theodos turned to Peter Modafferi, Rockland County's chief of detectives, for help.

"Pete, he won't talk to me. But you're the chief, he's *got* to talk to you," said Theodos.

Modafferi hadn't seemed fully engaged with the case, and there were rumors he was cooperating with the FBI on an investigation of his boss, Gribetz. Still, Modafferi and Zugibe were close, and that relationship could perhaps be leveraged to help the task force.

Modafferi agreed to play the intermediary, and to convince the medical examiner to, at the very least, turn the evidence over to his counterpart in New Jersey. Zugibe, though, did not care for this suggestion. He found the idea of giving up his jurisdiction to another medical examiner absurd, and his anger spilled over into the squad room, causing a scuffle.

"Hit me, hit me!" he taunted Modafferi, poking the younger man in the chest. Zugibe was much shorter, and stood on his tiptoes. "Hit me, hit me!"

Modafferi didn't laugh, but it took some effort. The two men would not speak to each other for the next year.

A couple of weeks later, Zugibe reported that Michael's blood alcohol was .18, which was high. Eventually he told investigators that the cause of death, which occurred nine to ten days before the legs and torso were discovered on August 8, was trauma to the head. In addition to stab wounds in the chest, inflicted while Michael's heart was still pumping, he had found ligature marks on the arms. The legs had been removed below the ball joint. The legs, like the arms, had been sawed off, he thought, with no attempt at disarticulation. Summoning up the Mulcahy case, Zugibe found a copy of *The New York Times* wrapped around the thigh. The Gray Lady had served, presumably, as a blotter.

Meanwhile, Zugibe still refused to relinquish the bags, so Colantonio contacted the FBI, which offered to dry and process them. On August 25, the evidence—a box with slimy, greasy bags—was extricated from Rockland County and driven to the FBI laboratory in Washington. Alas, the FBI proved no more responsive. Weeks went by with no results. Years later, Colantonio learned the FBI had not so much as taken the Sakara evidence out of the box. Any possibility of lifting fingerprints was gone.

"We lost a lot of credible evidence," Colantonio said.

For the first month, the investigatory pace bordered on frenetic. Nearly three hundred people were interviewed. It was rare for detectives to work a single case, and they embraced the unique circumstances. So long as they were awake, they worked, and were compensated accordingly. Overtime was plentiful—and lucrative.

Theoretically, there was enough work to do that an investigator shouldn't have had time to talk to a reporter. But at least one spoke to *Newsday,* presumably to generate leads and give readers a better sense of what, and who, to look out for. The newspaper painted a picture of "an intelligent, sophisticated con man who likely spent hours talking to his victims in order to lure them to their death." This was a man, noted the reporter, who deceived two businessmen and "a street-smart hustler." The killer was organized, with an ability to gain the confidence of his victims and blend in, whether at the Townhouse or Port Authority. Even the dismemberment, vicious as it was, had been done out of convenience. "You're not talking about some raving bizarre individual," offered the source.

At this point, the pool of potential suspects—chronicled each day in the task force updates, but never released to the general public—was small. William, a bearded librarian from Orange County, New York, caught the task force's attention after his name was found on a letter a few feet away from the hot dog vendor's trash barrel. He was elusive, which made investigators suspicious. "A squirrelly character," remembered one investigator. It took weeks to locate William and rule him out.

Gene, a cross-dresser known to occasionally drive Michael home from the Five Oaks, was looked into as well, but there was little of interest about him beyond his acquaintance with the victim.

Then there was Gabriel,[1] from Westchester County, whose collection of "homosexual magazines" had been dumped in Somers, New York, across the river from Haverstraw. Repsha and his partner drove to the address on the magazines. Counting off the numbers of the buildings, they pulled up to a house of worship.

"Oh, shit," said Repsha.

The men began to rationalize why they were idling in front of a church. *We're going to find out he cuts the grass. Maybe he's the cook. Maybe it's not . . .* that. Repsha went to the entrance. No one was in sight. He banged on a screen door. The monsignor, wearing a T-shirt, answered the door and asked how he might assist the detectives. They said they were looking for Gabriel.

"Ah," said the monsignor, "Father Gabriel!"

The investigators didn't disclose what they had found but asked to speak with the priest. It turned out, Father Gabriel simply had the misfortune to leave his stack of pornography where others might find it.

Most promising was the white man seen by the two panhandlers, who introduced himself to Lisa Hall as Mark or possibly John. So far as detectives knew, this fellow, who claimed to be a nurse at St. Vincent's Hospital, had been drinking with Michael and appeared to be the last person seen with him before his death.

The task force subpoenaed St. Vincent's for the names, addresses, and dates of birth of all nursing personnel with Mark or John as their first or middle names. (Once they realized there was a St. Vincent's on Staten Island, too, those records were also requested.) It was a narrow, specific

---

1 This name has been changed.

demand, unlikely to be challenged by an administrator. In an effort to find the nurse, one detective enlisted his own family. He and the kids stuffed envelopes with flyers of the composite sketches and sent them to employees at both hospitals.

Meanwhile, teams of investigators went to Greenwich Village to canvas and re-interview people, keeping the focus of their questions on Marks and Johns. Such work had gotten noticeably easier. Detective Malkentzos's presence was helpful, but the existence of a task force made queer witnesses more amenable to cooperating. There was a willingness to talk where before there had been silence. This was likely a result of the press coverage, too, which, while lurid and sensational, captured the attention of the Village. "A multi-state, multi-agency task force investi-gating a series of homicides—with that comes a little bit of clout," said Colantonio, who found he was now welcomed. Ocean County's Wood-field attributed the new openness to the Anti-Violence Project, whose staff convinced bar patrons to talk. "I remember having songs sung about me at the Five Oaks," he said.

Theodos called AVP each morning—to get them involved, sure, but also to forestall accusations of neglect. His state police colleagues ag-gressively availed themselves of AVP's help, in an effort to make inroads with potential witnesses. They were aware of how little they knew about the lives of queer New Yorkers. Foreman and Hanson functioned, in-formally, as tutors. Detectives would ask about the clientele of bars they planned to visit and about stories they'd heard, to gauge their veracity. For instance, word reached detectives that older gay men often pursued younger men, only to get rolled. *Was it true?* (It was.) AVP would separate fact from fiction. "They were like technical advisors," says Repsha.

On August 11, a Greenwich Village source gave detectives a name: Mark Holland, a nursing care coordinator at St. Vincent's in Greenwich Village.[2] In his midthirties and gay, his height and weight matched the

---

2 This name has been changed.

witness descriptions. He had homes in Manhattan and on Staten Island, and was rumored to have visited the Townhouse and the Five Oaks. Alas, Holland was on a nine-day vacation in Provincetown, Massachusetts. While they awaited his return, detectives left anonymous notes under Holland's door, informing him that he was wanted for questioning in Rockland County.

Three days later, Colantonio and New York City detective Raymond Pierce, who had undergone training at Quantico in the art and science of profiling, met Holland. It was Pierce's opinion that the man they were looking for hunted for victims in high places such as the Townhouse and low places such as Port Authority suggested an ability to ease between the two worlds.

Before Holland was driven to Rockland County, Colantonio and Pierce staged the interview room. This was a technique Pierce liked to use when there wasn't enough evidence for an arrest. They put a sign on the door that said MULTIPLE-HOMICIDE TASK FORCE. A file cabinet in the room had Holland's name on it. There were folders in plain sight similarly labeled. They wanted him to know immediately that, if he *had* murdered Michael, they knew he had also murdered the rest of the men. "The point was to use a limited amount of psychological stress to put some ammunition in *our* pockets during the interview—to put him on edge a bit," says Pierce.

Holland sat down. He was tall and thin, clean-shaven, with a head of full, thick hair. Nice white teeth, wore glasses. He looked a great deal like the composite sketch generated based on a panhandler's description. His interview followed the same format. They began by socializing, building rapport, asking "ground ball" questions—the answers to which require no thought and carry no criminal implications. *Where did you stay in Provincetown, Mark? Where did you go to school, Mark? Where do you work? Do you hang out in the Village?* Generally, such questions were asked casually by whomever drove the suspect to the DA's office, but Colantonio and Pierce wanted Holland to enter the interview cold. They waited for him to arrive and get situated before they began. Pedigree questions were next. They had nothing to do with the criminal matter under discussion: *What's your full name? Where do you live? What's your phone number? What's your Social Security number?* Then Holland was asked questions specifically designed to establish his timeline for Thursday, July 29, 1993. *What did you do that morning? Where did you have breakfast? What time did you eat lunch? Where did you eat lunch? Did you go to the Five Oaks? What did you have to drink?*

The questions never got difficult. The detectives didn't want to risk Holland shutting down. What they wanted was to gather information that could subsequently be confirmed or refuted. At times, Holland seemed nervous. But that didn't mean much. Most people get nervous being stuck in a small room with detectives. Holland asked how the detectives could believe he had done something so terrible. "Well, people do strange things for strange reasons," Pierce said.

For a couple of hours, the men talked. There was a large gap of time for which Holland couldn't account: Thursday morning to Friday morning. Where had he been? He refused to say. A detective observing the interview thought he was "fucking with us," and believed Holland was coy and evasive—refusing to give straight answers—and maybe even enjoying it. Finally, he admitted to sunning on the roof. But there were no witnesses, which caught Colantonio's attention.

After a few hours, they'd exhausted their questions. An interview only concludes, says Colantonio, "when you hear the crickets." Nothing Holland said was sufficient for an arrest. It had, in the end, been a fact-finding mission. The detectives took major-case fingerprints—the standard ten-print card as well as rolled impressions of the palms and the sides and tips of each finger—and allowed Holland to leave.

As the detectives awaited the personnel records and work schedules for the eleven St. Vincent's nurses named Mark and John, they tried to place

Holland in the Five Oaks on the morning of July 30. They had no luck. But maybe they could put him outside the bar? A search of motor vehicle summonses, warnings, and traffic stops during the week following July 29 was performed. (It was never far from anyone's mind that David Berkowitz, the Son of Sam, had been nailed by a parking ticket.) The results of the inquiry were negative.

In the end, Holland denied murdering the men. There was little to suggest otherwise: no criminal record, his fingerprints didn't match those on the bags that held Anthony's body parts, his friends and associates weren't suspicious, and he didn't own a car. There was nothing probative in his credit history or telephone records. Colantonio got a hold of Holland's dental X-rays and compared his bite impression with the one on Tom Mulcahy's neck—no match there, either. Eugene Williams, the panhandler in front of the Five Oaks, picked Holland out of a photo array, but Lisa Hall did not. She said there were a few headshots that were close, but no one who lined up with her memory of the man Michael left the bar with that night. "We did everything we could to eliminate [Holland]," said Matthew Kuehn, years later.

In mid-August, investigators met Tony Plaza. The task force notes describe him as "Sakara's last known lover," but that isn't quite right. Plaza, in his twenties and slight, worked at the Metropolitan Opera and drank at the Five Oaks after work. He loved watching Marie Blake and was exploring life as a quite-possibly-gay man. "It was a weird time in my life," he recalled. "I was in and out of the closet." He was just starting to realize he liked big, bearded men.

When Plaza first met Michael, he was so skittish that he introduced himself as John Díaz. He'd been going to the bar for several months. A mutual attraction had quickly been established. Long hugs, nudge-nudge, wink-wink. Never so much as a kiss. But eventually Plaza decided to tell Michael who he really was. *I've got to be honest with who I am*, he thought.

One night, the bar was almost empty, so they could have one-on-one time. Plaza sat down with Michael and said he had something to say.

He put his wallet on the bar and said, "Look at the ID."

"You're not one of those assholes who lies about his name . . ."

"I *am* one of those assholes!"

Michael opened the wallet. "*Tony*," he said. "Oh! That's better."

Michael laughed. He understood Plaza hadn't been ready, but now he was. They went back to the West End Avenue apartment and cuddled, Plaza in his underwear and Michael in nothing. Plaza likened the pairing to the Hanna-Barbera creations Yogi and Boo-Boo.

They had only one night together. The next Friday, Plaza didn't show up at the Five Oaks. He'd had a busy week. He learned of Michael's death from a headline in the *New York Post*.

When Plaza heard about the task force, he walked into the Sixth Precinct in the Village. He told a detective he knew Michael. They took his phone number.

In the decades since, Plaza wondered if, in a small way, he had left Michael vulnerable. *If I had been there,* he thought, *would I have made any kind of a difference, in terms of who he would've left with?*

"There are times when I really wish I was there that night," he says. "Maybe we could've spent more time together, and maybe none of that would've happened."

On August 26, a tip came in about a nurse at another hospital: Mount Sinai. This individual was into bondage, the source said. He had met the man at Julius'—one of the oldest gay bars in the city—and took him home. Sometime during the night, he awoke to find the nurse attempting to tie him up. In his update the next day, Theodos wrote:

The source states the subject had an uncontrollable compulsion to tie him up, however, he resisted and fled his apartment.

The source states he then met the subject again by chance in

"Townhouse" bar and restaurant. He states at that time the subject propositioned to go home again, however, he would not go home with him. The source states the subject is a nurse at Mount Sinai Hospital and has an apartment on Staten Island. The source could offer no further information regarding the subject, other than a physical description.

The source did not know the nurse's name. So investigators issued another subpoena, this time to Mount Sinai, for names, dates of birth, photographs, personnel records, and work schedules for all male nurses who lived on Staten Island. Matthew Kuehn showed Hall photos of the men. As she looked over the two dozen faces, one—a nurse whose photo had been snapped in 1979—stuck out. "This fellow," she said, "his hair is similar." But neither she nor the source of the tip itself could pick anyone out with certainty.

Despite a lack of conclusive leads or breakthroughs, the task force work had aided Mark Woodfield's investigation into the death of Anthony Marrero. He already had fingerprints off the bags, and now, Woodfield believed, he knew something about the mysterious perpetrator: he was a nurse, and he probably lived on Staten Island.

Woodfield had believed this for a while. The latex gloves and keyhole saw from the Mulcahy case were traced back to a CVS and a Pergament, respectively, on Staten Island. The plastic bag containing Anthony Marrero's head had been bought at an Acme on Staten Island. Woodfield's philosophy was *Stay home, until proven otherwise.* Detectives often have an inclination to cast a wide net, but in Woodfield's experience people lived where they shopped. This was doubly true of Staten Island. After all, he'd say, no one goes to Staten Island unless they have to. Had it been up to Woodfield, he said years later, that would've been the focus. But the task force investigators had to follow hundreds of leads, and Staten Island was one locale of many.

New Jersey's Jack Repsha acknowledges that, yes, Staten Island had been a nexus. But, he says, a large-scale shift of resources into a borough of four hundred thousand inhabitants would not have made sense. "You never want to start drawing conclusions: *He lives there. He goes there to shop.* You don't want to lock yourself into what this *probably* means." This was in line with what Theodos would tell his investigators: *Don't tell me what you think. Tell me what you know.*

A memorial for Michael was being planned. It would be held, naturally, at the Five Oaks. In the weeks prior, detectives interviewed his first lover, and nearly all of the patrons who were at the Five Oaks on his last night. Lisa Hall had been driven to the state police barracks near Newark Airport, where she met with a composite sketch artist. The rendering, she thought, looked nothing like the man who had been with Michael. "If I had drawn it myself, it would have been better," she testified.

The memorial was held on October 10. It was a balmy Sunday night, and patrons sang and traded stories. Remarks were wistful, but also angry, as mourners decried anti-queer violence. A small program was handed out. On the front was a pen-and-ink sketch of Michael done by Barbara Ross, his friend who read his horoscope each night. Inside was a passage from Robert Burns:

> I want someone to laugh with me, someone to be grave with me, someone to please me and help my discrimination with his or her own remark, and at times, no doubt, to admire my acuteness and penetration.

Among the accompaniment for the event was Kevin Fox, Michael's favorite piano player. He was alternating nights with Marie Blake, who had fallen ill. Michael had been in love with Fox and liked to sing "(Up A) Lazy River" with him. Fox knew Michael had troubles and remembered seeing him vomit in the bathroom, only to come back to the bar and order another round.

Detectives quietly attended. "Investigators are in the process of identifying the different people who attended this service," Theodos wrote the next day.

There was no formal announcement of the task force's end.

The first month or so, detectives worked around the clock, solely on the joint investigation. But in late September, once leads were exhausted, one by one they were called away to other cases. Slowly but surely, the message came down from on high that time was better spent working closer to home.

The last daily update, written on the morning of October 13, 1993, demonstrated the unresolved nature of the investigation. The detectives were still "looking at the possible linkages between these cases and the Peter Anderson Homicide." A day earlier, they received Mark Holland's telephone toll billing records.

Eventually all that remained was a core group of detectives, a skeleton crew from Rockland County and New Jersey.[3] They weren't disheartened. They knew they'd gotten close. One consolation, according to Woodfield, was that they probably "scared the dickens" out of the murderer. "I'm thinkin' I'm knocking on this guy's door, and he's a lucky son of a bitch because I'm in the neighborhood, but I just don't know which door to knock on."

Around Thanksgiving, the task force disbanded. But, said Repsha, "It's always with the codicil that, should something come up, we'll be up here tomorrow."

*   *   *

3 The NYPD had long since gone home, although Raymond Pierce remained involved with the case until his retirement.

In late 1993, detectives believed the man they were looking for—whose name, buried in a pile of subpoenaed hospital records, they didn't yet know—had stopped killing. Their case had more or less gone cold. What had once seemed like a surfeit of clues, witnesses, and tips trickled to nothing.

A New Jersey trooper, years later, would ruminate on how lucky detectives had already been with the investigation: "The thing with this particular killer, he was very good at disposing of the bodies." This was not an intuitive point. After all, detectives were aware of the four victims because their bodies had, indeed, been found. But, the trooper argued, each discovery was actually something of a fluke. Had an interior bag holding Thomas Mulcahy not ripped, "we never [would have] come across that one." Had an animal not dragged Anthony Marrero's arm onto the road, he would have been classified as a missing person. And had Michael Sakara's remains not been deposited in a fifty-five-gallon drum owned by a zealously observant hot dog vendor—"they're probably going to make its way to the landfill, and we don't have Michael Sakara. So, the question you ask yourself is, how many more are out there that we just don't know about?

"You don't just stop once you get a craving for this type of killing," the trooper continued. "The conclusions we arrived at is: either he's locked up, he's dead, or he's still out there and he's just getting a lot better at it."

At least two of these propositions proved wrong.

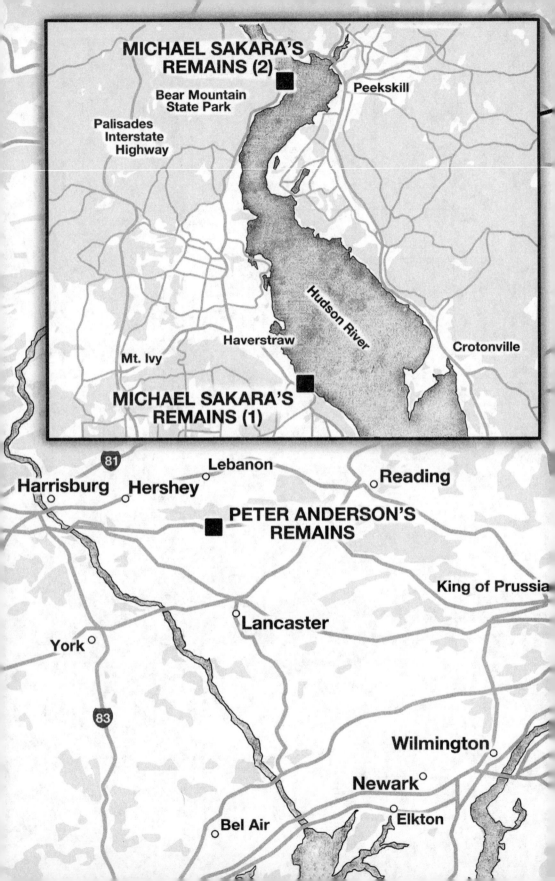

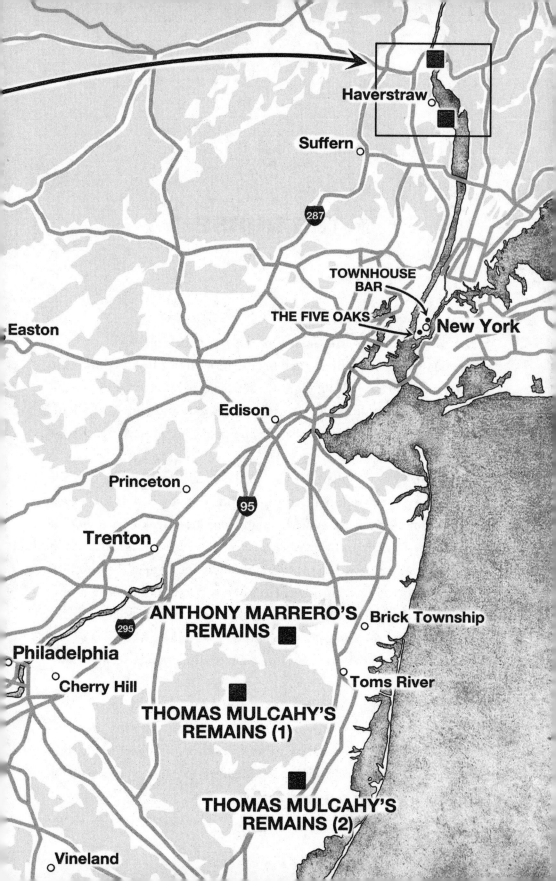

9

THE NURSE

He was a nurse in Mount Sinai Hospital's surgical intensive care unit, and had gone about his life—no longer shadowed by press accounts. The public's minimal fascination with the murders faded. He was sufficiently comfortable that, in June 1996, he turned to a date and said, "You should be careful who you are with because the police are looking for a serial killer."

Only a few weeks earlier, the surprised date, a short, demure Brit, was in New Hope, Pennsylvania, visiting friends. He stopped at the Raven, a gay bar, for a drink. In walked a man from New York City, taller but equally unassuming, and they struck up a conversation. As it happened, the fellow was a nurse, too. The Brit thought the man was quite nice, so they began seeing each other. He worked "strange" hours at Mount Sinai, recalled the Brit, often through the night, but soon enough they were commuting to visit each other—the New Yorker to the Brit's Connecticut home, and the Brit to Manhattan for dinner and overnight stays on Staten Island.

It was never terribly serious. "Towards the end," he said decades later, "I realized something wasn't quite right." One example: they were at a screening of *Titanic*. In the dark theater, another moviegoer made some noise. Nothing offensively loud, but he seemed to panic, with a palpable nervousness. They had to leave the theater.

The Brit thought that was strange, even then.

Not long after the relationship began, it ended, when the New York nurse ceased all communication.

He had worked for Mount Sinai since January 1979, hired right out of Pace University's nursing school. It was a fortuitous time to be on the job market, as the venerable hospital was halfway through a recruitment drive to bring in three hundred nurses. Commuting from Yonkers to Manhattan for the evening shift, he worked constantly, rarely taking more than a day off at a time. During his first year, he took a sick day in May, another in June, and in August, finally, a week's vacation.

In October, he was promoted to senior clinical nurse. With the added responsibility came more days off. In what would become his routine for the next twenty years, the nurse bunched his vacation days together: over three weeks in June 1980, he visited Quebec, West Virginia, and Sagamore Beach in Massachusetts.

The next year, he took four weeks off, commencing a cross-country trip in late April: Washington, D.C.; Mount Hood, Oregon; Jackson, Wyoming; the Grand Canyon; San Francisco; Boulder; and Niagara Falls.

Beginning in June 1981, he took little more than a sick day. Still on the evening shift, he worked from 8:30 P.M. to 8:00 A.M.

On March 22, 1982, he embarked on a four-week trip. There were excursions to North Carolina and Washington, D.C., but the bulk was spent on the east coast of Florida: St. Augustine, Daytona Beach, and Everglades National Park. There was, however, a detour to the middle of the state: Lakeland, home to Florida Southern College. It was his ten-year college reunion.

Richard Westall Rogers Jr. was born in Plymouth, Massachusetts, on June 16, 1950. His father was a lobsterman who, in the late fifties, moved the family to Florida for a better-paying machinist job in sheet metal manufacturing. The Rogerses had five kids, and Richard was the eldest.

A gangly, awkward teenager, Richard was "normal—normal as could be," said an older cousin, who remembered the straight-A student as neat and meticulous, and protective of his younger siblings. His classmates, though, more often remembered his perceived flaws—a high-pitched voice, an effeminate manner, a lack of friends. He was picked last in gym class and teased mercilessly about everything from his voice to the way he walked. Rather than play a sport, Richard was taken by his mother to Girl Scout meetings. In junior high, the self-conscious boy was a natural target: his refusal to strip and bathe after gym class drew the ire of his classmates, who once tossed him into a shower stall and turned on the water. He wept. Richard's lack of athleticism upset his father, who decided that teaching his eldest daughter to hunt and fish in his stead was a better use of time.

At Miami Palmetto High School, existence could be trying for students who weren't part of the in-crowd. Gay kids who were out, for example, would have been "persecuted," said a classmate. Being outside the mainstream incurred bullying as well. Richard, one of the few boys in French Club, was among the tormented.

The rumored nervous breakdown, about which classmates would gossip for decades, occurred after Richard allegedly took a knife from home and stabbed a neighbor. She was significantly older, and had perhaps rebuffed an advance. The incident resulted not in incarceration but, reportedly, in a brief institutionalization. "I thought," a classmate marveled, "that was the end of him."

Nevertheless, Richard graduated from Miami Palmetto in 1968 and matriculated to Florida Southern, a small college with a Methodist bent in Lakeland, more than two hundred miles northwest of where he grew up. Florida Southern was a politically and socially conservative liberal arts college not far from Tampa, known for its expansive collection of Frank Lloyd Wright architecture. When the famed architect first visited the campus in 1938, much of it was marked with citrus groves. Thirty years later, when Richard moved into Wofford Hall, the boys' freshman dorm, the trees were largely gone, and eight Wright buildings and structures were in their place.

To the extent Richard made an impression on campus, it was the absence of an impression—an achievement at such a small university. "He was somewhat of a loner, wasn't very assertive," said a classmate. "He didn't have a strong personality." Half the population was either in a fraternity or sorority, and there was mutual distrust between the Greeks and the GDIs ("goddamn independents") who fell outside the approved social scene. Richard, unsurprisingly, was a GDI.

During Richard's sophomore year, the United Methodist Church held its annual conference on campus. Understandably, Richard's sexuality was hidden from his peers, just as it had been from his family. More than one alum suggested that, had he been open about it, his life would have been endangered. In fact, a gay student who came out was reportedly moved into an off-campus apartment by the administration, for his own safety.

Yet, despite his peculiarity, Richard wasn't harried by fellow students. If anything, they felt sorry for him. One marveled that, on a Saturday afternoon, he could be seen aimlessly riding the bus, staring out the window: "I know about being lonely, but *wow*."

Richard had two roommates during his four years at Florida Southern. The first, Donald Cubberley, was from New Jersey. He'd been accepted to a half dozen colleges closer to home, but he wanted to escape the Northeast. The small campus with the Wright architecture was the perfect fit. It also felt like a different world; when he walked into the dorm room for the first time, he saw an "albino" palmetto cockroach sitting atop Richard's suitcase. Once the light was off, the insect scurried down the side of the suitcase and into a dark corner.

The morning of the first day of classes, tall and skinny Richard swung his legs over the side of the top bunk and jumped off. He hit the floor and crumpled—his stork legs unable to support his upper body—and crashed into his desk chair. Books went flying.

"Geez, man, are you all right?"

Richard, uninjured, rolled over. "Well," he said, "that didn't go the way I planned."

Richard was a nice guy, it seemed to Cubberley, but a bookworm who was "extremely introverted, very intelligent, but he wouldn't talk unless you talked to him first." Which Cubberley did, and they discussed politics, science, and goings-on around the college. Years later, he remembered the round shoulders, the sunken chest, the shaved head for ROTC that earned Richard the name the Human Q-Tip, and the strange way his roommate walked. "He didn't swing his arms at all, so it looked like he was gliding."

The rooming arrangement lasted no more than a couple of weeks. Once they split up, Richard moved in with a mathematics major. Richard and his new roommate were, by all accounts, joined at the hip for the duration of school.

Richard graduated in 1972 with a BA in French. He played no sports and joined no clubs of note, although he and a few friends joined Circle K, the Kiwanis-affiliated service organization. To most, he seemed like an outcast. But Richard appeared to enjoy his college years all the same, perhaps because, as a classmate told an alumni magazine, it's "where you begin to become yourself." In the years after graduation, Richard frequently returned to campus. He even took on the responsibility of the college's "liaison" for his class, serving as a host for homecoming events. "At least on the alumni side, he was very engaging," says a classmate. "Seemed to enjoy greeting people, getting events going."

It was, then, unsurprising that, during his four-week March vacation in 1982, Richard stayed in Lakeland for the reunion. Very little is remembered about the event, held in Orlando, but the violence that occurred in its proximity is notable.

A week before Richard returned to New York, a young man last seen in a Daytona Beach gay bar was found near Interstate 4 and Lake Mary Boulevard. Five foot eight, 140 pounds, with sandy-blond hair, Matthew

John Pierro had been stabbed six times and strangled. Pierro, twenty-two, had been on his way to visit his ex-wife, who lived an hour east in Cocoa Beach. He had come to Daytona Beach earlier in the year, reported the *Orlando Sentinel*, to help set up "a religion-based teen center for troubled youths." In the weeks before his death, he accumulated a short police record—getting scooped up for sleeping on a park bench and possession of marijuana.

The case has not been solved.[1]

In 1984, Richard began working the 6 P.M. to 7:30 A.M. shift at Mount Sinai.

Again, he took four weeks off from work, spending August in San Francisco, Salt Lake City, Boulder, and the Grand Canyon. Several months after his return, he was appointed operating-room nurse. Nearly a year later, in August 1985, Richard was transferred to Mount Sinai's cardiac surgical intensive care unit. Among his duties was to work with children.

Richard was one of a half-dozen nurses working with kids in recovery from heart surgery. It was a difficult job, particularly where newborns were concerned. Oftentimes, they came out of the operating room unconscious from the anesthesia. They were on a breathing machine hooked up to numerous monitors. Many had intravenous lines and received continuous infusions of drugs to treat the heart. Depending on the severity of the surgery, the newborns would have a nurse by the bedside at every moment of the first twenty-four to forty-eight hours, watching the monitors to ensure vitals remained stable and adjusting drips of adrenaline or epinephrine as necessary. Conditions could change in seconds.

---

1 According to a sergeant in the Lake Mary Police Department, as of November 2019, "The case is still open and is currently assigned as a cold case homicide in the Investigations Unit." I have found no evidence that Richard was considered a suspect in 1982, or even questioned in the matter.

Most of the time they were fine, and the care might consist of feeding them breakfast, changing bandages, or reading a story. But sometimes they went into cardiac arrest or bled after surgery, only to be rushed back to the operating room, with the nurses pumping blood in as they went.

Such a responsibility was given only to those who truly wanted it. Mount Sinai selected nurses who were highly skilled and motivated, who could ease the pain of frightened children, talk to nervous parents about life and death, and make judgments about whether a baby was stable enough to be in their presence. Another requisite of the job was tremendous empathy, and Richard had it. He and his colleagues in the cardiac intensive care unit were, a cardiac surgeon recalled, "considered elite."

In June 1986, Richard's commute to work changed. He moved from Yonkers to an apartment at 20 Merle Place, a five-story building on Staten Island, New York.

His new neighbors didn't know him very well. They saw him bring men home on occasion, but for the most part Richard was solitary and guarded. He never talked about his family or what was going on in life. He strictly rationed information, telling them about his long shifts at work and his love of Broadway, travel, and country music. Still, he was friendly and sometimes helpful. And, oh, was he tidy. A husband and wife in the building were struck by his exquisitely arranged collection of videos, and the never-ending hum of the vacuum.

For the next few years, he worked through the night into the early morning hours, leaving little time for visits to bars and clubs. On July 11, 1988, however, after three twelve-hour shifts the previous week, he took a day off.

That Monday evening, Richard went to G.H. Club on East Fifty-third Street. It served an older crowd, which is precisely what Richard looked for in a bar. He walked in and stood against the wall, scanning for a place to sit. He took a seat to the right of a businessman, a decade his senior, at the bar. The older man, whose name was Sandy Harrow, was talking with his friends about real estate and the stock markets, which were on the upswing.² Richard joined in the conversation.

After Sandy's friends left, Richard told him about the Merle Place apartment. It had recently gone co-op, he said, and he'd gotten it for an insider's price: $45,000. Cheap enough, he continued, that it could probably be flipped for nearly double that amount. Richard asked if he would like to come back to Staten Island to see the apartment. Sandy, who lived in Manhattan, initially refused. It was, after all, Staten Island—New Yorkers frequently look askance at the city's most conservative borough—and it was already eight o'clock. But after Richard volunteered to drive him there and then drive him back home to Midtown, he agreed to leave the bar. And so they did.

In the elevator, Richard warned Sandy that the fifth-floor apartment would be hot, and it was. Richard went to use the bathroom. Then he offered his guest a drink. Sandy requested a diet soda, but Richard returned with orange juice.

Sandy began to drink. The orange juice tasted fine. But the businessman began to lose consciousness. He could see himself fall forward on the dark blue rug.

When Sandy awoke, he realized he had been unconscious for hours. He was naked, lying on his back, and his hands and ankles were bound with more than a dozen hospital ID bracelets. He began to scream. Richard calmly injected a hypodermic needle into the vein on top of his hand.

"That will take care of you for a while," he said.

Sandy passed out.

It was vague, but Sandy would remember being threaded into his clothes and then pushed through the vestibule of his apartment building. When he awoke several hours later, on Tuesday morning, he called a friend who took him to the local police precinct. Sandy then went to

---

2 This name has been changed.

Roosevelt Hospital, where he was subjected to a series of tests. Doctors noted bruises on the vein in his hand. Terrified of contracting AIDS, he requested a rape kit. It came back negative.

Five weeks later, on August 18, Richard was arrested. He was back at work two days later.

Richard began 1989 by working either every other day or every third day. The job was demanding. It made sense, then, that he would seek relaxation in his off-hours.

That came in the form of the Townhouse, a new bar in the East Fifties. Richard had been a fan of its piano player, Rick Unterberg, since his days at Regent East. Richard set aside Thursdays and Sundays to see him perform.

It was late into the evening when Richard would settle into the Townhouse's back room, the domain of the pianists. Cocktail-hour shift had come and gone, and Unterberg was already in the middle of a set. Richard would inch up to the piano and banter with him during breaks. "He was always very pleasant," recalled Unterberg, who was aware of Richard's rigid schedule at Mount Sinai. "I never saw him overdrink. I never saw him rude." In fact, he didn't make much of an impression one way or the other on the piano player, who tended to remember big tippers or the real obnoxious types. Richard, who rarely drank to excess, was neither.

Richard was off work during much of February 1990. That month, he entered the Richmond County criminal court on Targee Street for a three-day bench trial, often favored by defendants who want to keep their private lives private. It had been a year and a half since the night at G.H. Club with Sandy Harrow.

Richard was represented by Christopher Nalley, a local lawyer, and prosecuted by Michael Clark, an assistant district attorney. He had been charged with misdemeanors under New York Penal Law sections 120.00 and 135.05—assault in the third degree and unlawful imprisonment in the second degree, respectively.

In a cavernous room filled with no more than a dozen people, including court officers, the trial began. Sandy was called to the stand. He introduced himself to the court, informing the judge that he'd worked for three years on a Japanese equity desk in Manhattan. He did not tell the judge that investment banking was a second career; years earlier, he'd been chaplain at a university in New York City.

Guided by Clark, he recounted the events of July 11, 1988.

"It was the hottest day of the year," said Harrow, forty-eight years old. After work, he went to the New York Health and Racquet Club on Fifty-first Street. It was too crowded, however, so after a few minutes he left. Harrow walked north up Third Avenue, then banked right on Fifty-third Street. On the corner of Fifty-third and First Avenue was the G.H. Club, a bar popular with gay professionals like Harrow—banking, real estate, and advertising. He settled into conversation with two friends and had a glass of white wine.

"After I was there about twenty-five minutes, I was sitting at the bar speaking to someone over an empty seat," he said. "The defendant came in and was standing against the wall." Harrow identified Richard—wearing a navy blue sweater and a red tie for his day in court—as the man in question. Richard "indicated he was looking for a place to sit," so Harrow made room for him to his right. Once Harrow's friends left, Richard told him about his Merle Place apartment and asked if he'd like to see it. It was now 8:00 in the evening.

HARROW: I remember entering the apartment and it was absolutely stifling hot. It was completely sealed. There was no air conditioning and he had warned me about that in the elevator. He said it would be hot. He also mentioned in the elevator that he had, immediately when we went into the apartment, he had to use the john.

I entered the apartment and he disappeared and he came back and offered me a drink. I said something soft like diet soda and he came back with orange juice or what seemed to be orange juice. I remember him saying he had something to do in the bedroom. He left and came back. I was drinking the orange juice. I didn't taste anything strange, but I remember passing out and as I fell forward, a very dark blue rug on the floor.

I awoke later. I had been unconscious for hours. I was stripped naked. My hands and ankles were bound with hospital I.D. bracelets. A lot of them. I started to scream and move my hands and feet and I couldn't move.

Harrow was subsequently diagnosed with post-traumatic stress syndrome, which hamstrung him socially. It had become difficult to trust people, to even get into cars with others. "I have enormous fears of any kind of intimacy with anybody," he told the court.

Nalley began cross-examination by asking Harrow to repeat the PTSD diagnosis. Then he asked, "Are you in fear of picking up any more men in bars now?"

"I did not pick Mr. Rogers up," replied Harrow.

Nalley turned to the timeline of events. He liked to preface his questions with *Sir*. "Sir, it is your testimony that you only had one glass of white wine; when did you get to the bar?"

Harrow guessed that if he got to the gym at 6:30 and the five-block walk up Third Avenue took fifteen minutes, he likely arrived at the bar by 7:30 or 7:45. He and Richard left the bar around 8:00.

Nalley handed Harrow a statement he had given to the police.

"Isn't it a fact that in your statement, you said that you got to the bar at 6 o'clock that night?"

Harrow said that was plausible, and conceded that his earlier estimate may have been wrong. He had been at the bar for two hours, during which he drank a white wine and, he told Nalley, "several Perriers."

Nalley asked Harrow if, on July 11, he carried a gym bag. *He had.* Was he wearing a watch? *No.* Harrow could not, in fact, be sure when he and Richard arrived on Staten Island. The lawyer switched gears, to the orange juice. "You're assuming then it was drugged," he said.

"I passed out because I drank the orange juice and it was drugged," countered Harrow. He had not had the juice chemically analyzed, he said. "I know it was drugged because I passed out."

NALLEY: What time did you wake up?
HARROW: I didn't have my watch on, Counsel. I had no idea approximately what time it was. I have no idea of time for that evening except when I got home.

The lawyer changed the subject, to Harrow's contention that, after Richard pushed him into his clothes and left him in the building's vestibule, he collapsed in his apartment. In a statement to police, Harrow had said his recollection was of "standing in the vestibule of my house fumbling with the key." He said nothing at the time about being pushed into his clothes. Of course, the Roosevelt Hospital psychiatric intern had told Harrow his memory might come back in stages.

Anyway, asked Nalley, how could Richard have navigated the stairs with Harrow's 140-pound limp body? "There is an elevator." But the lawyer talked past him. Even so, he said, how could Richard have possibly shoved him in a car, driven him to Manhattan, and dragged him into his own vestibule? Harrow presumed Richard had roused him long enough to produce his keys to the building. "I can remember standing at the door trying to get the keys in the lock," he said.

Nalley's questions were increasingly upsetting Harrow.

NALLEY: Do you know what time you got home?
HARROW: No. I know what time I woke up, which was at—
NALLEY: Didn't you tell the doctor you were home at 5:30?

HARROW: If I knew then, fine. I was home at 5:30. I called friends at 6 o'clock, as they will testify.

NALLEY: If you told the doctor you awoke at 4:30, if the hypodermic in your hand, and you told the doctor—

HARROW: There is a hell of a difference between knowing the time I was moving around during this episode and whether or not I was stuck with a goddamn hypodermic needle.

Harrow said Nalley was confused. In his statement to the doctor, Harrow had actually said, simply, that it was 4:30 "at some point." He was *not* pinpointing when Richard stuck him with the needle. In fact, the hypodermic needle was brandished a short while later.

Nalley asked, "By the way, you have a lot of problems with your right hand, don't you?" Harrow said he had been treated at Roosevelt Hospital for a dog bite a year or two before the incident. After a question about carrying his gym bag on the trip back to Manhattan, Nalley asked, "Sir, didn't you tell the hospital you thought you were sodomized?" Harrow said the rape test was a precaution because he was deeply afraid of contracting AIDS. *But hadn't Harrow gone to the bar to pick up a man? Wasn't he, in fact, a homosexual?*[3]

NALLEY: Have you been to apartments with male men?

HARROW: No.

NALLEY: Never?

HARROW: No.

NALLEY: Do you have them over to your apartment?

HARROW: No.

NALLEY: Do you have sex with them?

HARROW: This is the age of AIDS, Sir. Where have you been?

---

3 Such an insensitive line of questioning was not uncommon back then, particularly in the Staten Island criminal court. "It was like Mayberry," recalled a lawyer.

Harrow said he was now celibate, but the lawyer suggested that "the real reason" charges were brought against his client was because Richard refused to sleep with him. "Isn't it a fact," he said, "that you asked Mr. Rogers to tie you up?"

Clark objected, and was overruled.

Nalley turned to Harrow's injuries: "Besides the psychological trauma, you did not suffer any injury, if I may?"

"Psychological trauma should not be denigrated like that," replied Harrow.

When Nalley asked how post-traumatic stress syndrome manifested itself, Harrow said, again, that he had trouble getting into cars with strangers, had a fear of intimacy, had difficulty trusting people. This made everyday interactions with business associates trying. Then he uttered words that would be used against him: "Slight paranoia."

Nalley returned to the timeline, and Harrow's contention that he was "out cold" from about 8:40 P.M. to 4:30 A.M., and then, after the injection, for another hour. "And during that whole period of time," said Nalley, "you weren't sodomized?" In fact, that wasn't clear, Harrow said. If Richard used a condom, there would be no evidence in the rape test. "Did you suffer any bleeding from the anal cavity?" Not that he was aware of. "By the way, sir, they also did a test for sperm in your mouth; am I correct?" Harrow couldn't recall that from the medical record. Nalley told him that, as it happened, the test had been negative.

After a back-and-forth about Richard dressing a drugged Harrow ("It was fastidiously taken care of," the complainant observed), Nalley suggested the incident had been a product of Harrow's imagination. "Sir, isn't it a chance that, if you were drugged by the orange juice that you might—this might not have all happened?"

Absolutely not.

Nalley asked, "Do you dream?"

"We all dream, don't we?" replied Harrow.

Nalley asked if dreams sometimes seemed real. Sure, said Harrow.

"You're a reasonable man," said Nalley. "Isn't it possible that if you were drugged, that this incident might not have occurred?"

It was not, said Harrow; of that he had no doubt. Richard injected him, he said, because he had regained consciousness and saw what was happening to him.

On redirect, Clark tried to massage Harrow's timeline problems. Perhaps he'd left work for the gym earlier? (Sure.) Then he asked about his fear of AIDS. Was he still fearful? "I'm petrified of it. I have been for years," said Harrow. "I have had friends get very sick. Every gay man in New York City has friends who have had trouble with the disease. I do not engage in casual sex."

A few minutes later, the first day of trial ended.

On February 22, 1990, Richard was called to testify. His version of the events of July 11, 1988, bore little resemblance to Harrow's. In his telling, he entered the G.H. Club between 6 and 6:30 and ordered a light beer. Then he saw Harrow looking at him.

Harrow, now the aggressor, approached Richard and introduced himself—first name only. After some small talk about their respective professions, they began talking about real estate. As Richard remembered it, he told Harrow his apartment building was *going* co-op, not that it already had. Harrow moved close enough to Richard that their knees were touching.

ROGERS: Then he reached over and he put his arm around me and I kind of leaned back and I said—he said, what is the matter? I said, well, you know, I like to use a little discretion in public places.

Nalley interjected. "You're a homosexual, are you not?" Richard confirmed that he was.

The story continued: After Harrow backed off, the conversation resumed. Then Harrow asked if he could spend the night on Staten Island. *Sure*, Richard said, *but that's quite a hike. Wouldn't it make more sense to go to your place in Manhattan?* He estimated that a drive to Staten Island would take at least forty-five minutes, if there's no traffic. Harrow said his place was no good because his nephew was staying with him. But before they could head to Staten Island, Harrow had to go home to walk his dog and check on his nephew. They agreed to meet on the corner of Fifty-seventh Street and Ninth Avenue in forty-five minutes, at 7:30.

According to Richard, when Harrow got in the car, he was carrying a gym bag. "I said, what do you have in the bag, and he said a change of clothes."

Nalley walked Richard through his own version of the timeline. Contrary to his earlier testimony, Richard said he entered G.H. Club around 5:15. He began talking to Harrow ten minutes later. "Sir," said the lawyer, "did you notice whether Sandy was drinking anything?" Richard said Harrow appeared to be drinking white wine. He never saw Harrow drink Perrier.

Richard's recollection of the drive to Staten Island was at odds with Harrow's as well. In his telling, Harrow put his hand on Richard's leg. "When I'm driving, I keep my mind on the road," Richard said to him. "No offense."

When they pulled up to the apartment, Richard pointed toward some townhouses that were being built down the street. Then they went inside.

Richard turned on the air conditioner in the living room. Then, after using the bathroom, he offered Harrow a drink—regular beer, light beer, scotch, orange juice, or cranberry juice. No wine. Harrow requested orange juice. It was around that time, testified Richard, that he turned on the air conditioner in the bedroom. Then he poured them each a glass of juice and sat with Harrow on the living room couch. The men talked for ten or twenty minutes. Harrow leaned closer to Richard. They went into the bedroom.

ROGERS: Well, one thing led to another and at that point, he asked me if I was into bondage and I said no, I don't like that kind of stuff, and he said, oh, it's kind of fun. I said well, you know, I really don't care for that kind of stuff, it's not something I like. He said well, you ought to try it, and he said I brought some ropes with me, and he got his gym bag and he opened it up and he showed me inside the gym bag there were some ropes and there was also some condoms and there was also, it looked like a small shaving kit, and I didn't see any clothes in there like he said.

Richard wasn't comfortable with bondage, he told the court, and Harrow was "put off." As they lay on the bed, quite close to each other, Harrow requested "anal intercourse." Richard declined, citing the considerable health risk. "I don't do anything unsafe," he said. "I said you can't take chances."

Harrow was upset, and lay in silence. Then he sat up, and accused Richard of leading him on. "I didn't lead him on," Richard told the court. "We never discussed anything about what was going to happen when we got here." Even so, Harrow asked Richard to take him home.

When they got into the car, between 10:30 or 11:00, Harrow wasn't saying much; "the cold shoulder," as Richard put it. They crossed into Manhattan and drove up the West Side Highway. When Richard pulled up to the building on Fifty-fifth Street, Harrow grabbed his bag and got out.

According to Richard, that was the extent of their evening. They lay in bed together, yes, but he never tied up Harrow and certainly never injected him with a hypodermic needle. Under questioning from Nalley, Richard stressed that he couldn't have injected Harrow because narcotics were locked up tight at the hospital and accounted for between shifts. Furthermore, Richard was unfamiliar with any liquid narcotic that would knock a man out for eight hours.

"Did you put anything in the orange juice when you gave it to Mr. Harrow?"

Richard said he hadn't, and Nalley's questioning was over.

During cross-examination, Clark asked, "When a patient comes into the hospital, how is he identified? Is he identified by a tag? Is he identified by bracelets?"

"They have I.D. bracelets with their name on it," said Richard, who explained that they were made of a strong plastic, comparable to that which held together a six-pack of beer. Unfurled, a bracelet would be perhaps eight inches long.

Clark wanted to know more about Richard's medical training and asked if he had taken any "pharmaceutical courses." The defendant corrected him: "Pharmacology." Richard said he had considerable knowledge of drugs and the effects their ingestion would have on a person.

Clark said that Richard, by his own admission, sometimes brought home men without knowing their last name. Richard cheerfully confirmed this, and observed that, among gay men, anonymous affairs are common. He'd even brought home women, in the days before he realized he was gay: "You don't always know the person when you first meet them but you can tell if you like them or not."

On redirect, Nalley asked if being restrained in the manner described by Harrow would discolor the skin at the site of the wristbands. Yes, said Richard, but only if they were too tight or if a patient pulled against them. As for whether he would ever restrain a patient using hospital wristbands, he said no: the bands were not long enough.

It was now time for summations. Nalley delivered his first, informing the judge that the prosecution had not proven beyond a reasonable doubt that Richard intended to physically injure Harrow. According to Harrow himself, the swelling on his right hand went down after a week. As for the "so-called psychological trauma," said Nalley: why hadn't the prosecution entered a record of it into evidence?

The imprisonment charge, continued Nalley, was without merit, and the sole evidence for it was Harrow's testimony—which, he said, wasn't reliable.

NALLEY: I submit to the Court that it is incredible evidence. He admitted on the stand yesterday that he suffered from paranoia. . . . I submit to the Court that any evidence from his lips as of yesterday must be given no weight if he indeed admits that at this point he is suffering from paranoia.

Nor should the judge believe Harrow's testimony about being drugged, said the lawyer. It was implausible that Harrow could have reacted instantaneously to the narcotic. The timeline was suspect, too. There was a thirty-minute discrepancy: Harrow told the doctor he had awoken in his apartment at 5:30, but he testified that, in fact, it had been 6:00. Nalley speculated that Harrow tweaked his testimony because it dawned on him that, when one factored in the time it took to get Harrow dressed and transported to Manhattan, the story was "a practical impossibility."

Before asking the judge to dismiss the charges, Nalley again brought up Harrow's mental state: "The problem here is, Judge, that I believe Mr. Harrow is nuts."

In his own summation, the ADA noted Richard's access to hospital ID bracelets and said the inconsistencies in Harrow's version of the timeline were hardly evidence of Richard's innocence. "The People submit that these inconsistencies are all within an hour of what was originally said," said Clark. Any discrepancies "could be as a result of the drug that he received."

The next day, the judge rendered her verdict: "I find that the People have not proven the elements of the crime, either crime, beyond a reasonable doubt, and I acquit the defendant of the two counts against him."

Richard thanked her.

"Dismissed and sealed."

Eventually, Harrow left banking and returned to the priesthood.

After the trial, Richard's next few years were filled with work and travel. He was a good nurse, coworkers thought, and deceptively strong; he could lift an adult patient onto a gurney without assistance. And he was a perfectionist—intolerant of anyone he believed was falling short. Richard wouldn't mask his displeasure if questioned or challenged on his work.

Richard had the day off on May 4, 1991, the morning after Peter Anderson stumbled out of the Waldorf Astoria. He was also off on May 5, when Peter's body was found at a Pennsylvania Turnpike rest area.

In August, he purchased a new Toyota Corolla, and registered the car with the New Jersey Department of Motor Vehicles. He liked to drive, and by November had put nearly fourteen thousand miles on the car. By February 1992, he had driven another five thousand miles, and returned to New Jersey to have the Corolla serviced. In April, at twenty-four thousand miles, it was serviced again.

Richard then took off swaths of June and July. He wasn't working on July 7. On July 8, shortly after eleven o'clock that night, Thomas Mulcahy was last seen. He had gone to the Townhouse, closing out a successful business trip. Richard was off on July 9, and the next day, too, when Tom's body parts were found, spread across two rest areas in New Jersey.

In September, it was back to New Jersey; the Corolla now had just over thirty thousand miles on it.

The first week of 1993 began with three twelve-hour shifts.

In mid-March, the Corolla was serviced at thirty-five thousand miles. That month, Richard drove the car to a slew of Bass Hotels & Resorts, including franchises in Morehead, Kentucky; Valdosta, Georgia; Homestead, Florida; and, at the end of March, Lakeland.

On April 27, Richard used a vacation day, and then was off for the next week. On Tuesday, May 4, and Wednesday, May 5, he worked from 8:30 P.M. to 8:00 A.M. On May 6, when a Port Authority sex worker named Anthony Marrero was last seen, he had the day off. Richard had the day off on May 7, too, three days before Anthony's body was found on a dirt road in Ocean County, New Jersey, and one day before the dead man was supposed to attend a friend's birthday party.

During the next two months, Richard mostly worked on consecutive days and then took two or three days off.

In the early morning hours of July 30, Richard walked into the Five Oaks and was seen leaving with Michael Sakara, who told a panhandler they were "going upstate."

Richard was off that day and the next.

On August 8, two days before Richard had his Corolla serviced (at 44,326 miles), Michael's torso and legs were found off Route 9W in Stony Point, New York.

Richard never returned to the Five Oaks, whose business suffered after the murder. "It was grim," says Tony Plaza, for whom the relationship with Michael was so formative. "The Five Oaks was always a place where you had a good time. That was all missing."

On December 5, 1993, the bar was hobbled further when Marie Blake died at Mount Sinai. At seventy-four, downtown Manhattan's equivalent of Bobby Short had been in poor health for years—a long-ago coronary bypass, and in June she had polyps in her throat. Somehow, that had only marginally slowed her down. "Long as my health keeps up, I'll keep playing," she told a reporter that same month. "People tell me I'm a legend and now I'm starting to believe it."

Newspapers soon forgot the four dead men and the pursuit of a nurse. There were references here and there to the task force investigation in stories about current cases, generally involving dismemberment or a missing gay man. When a New Jersey schoolteacher disappeared, *The Philadelphia Inquirer* reported "a quickening of interest in the case among the group of investigators that has become interlocked in the probes of four dismemberment murders. . . ." But that was the extent of it. So in February 1994, when a plucky weekly called *Manhattan Spirit* looked into the story, it had an open field.

James Rutenberg, twenty-four, was already on his second tour at the paper—which, in a financial if not spiritual connection to Michael Sakara, happened to share a publisher with the *New York Law Journal*, where Michael had worked. Rutenberg was aware of the task force cases because, in addition to his editorial duties, he worked at a bar near the Stonewall Inn. There was plenty of chatter about the murders.

The idea for the story, however, came from a fellow reporter at "cop shop." Each week, Rutenberg went to One Police Plaza in Manhattan to gather material for the *Spirit*'s crime blotter. Colleagues from the *New York Post*, the *Daily News*, and *Newsday* hung around, too, and sometimes handed the young reporter stories they liked but, for one reason or another, couldn't cover. The "Last Call Killer" murders, as Mike McAlary called them, were an ideal topic for the *Spirit*, which often published stories other papers wouldn't touch. *It was a perfect story*, mused Rutenberg decades later. *A community that is under siege and is getting ignored—how could that not speak to your journalistic sensibilities?*

During the first week, Rutenberg found sources at the Five Oaks and around the Loop, a five- or six-block radius of East Fifties bars—including the Townhouse—catering to closeted, john-seeking men from the suburbs.[4] Rutenberg talked to NYPD detectives and Anti-Violence Project staff members, and he took the train to Rockland County to meet with the medical examiner, Dr. Frederick Zugibe.

Richard spent the latter part of the month driving through New Hampshire and working the 7 p.m. to 7 a.m. shift, unaware of these developments. He had not returned to the Five Oaks or the Townhouse. He was not whispered about as a suspect by task force investigators. Nor would Richard have noticed the publication of Rutenberg's story in early March, as he was driving through Allegheny County, Pennsylvania, where he was staying at Coraopolis's Holiday Inn.

The story was given the cover, which included a full-page photo of the

---

4 Eighteen years earlier, the Ramones recorded "53rd & 3rd," a song about the area: "53rd and 3rd, standing on the street / 53rd and 3rd, I'm trying to turn a trick / 53rd and 3rd, you're the one they never pick / 53rd and 3rd, don't it make you feel sick?"

Five Oaks exterior, over which were the words "THE STALKER." Deeply reported, the *Manhattan Spirit* story is a time capsule of the investigation during the first quarter of 1994. It reflects the broadly accepted body count—Peter Anderson, while vaguely referenced, is never mentioned by name.

Rutenberg also captured the NYPD's imagined position in the task force investigation; rather than playing an ancillary role, the city's police department believed it was leading the charge:

News of his exploits set the city's gay community on red alert, and politicians lined up to call for a region-wide manhunt. Just as the last mayoral campaign started heating up, then-Mayor David Dinkins went before the press with his police commissioner, Raymond Kelly, to put the city—predominantly its homosexuals—on notice that a killing machine in sheep's clothing was on the loose.

The NYPD put three full-time detectives on his trail. They were joined by cops from Westchester and New Jersey in a major police task force.

The city's queer activists had run out of patience with the investigators. "For Baby Jessica, they had a team for more than a year steady and they cracked it," AVP's Matt Foreman told Rutenberg. "Now we have three murdered men and dismembered gay men and we don't have anyone here—where the victims were last seen—working the case. All I can see is discrimination and homophobia."

Rutenberg synthesized the investigators' current thinking on the perpetrator, which hadn't changed much: "This is a man who is most likely white, who can hold an intelligent conversation with just about anyone, and has a good understanding of the gay pick-up scene."

That was true, to be sure, but the closest Richard got now to his old haunts was an occasional visit to the Townhouse Restaurant, half a block away from the bar. His off-hours were filled with concerts and museums. In the second half of April 1994, he visited the Carlyle Hotel in Manhattan, saw country singer Lorrie Morgan perform at the Westbury Music Fair, and (possibly out of nostalgia for Florida Southern) attended a Frank Lloyd Wright exhibit at the Museum of Modern Art. At the beginning of May, he went to Radio City Music Hall and the next day the Armory Antique Show.

The following weekend, Richard drove to Woburn, Massachusetts, where he attended the Northeast Pediatric Cardiology Nurses Association conference.

On the first day of June 1994, he had the Corolla serviced. Then off to more concerts: Bonnie Raitt at Radio City Music Hall, Suzy Bogguss at Carnegie Hall, Mary Chapin Carpenter at Avery Fisher Hall. Toward the end of the year, he took another vacation, this time to Provincetown.

Meanwhile, the Five Oaks closed. It had no doubt been hurt by Michael's death, but the bar had been badly managed. Still, the demise was sudden. Lisa Hall, the longtime bartender and friend of Michael's, had gotten no warning. She showed up to find padlocks on the doors and her personal belongings inside, including a trumpet. Hall played the instrument on *Gypsy*'s "You Gotta Have a Gimmick," which she performed while servers and bartenders pretended to be strippers.

"Nobody really got to say goodbye," she says.

It was now nearly five years since Thomas Mulcahy was last seen at the Townhouse, and four years since the investigators swarmed the bar looking for patrons to interview.

It was as if the murders had never happened.

In early May 1997, a handsome twentysomething began stationing himself by the piano at the Townhouse. Over the last month or so, he'd gained some weight but was impeccably dressed and appeared to have money. He seemed to have a job, though no one knew what it was.

The young man was a hit with the old men, of whom he was so enamored.

What they didn't know was that a week earlier, he had been in Minneapolis, where he'd beaten two men to death. Then he'd driven to Chicago and killed a real estate developer.

Now he was in Manhattan.

Soon enough, Andrew Cunanan would also kill a man in New Jersey.

Then, finally, in South Beach, Florida, Gianni Versace.

One night in autumn 1998, Richard went to Regents, a piano bar on East Fifty-third. He ran into Joe Gallagher, a white-haired, mustachioed legal proofreader with a pinkish complexion and a lot of white chest hair. Gallagher had for months been caring for an ex in treatment for colon cancer and, more recently, lung problems. This was his first time out of the house in months.

Richard and Gallagher had been friendly for a while. Gallagher knew him from Regents as well as the Townhouse. He found Richard to be quiet, but pleasant. Not physically affectionate beyond a hand on the shoulder. Not terribly opinionated. Never snippy. Not much of a talker, and almost never about himself. Gallagher knew what Richard did for a living—that he worked at Mount Sinai and did some private nursing work in his off-hours—but little else.[5] "If he was singing around the piano with the rest of the choir, he's not the one you would notice," Gallagher recalled. "Richard was one of those people who fades into the background. It wasn't so much that he was a Zelig, but he was someone without affect."

That night, Richard, to Gallagher's surprise, invited him home. Ordinarily, he might have declined, but it had been so long since he'd been anywhere. He appreciated the attention.

During the ride to Staten Island, Gallagher told Richard about his

---

5 I have not found documentation of the off-hours nursing work.

recent experiences as a caregiver. When they entered the apartment, Gallagher asked if he could use the phone to let his partner know he was okay. Then they talked more about the realities of taking care of a person who has been sick for a long time. As they chatted, Gallagher looked around the apartment; it was well kept, he decided, but not distinctive. The decor didn't betray any sense of Richard as a person.

The men had some wine, then went to the bedroom.

Decades later, Gallagher remembered Richard's paleness. His freckles. His dark hair. His long fingers. He remembered that Richard was measured in the bedroom, not energetic. How he was "more a watcher than a doer."

They slept together. Then Gallagher fell asleep.

He awoke around 4 A.M. to see Richard's expressionless face next to him, his hands snaking around his neck. It felt oddly clinical, as if the nurse was checking to see where everything was. Not menacing, exactly, but uncomfortable.

This isn't erotic, thought Gallagher.

"Richard, I'm not enjoying this," he said, in a low voice, as if he were reprimanding a dog. "Please stop."

Richard withdrew his hands. Once the moment passed, he was perfectly pleasant.

Hours later, Richard drove Gallagher to the ferry. This was the last time Gallagher went home with Richard.

In 1999, two events would change the course of the investigations.

Matthew Kuehn of the New Jersey State Police was contacted by a retired trooper turned private detective. Hired by Margaret Mulcahy, the PI was reinvestigating the murder of her husband. Then Mrs. Mulcahy contacted Kuehn herself. She wanted to meet and was invited to state police headquarters in West Trenton. There had been little progress, she was told, but detectives would take another look at the case. Kuehn didn't have many unsolved cases and felt obliged to see this one through.

In late April, as Richard slept off a twelve-hour shift at Mount Sinai, Nicholas Theodos was home in Iselin. The New Jersey State Police major crime unit supervisor was watching a forgettable television production called *The New Detectives*. But something caught his attention. A scientist on the show mentioned an unfamiliar fingerprinting process: vacuum metal deposition.

VMD, which had been around since the 1970s, was particularly useful for lifting old fingerprints from plastic surfaces—prints that more traditional methods, such as superglue fuming, might miss. Theodos was captivated. He knew that, despite the efforts of the respective labs in New Jersey and Rockland County, investigators still didn't have good latents off the garbage bags containing the remains of Mulcahy and Marrero. The prints lacked sufficient individual characteristics for a comparison— the arches, whorls, and loops that in sufficient number would allow a criminalist to say in court that the print had been left by one person only, to the exclusion of everyone else on the planet.

Without such a print, the likelihood of closing the cases was nil.

Theodos wrote himself a note:

Vacuum
Metal
Deposition
Process
RCMP-OTTOWA
Prints from garbage
bags

10

GOLD DUST

On Monday, Nicholas Theodos told Detective Matthew Kuehn about what he'd seen on TV. Only a few labs used vacuum metal deposition, he said, including the Toronto Police Service. As Theodos saw it, that was fortuitous, as both TPS and the New Jersey State Police ran homicide schools—annual gatherings at which law enforcement attendees paid for classes on forensics, case management, and interrogation technique. For years, New Jersey had sent investigators north to Canada and vice versa. The lieutenant colonel told Kuehn to contact Toronto and ask for a favor.

Kuehn called Allen Pollard, a detective in TPS's forensic identification services, a unit of fifty police officers and twenty civilians.

The Royal Canadian Mounted Police had used a VMD chamber for a decade. They assisted in solving more than a dozen cases brought by American law enforcement, including the 1986 strangulation of a San Diego woman found wrapped in garbage bags in a dumpster. RCMP lifted four partial fingerprints from the bags, which by then had been languishing in evidence for six years. The fingerprints were matched to a man already incarcerated.

Pollard said TPS would process evidence for North American law enforcement agencies at no charge. This was a godsend; the FBI had the technology, too, but its turnaround time for processing was a year and a half. Toronto's was a few months. Pollard told Kuehn that, once their busy season was over, he and his staff would come in on their days off to process the evidence.

In July 2000, seven years after the last known homicide, Kuehn drove an unmarked car to New York and picked up Rockland County detective Stephen Colantonio. In the trunk were two boxes of evidence from two jurisdictions, upward of forty bags from the investigations into the killings of Thomas Mulcahy and Michael Sakara. The men had taken the evidence they had at hand; there was no need, they felt, to overload the Canadian lab with the other cases. Kuehn's bags were dry, but Colantonio's, which had finally been returned by the FBI, were not, and were carefully sealed in clear plastic. They also took along a few pairs of state-police-branded sweatshirts, hats, and pants, a customary offering for fellow law enforcement.

As they sped northwest, Colantonio and Kuehn talked excitedly about the case, and the possibility that soon they might have a real suspect. They weren't exactly friends, but had known each other since 1993, when the investigative task force formed in the wake of the fourth homicide.

The task force was disbanded after a couple of months, but it was now re-formed. In a proposal from early March, Kuehn wrote that such a step would be worthwhile, in part because of "advances in forensic testing." Headed by Kuehn, the fourteen-member task force was based out of the state police barracks in Newark. Investigators hailed from the respective prosecutors' offices of Ocean County and Rockland County, as well as the Pennsylvania State Police, whose involvement was owed to the overdue inclusion of Peter Anderson among the official victims.

Kuehn began talking to newspapers about the re-formed task force, and the forensic weapon in its arsenal. "There is new technology out there," he told *Lesbian & Gay New York* in April. "There is technology that gets fingerprints off of plastic bags." That technology was the domain of Allen Pollard.

Pollard was a thirty-year veteran of the Toronto Police Service, nearing retirement. With an elegant, nicely maintained silver mustache and an easy laugh, he was a careful technician. He also was a trained cinematographer, who photographed/filmed/videotaped weddings as a hobby. Pollard charged his friends seventy-five dollars, which covered the cost of the film.

Pollard and a partner worked in Toronto's North York district, in TPS's Forensic Identification Services fingerprint lab. This was in a standalone building, on account of the contagions (including Dengue fever, rotavirus, and meningitis) handled therein. Consisting of two rooms, both kept at precisely sixty-six degrees Fahrenheit—not out of forensic necessity, but because Pollard's partner liked it that way—the lab was equipped with two state-of-the-art cyanoacrylate fuming chambers and a pricey VMD system, purchased recently for 100,000 Canadian dollars.

By October, the lab's busy season was finished and Pollard could finally attend to the evidence left by Kuehn. He and his partner opened the boxes and were pleased to notice the absence of a familiar smell: cyanoacrylate. More commonly known as superglue, cyanoacrylate was often used to develop latent fingerprints, and a lack of it meant that the processing of the bags eight years earlier, from the Mulcahy case, had been poorly executed. The detectives realized they could treat the evidence as if it had been untouched and start the process anew.

Pollard removed the bags from the plastic. He was impressed with the condition of the New Jersey evidence, how it had been dried and preserved. Unfortunately, the items from Rockland County—so neglected by the medical examiner and the FBI—were unusable and would be returned to Rockland County. "They hadn't been stored properly and we couldn't process them," recalled Pollard.

Pollard's method was to hang two bags at a time in the chamber and put a half-dozen drops of cyanoacrylate onto an aluminum dish. These dishes, of which Pollard bought thousands, were ordinarily used in the baking of butter tarts but worked well enough in the lab. The chamber was four feet high, four feet in depth, and three feet wide. A fan would circulate the fumes of cyanoacrylate, warming the glue to approximately three hundred degrees Fahrenheit. Ideally, as humidity flooded the chamber, the glue stuck to the fingerprints' substrate, which is approximately 99 percent moisture.

After twenty minutes, Pollard would extract the bags, but only after the air in the chamber was flushed out via a vent in the roof. This was of considerable importance because cyanoacrylate, when heated, produces cyanide gas. Pollard would spray the bags with alcohol and a hot-pink dye, which stuck only to the cyanoacrylate.

Last, Pollard would place the bags under an argon laser—an alternate light source—that caused the fingerprints to glow.

He would repeat this procedure with each bag.

Once it was processed with the cyanoacrylate, Pollard took the evidence to the VMD system. The machine was six feet high by five feet wide and made of inch-thick metal. A porthole in the front, four inches in diameter, allowed Pollard to monitor the progress. VMD, he liked to say, "was the ultimate process," and it was deployed in two hundred of the most serious cases a year: homicides, sexual assaults, and serial burglaries.

As before, Pollard would hang the bags, but this time he would drop into the ceramic crucible a tiny amount of twenty-four-karat gold, and zinc into another. The sealed chamber created a vacuum—"almost," he observed, "like in outer space." The gold would vaporize, which took but a moment. Then he warmed the zinc, which took on a gaseous state and adhered to the gold. The whole process took only a few minutes. If the process was successful, a silver fingerprint would be left in the absence of the substrate.

"We process a lot of material. We don't find fingerprints on the majority of stuff," Pollard recalled years later, estimating that fingerprints were found on only 11 percent of items analyzed in his lab.

Despite the odds, he always held out hope.

It took several weekends for Pollard to fume the bags with cyanoacrylate. On October 21, 2000, it was time for VMD. At the laboratory, Pollard removed his jacket and tie and donned a white lab coat and cotton gloves, over which he put blue nitrile gloves. It was Saturday, so he had the place to himself. He didn't listen to music, though, or allow himself any external distractions. Absolute concentration was required to avoid contaminating the evidence.

Pollard put the first couple of bags from the Mulcahy case into the VMD chamber. He flipped the switch to vaporize the gold and cranked up the dial. The first minute was just waiting. Then he threw the switch for the zinc. As he watched the progress through a porthole, Pollard kept his hand on the switch; he didn't want to overdevelop the latent. That could happen with VMD. There was a ten-second window where he could see a fingerprint develop, and he would have to halt the process. Otherwise, the print could be lost.

After ninety seconds, Pollard saw a fingerprint.

He threw the switch and smiled.

"When you find a fingerprint," he said years later, "it's a good day."

That Saturday, Pollard developed three prints in the VMD chamber. He was over the moon.

He had to tell someone what he'd done, what he'd found. He excitedly called his wife. Then he called Matthew Kuehn, who was ecstatic. Pollard heard cheers in the background.

All told, Pollard developed twenty-three fingerprints on four out of the forty or fifty bags put through the process. Twenty were developed using cyanoacrylate. The prints weren't all perfect; not all were sufficiently detailed or displayed ridge characteristics that could be searched in a database. Ultimately, on November 9, 2000, Pollard sent Kuehn copies of fifteen prints, which were entered into New Jersey's AFIS database.

Once Kuehn and Colantonio retrieved the Toronto evidence, including the negatives, they made seventy-five copies of the unidentified latent fingerprints. The pair then personally contacted each state crime lab—all fifty—as well as Army Criminal Investigation Command and Interpol, to discuss the case.

In April 2001, packages of evidence were mailed out. A month later, Colantonio got the call.

* * *

Kimberly Stevens, a forensic scientist in the Maine state crime lab's latent-print section, had been looking out for the package ever since she was contacted by Colantonio. She received it on May 11. Three days later, early on Monday morning, she opened the envelope and found black-and-white photographs—a contact sheet of ten fingerprints—and a cover letter on New Jersey State Police letterhead. It read, in part:

> *To Whom It May Concern:*
>
> *Please find enclosed nine (9) sets of unidentified latent fingerprints recovered from plastic bags used in the disposal of the dismembered body of victim #1, Thomas Mulcahy. The dismembered body of Thomas Mulcahy was discovered in Burlington County, New Jersey, on July 10, 1992. . . . Thomas Mulcahy was involved in international business for Bull Corporation and had traveled extensively throughout the world.*
>
> *There are two additional homicides which have been linked to the Thomas Mulcahy investigation. The two additional homicide victims are: Anthony Marrero and Michael Sakara. The dismembered body of Anthony Marrero was discovered on May 10, 1993, in Ocean County, New Jersey. The dismembered body of Michael Sakara was discovered on July 30 [sic], 1993, in Rockland County, New York.*

Once she digested it all, Stevens decided the chance of finding a match was close to zero.

Stevens, twenty-nine, had worked in the basement of the redbrick building for a year and a half. She was tall, wore an ocean-blue lab coat, and kept her brown hair in a loose bun. Her office, which had a view of the parking lot, was sparsely decorated. There was a potted palm tree, photos of her family on the wall, and a clock radio on the messy desk.

Stevens was well trained. She earned a bachelor's degree in biology from the University of San Diego and interned with the San Diego County Sheriff's Department crime lab, processing latent-fingerprint evidence. She loved the job, but after a few years she accepted an offer three thousand miles away in Augusta, Maine.

While Stevens went through the state lab's training and learned its protocols, she was limited to processing. Newly hired latent-print examiners were not tasked with AFIS comparisons until graduation. Going back decades, it had been the policy of the laboratory to make employment of the latent examiners contingent on passing a seven-week course in forensic identification at the Royal Canadian Police College.

Stevens was one of two international students admitted in 2000. The regimented course, taught by the Royal Canadian Mounted Police, included daily lectures on photography, print development, print comparisons, and even vacuum metal deposition. One instructor specialized in tire impressions; another, in blood spatter. The course was deep and rigid, and it instilled a sense of discipline in the attendees. For the final exam, students did a fingerprint-comparison test, and anything but a perfect score was unacceptable. Those who didn't measure up could be ejected, even on the last day of class.

At the time Stevens graduated, the FBI's Integrated Automated Fingerprint Identification System, or IAFIS, wasn't even a year old. The FBI had conducted comparison searches for years, and it could be an arduous exercise, taking months at a time. Now it was automated and quick, which left Stevens, in her short time in the lab, to perform many searches for outside agencies still reliant on regional AFIS systems.

Such searches were rarely successful, as the likelihood of a match largely hinged on the quality of fingerprints taken at the time of an arrest. "The patrolman or the sheriff, or what have you, often didn't have the expertise and didn't know how to take fingerprints," recalled Richard

Arnold, who had headed Maine's lab since 1974. All too frequently, there was too much ink on the pad, and the print would be smeared, or there wasn't enough ink, so the print lacked the necessary detail. As a consequence, many of the hundreds of thousands of ten-prints scanned into Maine's system, which also included New Hampshire and Vermont, were functionally useless, and the latent examiners were hamstrung.

Stevens could count on one hand the number of times she had gotten a hit. Which, more or less, is what she told a trainee on the morning of May 14. "We do this as a matter of routine, because this is what agencies do for one another, but this will not match anything in the system," she said.

Stevens set herself up in the small office adjacent to her own, which housed the AFIS computer, with its scanner and bulky monitor. There was little hanging on the wall other than photographs of tulips, which Stevens shot when she was in Ottawa.

As she scanned each contact sheet, Stevens determined if the latent fingerprints were of high enough quality for the AFIS. She trusted the judgment of the Toronto Police Service's forensic unit, but it was prudent to verify for oneself.

Stevens looked initially at the first-level detail, or the overall pattern: was it a whorl, which looked like a bird's-eye view of a tornado, or a loop, which resembled a wave on the ocean? The latent prints on the contact sheet, which she marked R1 through R10, looked like loops and arches. Then she looked at the second-level detail, or the ridges: How did the ridges flow? Where did they end? How thick were they? Where did they bifurcate?

The Canadian latents were indeed excellent, Stevens decided. Then she pulled them up on the monitor, adjusted each print's contrast, indicated to AFIS whether the pattern was a loop or a whorl, and plotted each fingerprint's ridge endings. She sent them off, one by one. All the while, she remained doubtful that anything would come of it.

"There's just no way," Stevens told the trainee.

At 10:51 A.M., the search was complete. For each of the ten individual prints Stevens fed into the system, AFIS produced thirty possible matches—each inked fingerprint had the same whorl, ridge endings, and bifurcations.

As each AFIS print appeared, Stevens compared it to the latents Toronto lifted off the garbage bags. Again, she looked at first-level and second-level details. Nearly all the recommendations were imperfect, for one reason or another. A ridge might slope in the same direction, but the number of ridges in the center of the pattern wouldn't agree. This wasn't a surprise to Stevens, who lived with the knowledge that inked fingerprints were buried in the system that would surely never be matched to latents.

However, on this particular morning, two of the prints stuck out: R1, an index finger, and R8, a ring finger.

They were from the same inked fingerprint card.

Stevens pulled up R1 first. She checked off the first-level similarities. Then the second-level. Stevens realized that, contrary to what she'd told the trainee, the details of the unknown and the inked were starting to agree.

"Well," she said, "maybe there's a possibility here."

She pulled up R8 next. That, too, agreed.

She was startled.

The inked print card by design contained neither name nor date of birth. Stevens needed more information, which meant requesting the physical inked fingerprint card from the State Bureau of Investigation.

Despite her growing excitement, a match was at that point still just a possibility; confirming an identification solely from AFIS was verboten. At the time, there was a pronounced disparity between the quality of a physical print card and an AFIS image, which was relatively blurry. "So at that point," she recalls, "it's just a person of interest, not *the* person."

Stevens wrote down the print-card number and called headquarters, housed in the neighboring building. The State Bureau of Identification was, like Stevens's office, in the basement. SBI had boxes and boxes of prints, taken through the years.

The card was ready within minutes.

The print card was nearly three decades old. On one side were the left-hand prints and right-hand prints. Text on the back revealed that the young man whose ridges and loops were so carefully documented had been arrested on May 1, 1973, by the Maine State Police. He was a student and lived in Orono, but his birthplace was Plymouth, Massachusetts. His crime: homicide.

Also on the back of the card were the telltale signs of an acquittal: EXPUNGED! DO NOT RELEASE.[1]

Stevens absorbed the contents of the print card and performed the final comparison of the latents and inked prints. Hunched over a long table, she looked through four-power magnifiers.

The fingerprints were a definite match.

Stevens couldn't wait to tell the detectives what had happened. But first, it was protocol to verify each latent match. Stevens called over a colleague to double-check her work.

He, too, bent over the four-power magnifiers. After a minute, he stood up and turned to Stevens: "Yeah, it's good."

"I was jumping up and down for joy and couldn't believe it," Stevens says.

Stevens called New Jersey first and asked for Matthew Kuehn. He wasn't available. Then she called Stephen Colantonio.

"I'm calling from Maine," she said. "I have some information for you. I have a name."

Colantonio told Stevens to hang on. He needed a pen, and he needed to sit down.

Stevens told the detective about an arrest and a homicide and an expunged record.

"His name," she said, "is Richard Rogers."

---

1 In an email to the author, responding to a query about why, despite the expungement, Rogers's print was in the AFIS system, the Maine State Police staff attorney wrote: "While I cannot answer your inquiry as it relates to the Rogers case specifically, I have inquired here and learned that, once prints are entered by the State of Maine into AFIS, the State of Maine does not remove them from that system."

11

THE EDGE OF THE WOODS

April 30, 1973

On Monday, Jason Manchester did his laundry.[1] Mondays were laundry day. Manchester, a graduate student at the University of Maine, walked out of a laundromat in nearby Old Town, a city of nine thousand best known for its eponymous canoe manufacturer.[2] As he held his clean clothes, an acquaintance of Manchester's entered with dirty clothes. Both studied French in the university's Foreign Languages and Classics Department. They'd hung out together the previous Friday evening, at the German Club's double feature of *The Cabinet of Dr. Caligari* and *Nosferatu*. Afterward, they went to Pat's Pizza and a pub a couple of doors down called Gambino's, both in Orono.

"Wait a minute," Manchester said. "You told me this morning that you did your laundry on Saturday."

"Oh," said Richard Rogers, stammering, "I, I did my whites on Saturday night."

Manchester went home and hung up his shirts. It was odd, he thought. That very morning, just before his nine o'clock class, he and Richard had

---

1 This name has been changed.
2 A year earlier, an Old Town canoe could be seen in *Deliverance*.

encountered each other on the steps of Little Hall, which housed the languages department. Manchester inquired about Richard's Saturday night. His own was uneventful—up late talking with his landlady.

"I, I did laundry," replied Richard.

The next morning, Tuesday, May 1, Manchester and Richard, both teaching assistants, were in the language lab together. Students had to sit at desks and listen to tapes for fifty minutes a week, while the TAs ensured they focused. Manchester told Richard that he heard Howard University was looking for French instructors for the following year.

A student ran in.

"Monsieur," he said. "There's been a murder. They found a body in Old Town!"

"Oh my God, Richard, did you hear this?" said Manchester. "Can you imagine? Something *exciting* finally happening in sleepy Old Town, Maine."

Richard seemed a little nervous, but not unusually so. Manchester continued to focus on his students.

At 10:45, fifteen minutes before the start of the next class, men in suits appeared outside the doorway. Richard got up and walked out. After a minute, he returned.

"Jason, if I'm not back when the class starts, would you turn the tape on for them?"

"Sure, absolutely," said Manchester. They frequently covered for each other.

Manchester finished his class, and Richard had not returned. The director of the language lab approached. He thought Richard was a strange guy.

"Hey, Monsieur. Where's your buddy?" he asked. "He's on duty."

Manchester told him about the men in suits and said he didn't know what happened to Richard.

In the afternoon, Manchester went home to his apartment. His phone rang.

"Richard! What happened? Where are you?"

"What are you doing?" Richard asked.

Manchester could hear an urgency in his classmate's voice and said he wasn't doing anything.

"Well, could you come to state police headquarters?"

State police headquarters was five minutes away, on Route 2 in Orono. During the drive, Manchester cycled through plausible reasons why Richard was with the police. Was it drugs? Maybe there had been a death back home and police had contacted Richard. Maybe his mother died. Or his sister.

When Manchester entered the tiny headquarters, there was a desk on the right-hand side of the room.

"Can I help you?" a woman asked.

"I got a telephone call from somebody who said he's here."

"Well, who would that be?"

"Richard Rogers."

The woman told Manchester to wait a moment. She hit a buzzer. A man, dressed in a suit, came down a dark hallway.

"State your name," he said.

Manchester, standing at attention, gave his full name.

"Where do you live?"

"Five Crystal Lane, Orono, Maine."[3]

The man, a district attorney, said to follow him. They walked down the hallway; then he opened the door to a small room.

Richard was sitting in a chair. He looked, Manchester thought, like a scared puppy. There was a small desk and a half-consumed bottle of ten-cent Coke.

On the desk was a paper that said JASON MANCHESTER and his phone number.

Manchester looked at Richard and said, "What—was I your one phone call?"

---

3 This address has been changed. There is no 5 Crystal Lane in Orono.

"We'll leave you two alone for a while," the district attorney said.

Manchester sat down diagonally across from Richard.

"Richard, what the hell is going on?"

On Saturday morning, said Richard, he went to his bedroom and found his housemate Fred rifling through his bureau. Fred had come at him with a hammer, "and now he's dead." Years later, Manchester recalled he had seen "no indication of a struggle" on Richard.

Manchester asked if Richard had called the police.

"No, I was afraid to."

What had he done with the body?

"Well, I waited until the nighttime, and I wrapped his body in my Boy Scout tent. And when nobody else was home, I dragged his body out of the house and across the parking lot and into my car. And I drove into Old Town, into the woods."

Manchester imagined Fred's body going down the staircase, his head bouncing, step after step.

Richard said the police had confiscated his bedroom rug.

"Oh," said Manchester, "you weren't able to wash Fred's blood out of it?"

Richard blanched.

"Don't tell anybody," Richard said. "I'll be back in school on Thursday, and no one will know that anything happened." The next day was Maine Day, so there were no classes.

"Richard, I hate to burst your bubble, but this is bigger than Watergate," said Manchester (John Dean had been fired a week earlier). "If you don't think this is going to be all over the newspapers, and all over the radio, and all over television, you're out of your mind."

A reporter from the *Bangor Daily News* accompanied the Old Town police to the scene. The area was recovering from the worst flooding seen in a half century, which just a few days earlier left Old Town looking like a lake. When they arrived at Route 116, the reporter thought to himself,

Do I really want to see this? He had never seen a dead body. But he got out of the car and stopped fifty feet away from the victim, who lay by the side of the road. It was shocking to see the body, he recalled, because he could not see any obvious injury.

Earlier that afternoon, two cyclists found the deceased young man at the edge of the woods, twenty feet from the road. He was shirtless, covered in blood, and wrapped in green canvaslike material resembling a tent. Nearby were tire marks, which, police surmised, had been left by the car from which he was dumped. There was no identification on the body, but in his clothing detectives found a key.

The key was traced to a post office box in Orono rented by a student at the University of Maine: Frederic Alan Spencer.

Fred Spencer's parents, Claude Spencer and Louise Wible, met at the University of Michigan during the latter half of World War II. They fell in love, married, and each earned a degree in chemistry. After a move to Boston in 1946, Claude earned a Ph.D. in chemistry from the Massachusetts Institute of Technology. A son, Fred, was born on May 13, 1950. After a decade at Merck, by which time Fred was nine, Claude was hired as a chemist by the Norwich Pharmacal Company in Chenango County, New York. The Spencers moved to a big blue house in a nice part of town.

Sixty miles from Syracuse and two hundred miles from Manhattan, Chenango was the northern end of Appalachia. Norwich, the county seat, was bordered to the west by a creek and to the east by a river. It was insulated from current events, and during the turbulent 1960s was more or less untouched by antiwar sentiment or the civil rights movement. Like surrounding cities and towns, Norwich was religious, white, and conservative. But it was also, in a sense, an outlier: relative to the rest of the county, Norwich's population of eight thousand was well off and educated. To the extent there was a divide in Norwich, it was between those who worked for Norwich Pharmacal, known as the Pharmacy, and those who did not.

The Pharmacy was founded in 1887. The company introduced the first antiseptic surgical dressing in 1893, and then a wildly successful antacid eight years later called Pepto-Bismol. By the 1950s, the Pharmacy employed thousands, including Claude.

Claude and Louise were encouraging, affectionate parents. They didn't push Fred academically, but he did well anyway. He is remembered as assiduously neat, well groomed, and fond of green pants, which he wore every day. A sense of humor, yes, but not outwardly funny. He was quiet, too—gentle, soft-spoken. Possessing considerable intelligence, Fred did not flaunt it. He studied hard and remained humble. Fred's physics teacher described him as "well-mannered, well-behaved, very bright," and said his labs were well written and completed on time. Fred, like his parents, excelled in science. In his senior year, he won an award from the American Chemical Society.

Fred wasn't tall, maybe five foot six, but he was in good shape. He enjoyed table tennis, which he played in his parents' basement. Contact sports didn't hold his attention. What he really loved was the outdoors. When the Spencers vacationed in Maine, he solo hiked sections of the Appalachian Trail. Back home, he was an enthusiastic Boy Scout. Indeed, the Spencers sent him to a monthlong Scout camp in the Rocky Mountains, where he hiked trails, rode horses, and tended cattle. Fred was one of two Norwich kids from troop 63 to make the trip. He and a classmate shared a tent and cooking responsibilities.

The smart kids at school tended to keep each other's company. This included Jenny Riley, a dark-haired girl with a frequently intense expression, who wore Fred's class ring around her neck.[4] They met in homeroom junior year. "I think I've always been intrigued by people's brains, and he was a smart guy," she says. "This is going to sound presumptuous on my part, but I thought I was his match."

Fred and Jenny began dating, which, because this was sleepy Norwich,

---

4 This name has been changed.

consisted mostly of once-a-month dances and movies. She remembers seeing *The Lion in Winter*. One Christmas, she baked Fred 365 chocolate chip cookies—his favorite.

For the junior prom, Fred picked up Jenny in the family station wagon. It was customary to go out to dinner prior to the dance, but that year the Spencers hosted a meal for their Turkish exchange student and his date. Louise fixed a fancy dinner, then left the foursome to eat without the intrusion of meddling parents. Afterward, Fred, clad in his tux, escorted Jenny in her long pink linen dress to the high school. The dance was in the gym, decorated in accordance with the theme: under the sea. In a large clamshell sat the prom king and queen.

"He was my first love, and he was wonderful," says Jenny. They never really broke up, continuing to see each other when Fred went off to college—to the University of Michigan, like his parents. Jenny went to a Catholic college in South Bend, Indiana. He wrote her letters daily and visited a couple of times freshman year. She went to see him in Michigan, too. But Jenny spent the entire sophomore year studying in France, so they didn't see each other for a while. The summer before senior year, they drove together from Norwich to Ann Arbor.

Fred and Jenny began to grow apart. Still, they kept in touch. In high school, he had given her a black-and-white photograph he'd taken of a tree she loved. In the spring of 1973, he sent her another photo of a similar tree, but in color. By then, she had been in love with someone else for almost a year.

Senior year, Fred asked if he could visit over Thanksgiving weekend. Jenny said no. "I just felt like I was moving on and didn't want to lead him on."

Jenny remained close with the Spencers. After she got the call that Fred had been killed, she rushed to the Summit Street house to be with them. She had been an important part of Fred's life and felt a need to comfort his parents. The Spencers had harbored hopes Jenny would marry Fred, but as far as she could tell there was no resentment that the union hadn't come to pass. They embraced her, and for three days their son's ex-girlfriend kept them company amid the grief. There were tears, of course, and confusion. *How did this happen?* they asked. *Who did it? What in the world is going on?* Losing a child is horrendous enough, but to murder? It's almost impossible to fathom. The Spencers never recovered.

In the days after Fred was killed, neither Jenny nor the Spencers concerned themselves with the police investigation. They knew very little of what was going on in Orono. But the fact of Fred's sudden death provided his high school girlfriend with a grim epiphany. At twenty-three, she learned "that everything can change on a dime, and it doesn't matter who you are or what you are."

On Tuesday morning, May 1, the state police had visited 10 Main Street, a two-story house in Orono. They pounded on the front and rear doors. William Mazerolle, a philosophy major, was home, and rattled. Over the weekend, he saw stains on the red carpet in the stairwell. He noticed such things, because the landlords gave him a discount on the rent if he cleaned the place. The stains were dark, and he assumed they were grease. His housemate, Fred, liked to work on his car. He was still thinking about the stains when he heard the door knocks.

"Is Fred here?"

Mazerolle invited the police in.

He walked upstairs, knocked on a bedroom door, and yelled, "*Fred! Fred!*"

No response. This was somewhat troubling to Mazerolle because he hadn't seen his housemate in a while.

He came back downstairs. The police produced two photos of Fred's face and shoulders. He looked black and blue, but not seriously injured. "That's Fred," Mazerolle said. He put on shoes and accompanied the police to the Orono barracks for further conversation.

Investigators didn't pressure the student. They asked him to draw a floorplan of the house. Fred lived at one end of the upstairs hallway, Richard in the center, and Mazerolle had the third bedroom on the other end, across from the bathroom. A fourth housemate lived in the basement.

Mazerolle told them about his roommates. Richard was a quiet, odd guy who taught French and sang in the Newman Center church folk group. He was outwardly squeamish and covered his eyes during the violent Ludovico technique scene in *A Clockwork Orange*. Fred was an easygoing, long-haired graduate student who spent weekends in the wilderness of western Maine and New Hampshire. He had been recruited to the College of Life Sciences and Agriculture, an advisor wrote, "based on his outstanding academic record and future promise as a research scientist."

The three men were not close, Mazerolle said, just acquaintances. What little time they spent together was in the kitchen, preparing meals for themselves. A guest remembers Fred once offering Richard leftovers as he was cleaning up. "Do you want this? Because otherwise, I'm going to throw it out," he said.

"It makes me feel so good to know that I was one step ahead of the garbage can," Richard replied.

Fred and Richard didn't care for each other. Mazerolle sensed a certain tension. Fred found Richard curious. He seemed so nervous and tightly wound. When he talked, his breathing would get labored. He breathed through his mouth, which was disconcerting. It seemed to Mazerolle that Richard, with his short hair, his effeminate nature, and general quirkiness, was a source of amusement for Fred. But that's all it was, he thought. There was no history of violence, no indication that one man would attack the other.

Detectives took Mazerolle to lunch at Pat's Pizza. Pat's was famous; it was believed no student had ever graduated from the University of Maine without eating there at least once.[5] Then a trio of officers escorted him

---

5 A few years earlier, an English major named Stephen King sat at the counter and drank beer.

back to 10 Main Street. They walked upstairs and found some spongy material in the hallway. They had seen this before, the prior evening, in the canvas that held Fred's body. They followed its trail to the room of Richard Rogers. There were blood droplets on the wall and bloody fingerprints on the door near the entrance to the bedroom. On the floor in front of the bathroom was a hexagon-shaped imprint of the sole of a shoe. That, too, was blood.

In Richard's room was a hammer.

Richard was brought to the police barracks and, under interrogation, confessed to killing Fred. Fred suffered eight blows to the back of the skull and, as a further indignity, Richard had placed a plastic bag over his face. Any of the blows would have been fatal.

The next afternoon, hours after Fred's body was flown home to Norwich, Richard was arraigned, and he pled not guilty. He was held without bail at the county jail in Bangor. His fingerprints, height, and weight were taken. Richard was six foot one and only 140 pounds. Jail records note his brown eyes and an abdominal scar.

Not noted: his lack of defensive wounds.

On Saturday, five days after Fred's body was discovered, Jason Manchester visited Richard at the county jail. As Manchester sat in the waiting area, Margaret and Earle Baker, Richard's mother and stepfather, arrived. He introduced himself. She told Manchester that Richard was allowed only one visitor at a time, so he had been bumped. "I hope you understand. He needs to see his mother more than he needs to see you."

After the thirty-minute visit, the Bakers asked if Manchester would help them sort through Richard's books and food.

After seeing Richard himself, Manchester went to 10 Main Street. Mrs. Baker was in the kitchen. Each resident had his own cabinet of food, and she was going through her son's. Manchester was startled by her apparent calm. As she picked up each can, she'd chatter to Manchester. *Oh, my kids will eat this. My kids will eat that . . . Oh, peanut butter. My kids love peanut butter. Will you eat this?*

Manchester thought about his own mother. Had she been in Mrs. Baker's position, she'd have been inconsolable. He got the sense that Richard's mother was in self-preservation mode.

Other classmates had come to see Richard, including a member of the Newman Center folk group. During the six months he was incarcerated at the county jail, she saw Richard two or three Saturdays a month. He was thrilled to have the company. They weren't allowed to discuss the case, so the conversation was light—restricted to books, movies, and their respective activities. They didn't know each other well.

"It was very awkward," she recalls.

On Monday, October 29, the trial for the murder of Fred Spencer began in Bangor's superior court. Foahd Saliem, the assistant attorney general, represented the state. He was considered a decent man, and a calm, competent lawyer. Richard was represented by Errol K. Paine, a locally prominent trial attorney who gravitated toward controversial cases. He didn't, as a rule, do much pretrial preparation. He didn't share strategy with associates and chose to keep everything in his head. Oftentimes, he entered the courtroom with little more than a copy of the indictment. In at least one instance, said William Cohen—who met Paine during law school and cofounded the firm with him in 1967—he walked into a federal court "without a note in his hand."[6]

There had been an attempt to avoid a trial. In chambers, the judge tried to broker a plea agreement between Paine and Saliem. But Richard could not be persuaded. Asked if there was any offense to which his client would be willing to plea, Paine replied, "Littering."

Testimony commenced on Wednesday, October 31.[7] The medical examiner told the court Fred had died of "massive head injuries." The jury

6 Many years later, Cohen was appointed secretary of defense by President Bill Clinton.
7 The court transcript wasn't preserved, and there is no record in the newspapers of opening statements.

was shown color slides of eight moon-shaped wounds, and presumably informed that Fred's pinky broke during the struggle with Richard.

Saliem called Manchester, who by then had graduated and was living in another state. He recounted his conversation with Richard at the barracks. Manchester recalled Richard telling him that, when he entered his bedroom, Fred was standing near the dresser with a roofing hammer. After Richard hit him repeatedly with the hammer, Manchester said, Richard claimed Fred hadn't seemed dead—just unconscious.

The state continued its case on Thursday. The atmosphere in the courtroom was relaxed. Saliem seemed confident in the strength of his case. Paine was confident in his own.

Police, from both the campus and state, testified. A professor in the entomology department attested to Fred's good character. He found the questions "inane." Paine declined to question the state's witnesses. "No questions, no questions," he'd say to the judge.

His associates were befuddled. *You're trying a murder case and you have no questions?* "It's expected that you would ask questions, even if they don't get you anywhere," said an associate years later.

At the day's conclusion, Paine made a motion to reduce the charges from murder to manslaughter. The motion was granted. The state's evidence, said the judge, showed that Richard had been provoked, and thus "the jury could not find that the actions of the defendant exceeded the crime of manslaughter."

After several witnesses spoke of Richard's good reputation, the defendant himself testified. "Errol had the opinion that he would not have to prep this kid," remembered the court reporter.

Echoing Manchester, Richard said Fred had been standing near his dresser when he attacked with a hammer. Wrote the *Bangor Daily News* reporter:

Rogers said that he wrestled the hammer away from Spencer and in self-defense inflicted eight blows to Spencer's head. Rogers testified that after that Spencer was still "struggling" and that he put a plastic bag on Spencer's face to knock him out.

Spectators felt Richard did an excellent job on the stand. He had been calm, concise, and persuasive. He argued the bludgeoning of Fred had been done, as his lawyer put it, "in passion under sudden provocation." Even so, Richard's case discomforted Paine's associates. "Putting the plastic bag over his head takes self-defense out of it, it seemed to me," one observed.

During cross-examination, Richard told the court he had not intended to kill Fred. In a "daze," he said, he attempted to clean the room and the bloodstained rug. "I just didn't know what to do. I wanted very much to go to the police, but by then I felt it would look very suspicious." Instead, in the middle of the night, Richard put Fred's body into his 1968 Dodge Dart, drove across the Stillwater River, and made a sharp right onto Route 16. This was a dark, residential, untrafficked stretch of road. He stayed on 16 for fifteen minutes until he made another right, this time onto 116. By then he had entered Old Town. After a minute or two he got to Birch Stream, which fed into the Stillwater. It was around here that Richard unloaded Fred's body. Surrounded by trees and water and not a house in sight, this must've seemed, to Richard, like the middle of nowhere.

On Friday morning, six months and a day after Richard's arrest, the judge gave directions to the jury of six men and six women. *In order to find the defendant not guilty,* he said, *they must be convinced he had not acted in self-defense.*

Without a transcript, it's hard to ascertain what set of facts the jury was working with. None of the newspaper coverage suggests Paine used a gay panic defense. But at least one spectator remembers something to that effect. Decades later, Orono residents recalled a "gay angle" to the tragic event. They heard Fred had come on to Richard, that this act precipitated the killing. "It was in the rumor mill," said the wife of a professor. "There was speculation."

The jury deliberated for only three hours. A guilty verdict was anticipated.[8]

The jury foreman stood up and announced that Richard had been found not guilty of manslaughter. Richard smiled, turned to Errol Paine, and said, "I can't thank you enough. I can't thank you enough."

Paine, according to his associates, was the only person in the room not surprised by the verdict.

As a juror walked out of the courtroom, Richard had something to say to him: "Thank you very much. I assure you that you did the right thing."

The last time Manchester saw Richard was in February 1978. They met in Manhattan, which was recovering from its most severe blizzard in decades. Manchester wanted to meet in a public place, and they agreed on a restaurant by Rockefeller Center.

The former acquaintances sat down and ordered drinks. Manchester had something weighing on him. He mused that the double jeopardy clause was a wonderful aspect of the American legal system. Then he said, "I have one question: what really happened?"

Richard began quickly inhaling and exhaling.

"Just, just, *just like I said.*"

Manchester picked up his drink.

"Oh, really?" he said. "Let me tell you something. I didn't believe it then and I don't believe it now."

Manchester felt Richard owed him. He had, after all, been dragged into the middle of a legal proceeding. Manchester could see, however, that Richard would exhibit neither honesty nor contrition. He'd con-

---

8 And, for the court reporter, hoped for. A guilty verdict meant that multiple copies of the transcript would need to be typed up, and he would earn enough money typing them to build himself a garage.

vinced himself of his own innocence. Even so, Manchester didn't leave the table, and they ordered dinner.

"Richard," he continued, "when we were in graduate school, it seemed to me that you were a little bit confused about your sexuality. Have you made a decision? Are you gay, are you straight?"

Looking to the left, then the right, Richard whispered, "Straight."

Manchester didn't believe that, either. He didn't care that Richard was gay, but he resented being lied to about it.

They finished dinner and walked around Manhattan, ending up at a bar two blocks from the Port Authority Bus Terminal. They ordered more drinks. Even with the assistance of alcohol, they had nothing to say to each other and lapsed into French. After a while, Manchester called it a night. They exchanged goodbyes in front of the bar. Maybe they hugged; maybe they shook hands. Manchester isn't certain. He walked toward Port Authority. "We're never going to see each other again," Manchester said, but he wasn't sure if Richard heard him.

12

INDISPUTABLE EVIDENCE

May 14, 2001

At six o'clock in the evening, Rockland County detective Stephen Colantonio called a detective in the New Jersey State Police. That Monday, minutes earlier, he'd learned that the likely murderer of four men in New York over a three-year period—the man investigators across multiple states and jurisdictions had been pursuing for eight years—was Richard W. Rogers, a nurse at Mount Sinai Hospital. Colantonio sought to inform Matthew Kuehn. The problem, he learned, was that Kuehn was celebrating his twenty-fifth wedding anniversary, and he was encouraged not to interrupt the man. But *of course* he would. When you work shoulder to shoulder with a man all these years, you don't want him to read about an identification as significant as this in the newspaper.

Colantonio called. Kuehn wasn't a bit upset.

Ten days later, the Thursday before Memorial Day weekend, Kuehn and Colantonio met with a captain at One Police Plaza, the NYPD's brutalist headquarters by the Brooklyn Bridge in Manhattan. They proposed a plan: beginning on Monday, May 27, the department's major case squad and Joint Terrorist Task Force would surveil Rogers. He was working the 7:30 P.M. to 7:00 A.M. shift and could be shadowed the moment he left the hospital. The surveillance would last for at least one week.

From the beginning—the investigation of Peter Anderson's homicide by the Pennsylvania State Police in 1991—the NYPD had taken, at best, a secondary role. However, Rockland County and New Jersey detectives didn't hesitate to turn over the surveillance operation to the NYPD. It was a no-brainer, really. A crime scene still hadn't been found, and it was entirely possible the men were killed within New York City limits. Furthermore, it was common sense for such a fluid, unpredictable operation to be run by actual New Yorkers, who worked in the five boroughs every day. It was vital that such men, zipping around in undercover vehicles, not look like tourists or out-of-town cops; just one mistake could spook the target.

Sure, there was a modicum of disappointment regarding the NYPD's role, recalled Ocean County's Thomas Hayes. "That's the way it's gotta be. It's their backyard."

The hope was that Richard would lead investigators to an as-yet-unknown property, either rented or owned. Perhaps it was another home or even a dungeon—a possibility that, while seemingly preposterous, couldn't be discounted. The murders, after all, had to take place *somewhere*. But it was more likely that Richard would tip them off to an elusive bank account or post office box. Or, at the very least, reveal basic facts: where he ate breakfast, shopped, did laundry. Mundane as it was, all this could provide leads that would assist an eventual prosecution.

If nothing else, knowing where Richard was at any given moment would allow investigators to arrest him on their own terms—on the way to a black-tie function, maybe, or after a night out at a bar. The idea was to retain the element of surprise, but simultaneously keep him calm. No one wanted Richard to be defensive or upset. "You wanted to be low-key, without rattling him," says Jack Repsha, who was in charge of the New Jersey State Police's major crime unit.

The NYPD captain liked the plan. Despite the minimal odds of success, he figured, *How can you justify not taking the chance?* He promised the surveillance would take effect Monday morning.

Sunday evening, May 27—twelve hours before surveillance was set to commence—the investigators were finally relaxing. Thomas Hayes and his wife were at the Jersey Shore, just about to start dinner. Michael Mohel, Hayes's boss, was at a barbecue. Repsha was barefoot in his backyard, cradling a gin and tonic. Colantonio was in his backyard, too, hosting his annual Memorial Day celebration.

At around six, Colantonio got a phone call from the NYPD captain. He didn't waste words: *Richard Rogers was on his way to One Police Plaza.* Two of his major case detectives, he said, visited Rogers at Mount Sinai and requested his presence at headquarters. They told him he'd been a victim of credit card fraud. He was about to be arrested.

"For what?" said Colantonio. "You have no charges."

The captain didn't have an answer for him. His hands were tied.

Everyone mobilized. Colantonio drove in from Rockland County, the others from New Jersey.

Upon arrival, Colantonio, Mohel, and Repsha were summoned to a conference room. A painting of Theodore Roosevelt, New York City's one-time police commissioner, hung on the wall. They were greeted by William Allee, the NYPD's walrusy chief of detectives. Acknowledging the detectives' anger, Allee took responsibility for the decision and stood by it. The NYPD was just being cautious, he said. Three days earlier, they'd released a suspect from custody, only to see him kill and dismember a man.

Mohel could barely contain himself. "This is all bullshit," he told the chief.

The investigators had been working on this case for a decade. Not unreasonably, they were livid. A few even conducted a thought experiment: *What if New Jersey pulled back and told their brothers in blue—who lacked any evidence linking Rogers to the crimes, or even a justification to keep him in custody—they were on their own? Well, what then?* The decision to short-circuit the investigation had put the NYPD in a potentially precarious position. But only in theory, of course; New Jersey wouldn't actually undermine New York. The case was more important than a ham-handed move by the NYPD.

Eventually, investigators learned the rest of the story from the detectives who escorted Richard to One Police Plaza: the unwitting catalyst for the disaster was Rudolph Giuliani, the mayor of New York City, whose mother, Helen, had been a patient at Mount Sinai since May 21. Giuliani himself wasn't concerned about his mother being in relative proximity to a suspected murderer—indeed, nothing suggests he was even aware of it—and given Rogers's targets, he had no reason to be.[1] But the upper echelon of the NYPD were worried on his behalf. The order to arrest Richard had come from the commissioner himself, Bernard Kerik.

Years later, asked about the NYPD's actions, Kerik denied it: "This really doesn't make any sense to me. I don't remember any of this. It couldn't have been that big of a deal, or I would remember." In another interview, he said, "Here's what I *do* know: If Giuliani's mother was at the hospital, and we had some psychopath at the same hospital, and they wanted to make sure there was some separation of the two, I can *promise* you Chief Allee would have come to my office and told me personally. Period. There's no way around that. That never happened."[2]

It was another week before news of what transpired seeped into the press. "Members of the task force that tracked down gay-slay suspect Richard Rogers believe the NYPD moved in too soon to arrest him—dashing hopes of tying him to other killings," reported the *Daily News*. The tabloid, with the help of NYPD and New Jersey sources, revealed the surveillance, the matter of Helen Giuliani, and how Allee was to blame. Sources made sure to get across what had been lost by the NYPD's decision:

> "The questions we wanted answered were . . . What has he been doing since 1993? Who does he associate with? Did he have a place upstate or in Jersey under an assumed name?" the source said. "He could have led a whole separate life, and now we may never know about it."

---

1 When I asked Giuliani about this in October 2019, he replied, "Crazy."
2 Later, after further inquiry, but off the record, Kerik said something different.

"We lost the opportunity to conduct a thorough interview and learn about any unknown cases he may be responsible for," agreed a second task force source.

The investigators didn't talk publicly about it at the time, but they all believed Richard had killed dozens of men. In fact, they assumed he killed people whenever he went on vacation.

"The public and the gay community don't really know the damage that may have been done to the investigation," a source told the paper.

Thomas Hayes, now a sergeant with the Ocean County Prosecutor's Office, and David Dalrymple, a New Jersey State Police detective, were chosen to interview Richard. Dalrymple, tall, lean, and sharply dressed, had a reputation as a calm, methodical interrogator, just as comfortable talking to a homeless man as to a CEO.

Hayes thought the odds of Richard telling them anything useful were low. Richard had been sitting in NYPD headquarters for hours, and presumably realized that victims of credit card fraud are not ordinarily invited to One Police Plaza. As Mohel would note, "He's a serial killer, but he's not stupid."

At 12:03 A.M. on May 28, Hayes and Dalrymple, both in suits, entered room 1108-A. The tiny space on the eleventh floor wasn't a real interrogation room. It was equipped with a small table, a few chairs, and some lockers. Richard was sitting at the table, uncuffed, wearing a pink Oxford shirt, khaki pants, penny loafers, and glasses. He was nervous, but polite. The detectives introduced themselves and shook Richard's hand. To Hayes, he seemed soft, not in particularly good shape. *How the hell did this guy do what he did?* Another detective, who peeked in before the interview began, thought Richard looked like the uniquely timid comic book character from the 1920s Caspar Milquetoast.

Dalrymple read Richard his Miranda rights off a card—a signal that, even absent an arrest warrant, Richard was not free to simply walk out. Dalrymple asked Richard if he understood. Richard wrote his initials next to each right. Dalrymple and Hayes signed the card, too. Hayes expected that would be the end of it, that Richard would invoke his rights immediately. But he didn't, and to this day the retired detective doesn't know why.

It was curious, said Richard, that detectives from New Jersey would come to New York to interview him. What would they want with him?

The detectives threw the question back at him: *What do you think we want with you?*

Richard said that perhaps they wanted to discuss an arrest from 1988. A man named Sandy or Fred, he wasn't really sure, accused him of assault. There had been a trial.

Well, no. In fact, what they wanted to talk about were the killings of four gay men between 1991 and 1993. Dalrymple showed Richard a flyer with faces on it: Thomas Mulcahy, Anthony Marrero, and Michael Sakara.[3] They asked if any of the men looked familiar. Richard pointed to the photo of Michael, and said he knew him, that they were both patrons of the Five Oaks. He denied knowing either Anthony or Tom.

The detectives took Richard's pedigree information: He was born in Plymouth, Massachusetts, and moved to Florida, where he went to high school. Then he attended Florida Southern College, graduating in 1972. Jumping forward some years chronologically, Richard said he moved to New York and earned a degree from Pace University's school of nursing in 1978. He was hired by Mount Sinai the following year, and had been happily employed ever since.

Richard did not mention his time at the University of Maine.

The detectives found Rogers polite, even cooperative. They asked if he traveled. Quite a lot, he said, frequently driving all over the country: California, Florida, Massachusetts, West Virginia, Atlantic City, and Blytheville, Arkansas, where he visited his mother and stepfather.

---

3 None of the investigators are sure why Peter Anderson's photo wasn't among them.

The detectives returned to the homicides. That's when Richard began to get impatient.

"Other than recognizing Mr. Sakara, I don't know if I can help you with anything else."

"Richard," Hayes replied, looking straight at him, "we're not here looking for your help tonight. You're here because we have indisputable evidence, both physical and circumstantial, that links you to these four homicides."

Richard had been sitting with both feet on the floor, hands on his lap. Now, though, he crossed his legs and arms and sat straight back in his chair. It seemed to the detectives he had become guarded.

"We're going to tell you now—we're going to go through each homicide in the order they occurred, and we're going to tell you what physical evidence we have that links you to each crime," said Hayes.

They started with Peter Anderson: On May 5, 1991, Peter's body was found in Lancaster County, Pennsylvania, in a large garbage bag. On that bag were numerous fingerprints that were positively identified as Richard's.

Richard nodded his head up and down. He began audibly swallowing, taking large gulps of air. Dalrymple believed Richard gulped at points in the conversation where one might normally respond to a question or accusation. He also began to pass gas. "He kept excusing himself," Hayes testified.

The detectives asked Richard if he would explain why he committed the murders. He wouldn't. Fine, they said, and moved on.

"We're going to discuss another homicide that occurred in July of 1992," said Dalrymple. "The body of Thomas Mulcahy was found. His head, arms, and upper torso were dismembered and found in Burlington County, and his legs were found later that day in Ocean County right off of the parkway at a rest stop."

Fingerprints were recovered from the bags containing the body parts, and were unquestionably Richard's.

They told Richard about the surgical gloves and the keyhole saw and how the items had been traced back to Staten Island—and how the nexus between the victims was piano bars in Manhattan.

Once the review of the Mulcahy evidence was over, Richard nodded.

Hayes told Richard it was time to talk about another crime, this one from May 1993: the murder of Anthony Marrero. They went through victimology. Anthony, they said, was a known sex worker, last seen around the Port Authority Bus Terminal. They reviewed the physical evidence: fingerprints found on the bags were Richard's.

The Acme bag containing Anthony's head had been traced to Staten Island.

Richard listened. Then he nodded and gulped.

Finally, the detectives moved on to Michael Sakara, whose body was found in Rockland County in July 1993. Investigators had blanketed the Five Oaks, where Michael was last seen alive, and talked to everyone. *As Michael was leaving the bar,* Hayes and Dalrymple said, *he had been seen with a man that fit your description. We know you told the bartender you were a nurse, even if you lied about your name and where you worked. Witnesses saw you and Michael get into a light-colored vehicle.* Earlier in the interview, Richard said he drove a 1991 light gray Toyota Corolla at the time of the homicide.

Richard nodded and stared straight ahead. He did not deny involvement in the crimes. He never said, *I did not do this.*

"Do you think I need a lawyer?" he said. "Should I consult with an attorney?"

"You've been advised of your rights," said Hayes. "You can invoke your right to counsel at any time you want."

"We can't make that decision for you," said Dalrymple.

The detectives continued reviewing the physical evidence.

Finally, at 12:33 A.M., thirty minutes after the interview began, Richard invoked his right to counsel.

An arrest, however, would have to wait. At the conclusion of the interview, Matthew Kuehn boarded an NYPD helicopter to New Jersey to procure a warrant. A judge signed it in the middle of the night.

The next day, Richard was charged by Ocean County in the murders of Thomas Mulcahy and Anthony Marrero, and search warrants were executed on Richard's car, his locker at Mount Sinai, and his homes, past and present. He'd sold the apartment at Merle Place the year before and moved around the corner to 62 Bridge Court, a two-story house. In the application for the search warrant, an NYPD detective stressed the importance of Merle Place: "The dismemberments of the [sic] Mulcahy and Marrero had to have occurred in a place not only secluded, but where Richard W. Rogers, Junior, felt confident that he would avoid detection. . . . Additionally, parts of Thomas Mulcahy's body were found wrapped in designer sheets and shower curtain of the kind not typically found in commercial lodging." New Jersey detectives and crime scene technicians were authorized to look for physical evidence of homicide, such as bone fragments, blood—bodily fluids of any kind—and the personal property or clothing of the four men.

Before the search began, John Halliday, a senior detective, walked through the house, snapping photos of every corner and cranny while the home was still pristine. This was a bookend of sorts; he'd documented Tom's crime scene nine years earlier. Halliday was unnerved by the state of the house. "It was *immaculate*," he said nearly twenty years later. "He would give my wife a run for her money. That house was fucking clean."

The rest of the detectives proceeded slowly from room to room. They could see grooves in the living room carpet where Richard fanatically vacuumed; remote controls, evenly spaced, along the back of the couch; lobby posters for *Charade*, *Dial M for Murder*, and *Love in the Afternoon* hung in perfect symmetry on the wall. Hundreds of VHS recordings, alphabetized and separated by genre. (Fifteen years later, detectives marveled about the number of *Golden Girls* episodes.) Nothing out of place.

In the bedroom they found a pair of handcuffs, books, a copy of the porn film *Boys Will Be Boys,* a stack of *National Geographic* magazines, records, movies. Hardcovers of *Gray's Anatomy* and Ronald Haver's *David O. Selznick's Hollywood.* On a nightstand was a copy of the Hebrew Bible, in which certain passages were marked:

And his nurse took him up and fled. And as she made haste to flee, he fell and became lame. (2 Samuel 4:4)

When they came into the house he was sleeping upon his bed in the parlor and they struck him and killed him; and taking away his head, they went off by way of the wilderness walking all night. (2 Samuel 4:7)

And David commanded his servants and they slew them; and cutting off their hands and feet, hanged them over the pool in Hebron; but the head of Isboseth they took and buried in the sepulcher of Abner in Hebron. (2 Samuel 4:12)

The basement was strewn with boxes. An ironing board leaned against the wall, a plaid shirt hung off a drying line. Detectives found a brown bag on which was written *Thank you for shopping here,* identical to the one found near Tom Mulcahy's body in 1992.

They found a bottle of potassium chloride, a bottle of Versed, a two-milligram tablet of diazepam, and a two-milligram bottle of morphine sulfate, which was under the couch. (In Richard's employee locker at Mount Sinai, detectives found more drugs, including a bottle of potassium chloride and a two-milligram bottle of Versed.) Potassium chloride is a prescription medication frequently used in lethal injections; Versed, a presurgery sedative, was another shot in the execution cocktail; diazepam is a calming substance better known as Valium; morphine sulfate is a prescription pain reliever.

Elsewhere: a carousel of photo slides from 1982, documenting Richard's college reunion, Disney trip, and ventures to, among other places, Daytona Beach—where Matthew John Pierro was last seen that April.

There was at least one awkward moment. During a search of Richard's upstairs bedroom, New Jersey detectives found an address book. An NYPD detective flipped through it and found the name of a New York City district attorney. This prompted a brief turf war over the evidence, which ended only when New Jersey reiterated that, although the NYPD obtained the search warrant, any evidence found was the property of the Garden State. The address book could not be removed from the premises by the NYPD.

Ultimately, investigators "carted out 15 large cardboard boxes, a footlocker, two vacuum cleaners and a toolbox," reported the *Daily News*. A concurrent search executed on 20 Merle Place yielded nothing of value. But that was expected.

Neither search provided investigators with additional physical evidence linking Richard to the four murders.

Richard was held under suicide watch in Rikers, while he fought extradition to New Jersey.

Several months later, he lost.

Meanwhile, reporters from the victims' hometowns began contacting family and friends. The *Bangor Daily News* found Fred Spencer's mother, Louise, who now lived in Maine. "This just renews the pain that we have felt all of these years," she said. "We have been in such pain, and this opens the wound and makes it fresh again." A First Troop colleague of Peter Anderson's talked to the *Philadelphia Daily News*: "We're glad there appears to be an answer, and we're obviously relieved." Margaret Mulcahy, wife of Tom, told *The Boston Globe,* "We're pleased an arrest has been made." *The Star-Ledger* found Michael's mother, Mary Jane, who had left Youngstown for Florida. "I'm not out for blood. But if it's him, I'd like him to be charged," she said. "I feel like I'm hanging in midair."

But it would be another four years before the trial began.

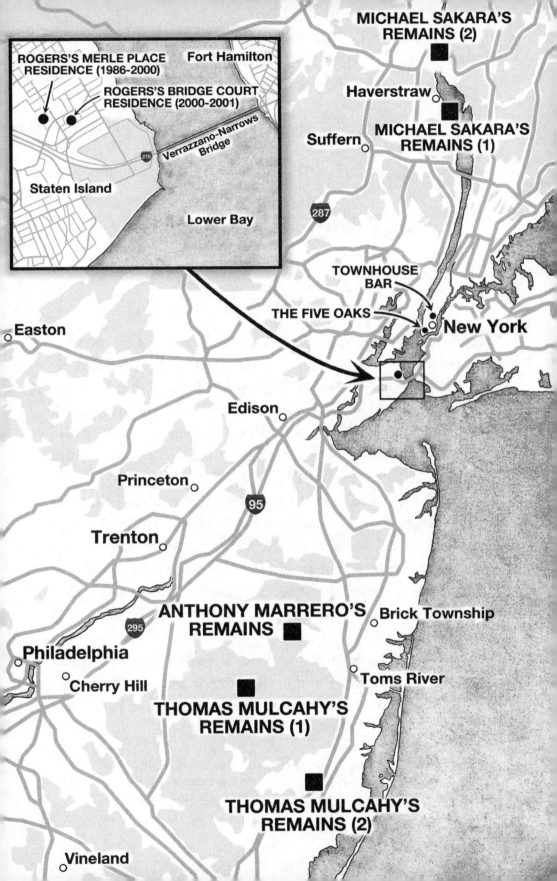

MICHAEL SAKARA'S
REMAINS (2)

ROGERS'S MERLE PLACE
RESIDENCE (1986–2000)

ROGERS'S BRIDGE COURT
RESIDENCE (2000–2001)

Fort Hamilton

Haverstraw

MICHAEL SAKARA'S
REMAINS (1)

Suffern

Verrazzano-Narrows
Bridge

278

Staten Island

Lower Bay

287

TOWNHOUSE
BAR

THE FIVE OAKS

New York

Easton

Edison

Princeton

95

Trenton

ANTHONY MARRERO'S
REMAINS

Brick Township

295

Philadelphia

Toms River

Cherry Hill

THOMAS MULCAHY'S
REMAINS (1)

THOMAS MULCAHY'S
REMAINS (2)

Vineland

13

GET HIM OUT OF HERE

The extradition to Ocean County hadn't been the end of the investigation, but simply the beginning of a new phase. Detectives, reported *The Star-Ledger*, interviewed "scores" of people, including Richard's Mount Sinai colleagues and bar employees and patrons. That was largely why it wasn't until 2003 that Richard was indicted. In those days, recalled William Heisler, the dashing Ocean County prosecutor, "it wasn't unusual for a homicide indictment to take two years."

Richard was charged with the murders of Thomas Mulcahy and Anthony Marrero, as well as two counts of hindering apprehension—on account of the dismemberments.[1] He wasn't facing the death penalty. He had been ruled ineligible because the review committee determined, according to the *Asbury Park Press*, that "the fact that the bodies were cut up does not constitute an aggravating factor because the mutilations occurred after death."

In October 2005, Richard was offered a plea. If accepted, he would serve no more than thirty years—the sentences imposed for the two murders would run concurrently—and would be eligible for parole after

---

1 The Mulcahy and Marrero homicides were the only cases in Heisler's jurisdiction. Pennsylvania could have indicted Richard for Peter Anderson's murder but chose not to, and New York did not have sufficient evidence to move forward for Michael Sakara's murder.

fifteen years. Pennsylvania and Rockland County promised he would not be charged for the killings in their jurisdictions.

Just as in 1973, Richard declined to take the plea. He was fifty-five years old, and at his age it was a probable life sentence. But he may also have expected an acquittal. "They found DNA on the victims that didn't match mine—big surprise—and they didn't find any evidence of a crime scene in my house or my apartment that I was living in at the time," he'd written to a college friend in February. In 2003, in another letter, he speculated the case against him would fall apart entirely. "I'm hoping there will be a pre-trial hearing and it won't go to trial for lack of evidence," he wrote.

The trial began in October, in Toms River. Prospective jurors were queried, in part, on their opinion of homosexuality. "We want to know if you have any biases or prejudices that would impair your ability to be fair and impartial," the judge informed them. The jury would be hearing only part of the story; the killings of Fred Spencer and Matthew John Pierro, and the assault of Sandy Harrow, were off-limits. However, the judge did allow the prosecutor to bring in evidence of the murders of Peter Anderson and Michael Sakara. This was a small victory for the families, as neither case would be prosecuted and both remain, to this day, open.

In his opening statement, Heisler summed up the evidence against the defendant: "Thomas Mulcahy, sixteen fingerprints, nine different fingers. Anthony Marrero, two fingerprints on the bag containing his head, and another palm print. Peter Anderson, seventeen fingerprints and a palm print. Michael Sakara turns up dead twenty-seven hours after he's seen with him."

Over the next two weeks, the jury heard testimony from Margaret Mulcahy, Tom's wife; Cynthia Anderson, Peter's wife; Carlos Santiago, a friend of Anthony's; Lisa Hall, the Five Oaks bartender and confidante of Michael's; and Rick Unterberg, who still played every Saturday night at the Townhouse. They also heard from New Jersey, Rockland County, and Pennsylvania investigators, some of whom had since retired.

The state's case was strong.

In a departure from his trials of 1973 and 1990, Richard did not testify on his own behalf. ("Meek like a mouse," recalls the court reporter. "Didn't say a word.") His attorney put forth a solid defense, given the circumstances. He didn't dispute the presence of his client's fingerprints on the bags but argued the state's experts couldn't be certain when, exactly, they were left. He argued, further, that there was no proof the murders had even been committed in New Jersey. That was certainly true; the location of the primary crime scene was, and would remain, one of the mysteries of the case.

In the end, this wasn't sufficient for reasonable doubt. Jurors deliberated for only a few hours. As far as they were concerned, Richard's culpability was not in question. They'd been swayed by the eyewitnesses and fingerprints; the defense's closing argument, resting largely on territorial jurisdiction, wasn't persuasive. "It seemed kind of weak on his part," a juror said of Richard's attorney.

On November 10, 2005, a teary-eyed forewoman rose to address the crowded courtroom. Another juror held her hand.

"On the first count of the indictment presented for deliberation charging the defendant, Richard W. Rogers, with the murder of Thomas Mulcahy, how do you find, guilty or not guilty?" the judge asked her.

"Guilty," she said.

"On the third count of the indictment presented for deliberation charging the defendant, Richard W. Rogers, with the murder of Anthony Marrero, how do you find, guilty or not guilty?" he asked.[2]

"Guilty," she said.

The former nurse's face betrayed no emotion.

In January 2006, Richard stood in the packed courtroom as the judge imposed a sentence. The judge had absorbed a presentencing statement

---

2 In the second count of the indictment, Richard had been charged with "hindering apprehension" in connection with the murder of Tom.

by Tracey Mulcahy, who told him what had been lost when Richard snuffed out her father's life. She concluded:

> His innate ability to relate with other people from all parts of the globe and his compassion for humanity as a whole enabled him to provide a life for me, my siblings and my mother that he never had growing up. He was a good man who worked hard, and he deserved the best from life. For me that's what made—that's what made what Richard Rogers did all the more tragic.

Richard was sentenced to two consecutive life terms in prison plus ten years, a penalty for hindering apprehension.

"To do less would diminish the horror of the offenses that you've committed, sir," said the judge, glaring at Richard. "It's the purpose of this sentence to do everything within my power to assure society that you never walk free again and that you die in some hole in some prison without ever having freedom again. And hopefully society will find some modicum of justice in that, because there's nothing else I can do.

"We're done," he continued. "Get him out of here."[3]

---

3 Richard Rogers would not talk to me. He declined to reply to letters I sent in May 2018, May 2019, and November 2019. In July 2019, he rejected my request to talk to him in person.

EPILOGUE

January 18, 2020

It's been nearly thirty years since Peter Anderson was murdered and left on the side of the road in Lancaster County, fifteen years since the sentencing, and just over three years since I began working on this book.

I'd found the story by accident, surfaced by an errant Web search. Most of these so-called true crime cases don't stay with me, but this one I couldn't let go. Once I got past the murders and the investigations, and my own disbelief that it had all been forgotten—a string of killings in New York City didn't merit so much as a Wikipedia entry?—I became obsessed with the lives of the victims. I became obsessed with the lives they *wanted* but couldn't have. Here was a generation of men, more or less, for whom it was difficult to be visibly gay. To be visibly *whole*.

For more than a year, I talked to their family members, friends, colleagues, and lovers. I talked to the men and women who had investigated their deaths, and in doing so had gotten a sense of their lives. I talked to queer activists who tried to convince the New York courts and cops—and all New Yorkers and Americans—to take anti-queer violence seriously, to investigate these crimes.

None of the people I contacted had heard from a journalist in more than a decade. We often talked about why that was so. *Did no one care about the victims? Was the multijurisdictional nature of the investigation too much to properly absorb? Were there just too many other murders in those days for anyone to notice? Had the events of September 11, 2001, conspired to make everyone miss the fact that, after a decade, the perpetrator had been caught?*

We didn't know the answers to these questions. After years of thinking about it, I've decided it's probably a little of each.

Eventually, I had enough for a book proposal. When I met with editors, I told them my plan. Essentially, I wanted to be the friar from Thornton Wilder's *The Bridge of San Luis Rey*. In Wilder's novel, Brother Juniper watches people on a Peruvian rope bridge fall to their deaths when it collapses. He, in turn, decides to "inquire into the secret lives of those five persons."

Why, he asked, were they on that bridge?

Wilder's monk endeavored to divine the intentions of God. On that count I was indifferent. I simply wanted to know about Anthony Marrero, Michael Sakara, Tom Mulcahy, Fred Spencer, and Peter Anderson before they became victims. Who were they? What brought each of the men into the path of Richard Rogers? What brought them to New York? to Port Authority? to the Five Oaks? to Orono? to the Townhouse?

The Townhouse—where Peter spent part of his last night alive—has forgotten Richard Westall Rogers Jr., who for fourteen years has been locked away in the New Jersey State Prison. Rogers spends his time watching movies, keeping abreast of current events, and writing letters. In a letter sent earlier in the month to an acquaintance, he wrote about his feelings on soon turning seventy, staying up to watch the ball drop in Times Square ("We had a *really* good roast beef dinner, then a better-than-average spaghetti supper . . ."), and the impeachment of Donald Trump. "With the recent E-Mails and documents that have come to the surface, I don't see how the Republicans can save face without having a proper impeachment trial," he wrote, but allowed that "some of these Republicans will continue doing for Trump what toilet paper does for the rest of us." He's eligible for parole on September 18, 2066; he would be 116 years old. There is no chance Rogers will set foot in the Townhouse again.

But if he did, the former Mount Sinai nurse wouldn't find the bar much different than he left it.

In January, as I was working on a book revision, I went to the Townhouse to see Rick Unterberg, who, improbably, still played every Saturday night. I'd come to love the place and would visit even when I wasn't looking for interviews.

Sometimes, as I talked to the regulars—many of whom offered to pick up the tab—I wondered if, in fact, this was my story to tell. Could I do right by the queer community and its history? That's not for me to say. What I tried to do in this book was let my sources tell the story.

On this particular Saturday, I was here to talk to Rick and bar patrons about how, over the past two decades, the place had changed.

The ways in which it remained the same were obvious. When I asked Michael Musto, then a *Village Voice* columnist, about the Townhouse a few years back, he remarked that the clientele was still largely composed of older men. This was in keeping, he said, with the decor. "It's elegant, and it almost looks like a funeral home."

This is true. As Rick once observed, only the placement of the paintings on the wall is noticeably different from the night the bar opened in 1989. The liquor is still high-end, the pours still heavy.

When I got to the Townhouse, it was still an hour before Rick's shift. The back room was dark, so I sat at the bar in the front. Across the way I saw Mitch Kahn, a piano player who has logged four decades of gigs and somehow doesn't look the worse for wear. Mitch was at the Townhouse the week it opened.

"It's mostly unchanged," he said. Then he paused. "It was always a bar that attracted younger men who were into older guys and vice versa. Many of the older guys who patronize the bar today were the younger guys thirty years ago. And they're in a sad position because they're always attracted to older guys. Now *they're* the old guys."

Food for thought, Mitch added.

"The Townhouse," he noted, "is the last man standing." Even the context in which it flourished is gone; the once-bustling Loop—that hustler buffet orbiting East Fifty-third Street—was barely a shadow.

We talked for a while, mostly about the declining number of gay bars but also about the Five Oaks. Mitch was there the night Michael Sakara met Richard Rogers, but had left earlier in the evening. He took out his phone and showed me a Five Oaks menu from 1989, inscribed by the staff and regulars. "Much love for the holidays," Michael had written. "Thanks for the Chopin."

I made my way to the back room and sat on the couch near the piano. It was almost time for Rick. Two elderly men sat together, catty-corner from me. Both were from out of town and had been visiting the Townhouse for decades during business trips. They'd met that night and quickly established that they weren't each other's type.

I drank scotch and watched Rick noodling an old standard, his fingerprint-covered fishbowl tip jar on the piano. Then I asked the older man, who was in his late seventies but spry, about the bar.

"When I first started coming here, in 1992, there was a wonderful range of ages, and age-wise it was very egalitarian," he said, sipping a rum screwdriver. "It was like heaven, from both ends of the age spectrum.

"It had only been a few years before that I thought it all ended at age fifty—and after that you just didn't do anything anymore. Then at about fifty-five or sixty, I discovered, *Hey, there's a whole new world out there!*" Young guys, he found, were into old guys. His sweet spot was Asians between twenty-five and thirty-five. "Under twenty-five, they're too dumb, and over thirty-five, *eeeeeeeehhhhhh.*" He was rigid about this and shrugged off the advances of a nice-looking Asian man next to us. "Five years too old."

His new friend, a few years younger, saw the changes, too. "You used to get a lot more foreign guys—international types," he said. There was a man from Connecticut who pursued him every time he was at the bar, and it was starting to get annoying. "That's been a little unsettling, but he's harmless."

The men agreed the Townhouse peaked about a decade ago, and there'd been some missteps since then. For a spell, a couple of years ago, the owners installed go-go dancers in the downstairs bar. They were gone now and not missed. And, of course, the hustlers were gone, too. In Musto's words: "Now there isn't that charge in the air of entrepreneurism."

After an hour or so, Rick took a break. We headed downstairs. Downstairs was where Douglas Gibson, all those years ago, had gone after Tom Mulcahy's gentle rejection.

Rick and I settled into a corner. There weren't more than a half dozen men around us.

We talked about how the sartorial formality had basically vanished. The suit and button-down was no longer mandatory, but some patrons still adhered to it out of habit. Anyway, the herd had thinned. A bunch of customers never came back after the smoking ban took effect in 2003. Dating apps, certainly, hadn't helped matters. Those who remain are trending younger. "Somebody called me daddy last night, and I just wanted to *die*," said Rick. "But that's the difference; in thirty years, you're old enough to be somebody's dad. I could be somebody's grandfather now."

We talked about how the terror of AIDS has vanished. "I have friends who, now that they take PrEP, they just don't think it's going to happen to them," said Rick. "They think that being undetectable is the same thing as being negative. They don't realize how many drugs they have to take to stay undetectable.

"I sort of equate it with 9/11. It's so long in the past that now it's in the history books. And this new generation wasn't here for it."

AIDS, he recalled, took two of the Townhouse's first three piano players.

We talked for ten minutes, and then Rick's break was over. He would be dead just over three months later, when an unchecked pandemic devastated the planet.

But not yet. He gingerly walked back up the stairs, and played on.

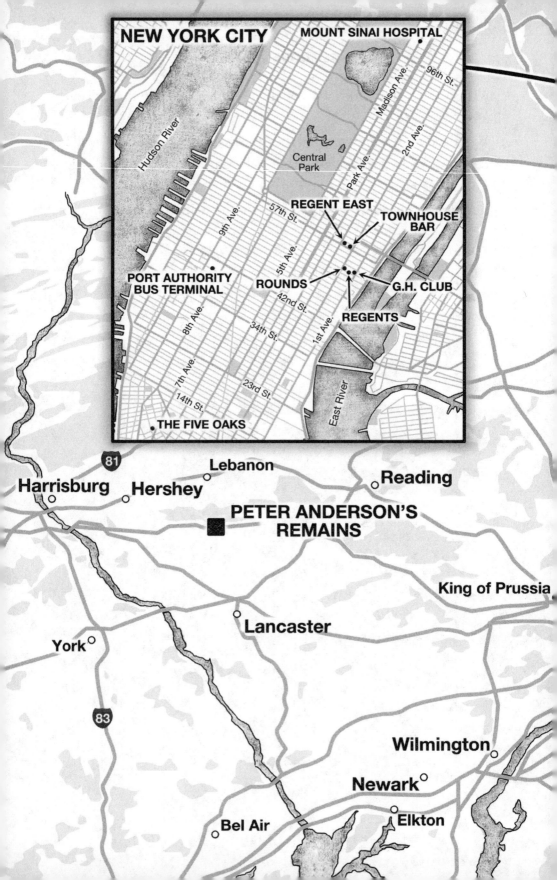

NEW YORK CITY

MOUNT SINAI HOSPITAL

Hudson River

Central Park

Madison Ave.

96th St.

2nd Ave.

Park Ave.

57th St.

9th Ave.

5th Ave.

REGENT EAST

TOWNHOUSE BAR

PORT AUTHORITY BUS TERMINAL

ROUNDS

G.H. CLUB

REGENTS

8th Ave.

42nd St.

34th St.

1st Ave.

7th Ave.

23rd St.

14th St.

East River

THE FIVE OAKS

81

Lebanon

Reading

Harrisburg

Hershey

PETER ANDERSON'S
REMAINS

King of Prussia

York

Lancaster

83

Wilmington

Newark

Bel Air

Elkton

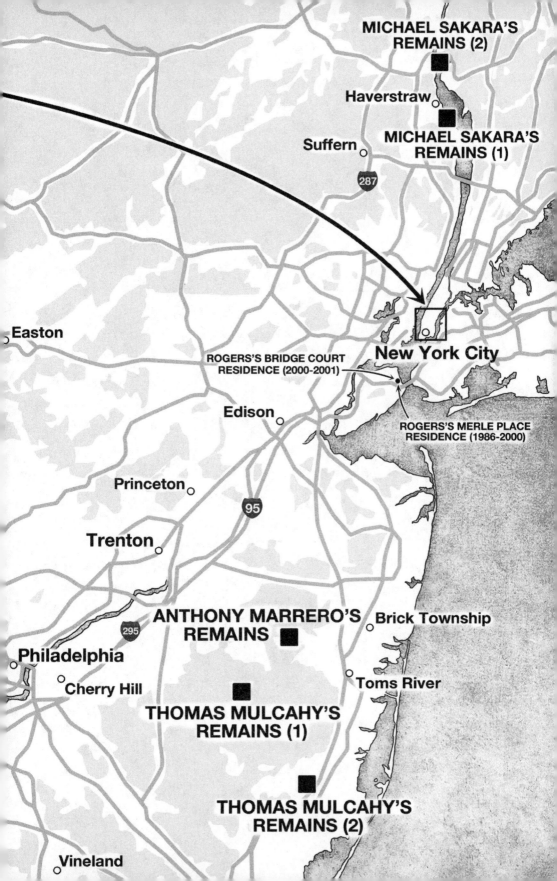

MICHAEL SAKARA'S
REMAINS (2)

Haverstraw

MICHAEL SAKARA'S
REMAINS (1)

Suffern

287

Easton

ROGERS'S BRIDGE COURT
RESIDENCE (2000-2001)

New York City

ROGERS'S MERLE PLACE
RESIDENCE (1986-2000)

Edison

Princeton

95

Trenton

ANTHONY MARRERO'S
REMAINS

Brick Township

Philadelphia

295

Toms River

Cherry Hill

THOMAS MULCAHY'S
REMAINS (1)

THOMAS MULCAHY'S
REMAINS (2)

Vineland

ACKNOWLEDGMENTS

Last Call would've been unthinkable without my parents, Hank and Diane, and my in-laws, Laykoon and Eugene, each of whom gave me the time and freedom to write it. My sister, Rachel; my brother-in-law, Mike; and my wonderful nephews, Adam and Dylan, frequently provided a spark. My other brother-in-law, Sherng-Lee, sister-in-law, Livia, and nephew, Luca, were encouraging from afar. I'd like to think that my grandparents, Martin and Annette, Arnold and Muriel, and Irene Schultz, would be proud.

This was a research-heavy book, and it was made easier by folks who went above and beyond to get me documents, sources, and such. Where would I be without librarians and archivists? I am particularly grateful to Jen Bonnet and Desiree Butterfield-Nagy of the University of Maine's Fogler Library, Marta Crilly of the Boston Public Library, Madeleine Bradford of the University of Michigan's Bentley Historical Library, Betsy Paradis of the Bangor Public Library, Lorraine Chwazik of the Norwich City School District, Kathryn Greene of the Guernsey Memorial Library, and the Public Library of Youngstown and Mahoning County's Rebekah Davis.

In a similar vein, William Heisler, the former Ocean County prosecutor, gave me a complete trial transcript. Sam Katz of Detectives' Endowment Association connected me to helpful sources. Brent Cox was a whiz with real estate records. Matt Katz hooked me up with the book's best unnamed source. Tracy Quan, whose generosity was a gift, made invaluable introductions. Without Jamie Marich, I would not have met Dharl and Mike. Robert Silverman got Port Authority to be more forthcoming than it should've been. David Gever connected me to the Norwich diaspora. Olivia Nuzzi plundered her Rolodex. Donna Prestia, the chief clerk of the Ocean County Prosecutor's Office, returned to the storage room multiple times to procure the most important document I ever got.

Paul Dowling, the creator of *Forensic Files,* deserves his own paragraph. Without access to information from the show's raw transcripts, many of which contained interviews with sources who've since gone quiet, the book would've been impossible.

Matthew Bank, the founding editor of *HX,* was similarly invaluable. Much of his help, which was exhaustive and generous, is mostly invisible in the book. However, without him—and the stacks of *HX* he gave me—I would've had no real sense of Manhattan's gay nightlife. There is surely no one alive as knowledgeable as Matthew.

Much, if not most, of the work in this book is a reflection of my learning as I went along. I would've been lost without the kindness of people who know the terrain. This includes Ames Grawert and his wisdom on New York City courts; Emily Loyd, who provided the particulars of autopsies; Vince Guerrieri, an extraordinary Youngstown tour guide; and Kevin Walsh, who spotted a footnote in a 404(b) brief that changed *Last Call* for the better. Hugh Ryan, Michael Bronski, Betsy Arnold-Leahy, Burt Lazarin, Michael McKee, Christy Mallory, David Krajicek, Charles Scaglione, Gloria Brame, and Andy Humm all took the time to get on the phone, and I am deeply appreciative.

Thanks, too, to Matthew Gabriele, Benjamin Moser, and to Marcia Loher—who gave my wife and me an exceedingly informative tour of gorgeous Florida Southern.

To the extent the book succeeds, it is in no small part thanks to the editors I've had over the years, all of whom made me a better writer. Paige Williams and Cory Shouten each took a chance by asking me to interview journalism's finest—the former for *Nieman Storyboard*, the latter for *Columbia Journalism Review*. Choire Sicha and Alex Balk let me write for the inimitable *Awl*. Jason Diamond has brought me with him from publication to publication. Kip McDaniel assigned my first and last cover story. Michael Agger is surely the only editor who'd let me interview Mavis Staples for three separate stories. Jazmine Hughes took my pitch on adult adoption. Serena Golden didn't blink when I asked to write about a music video and some missing kids.

I was never edited directly by the late Peter Kaplan, but he was my boss at the *New York Observer*. He taught me a hell of a lot about reporting and writing, and I hope this book reflects that. Peter's love of Manhattan and all its nooks and crannies was contagious, and his ardor for it became my own.

This book pretty quickly became an obsession, and I remain indebted to friends for their patience. Alex Hammond, Max Cavanaugh, Ian Markiewicz, and Maya Mumma were always there when I needed them, as were Ben Harper, Kierin Baldwin, Erica Tsao Hill, Mark Savino, Ashley Ley, Megan Hall, Matthew Parker, Jessica Bizer, Brynna Kaulback, and Rosemary Talmadge. Thank you to David Yaffe, Brian Schmitz, Ekaterina Smirnova, Caroline Ashby, Dan Chuzmir, Lee Feldman, Chris Tokar, Wendy Chamberlain, James Leet, Jay Friedman, Lauren Baskins, and Margaret Levine.

There's also no book without Erik Malinowski, Joe Hagan, Josh Sternberg, Esmé Weijun Wang, Laura Lippman, Zandy Hartig, Jordan Davis, Dr. Steven Thrasher, Sam Sanders, Nicole Chung, Isaac Butler, Alex MacPherson, Adam Begley, Alex Vadukul, Robert Arbuckle, Rebecca Pilar Buckwalter-Poza, Sridhar Pappu, Haley Joel Osment, Kyra Darnton, Sarah Schulman, Michele Catalano, Rumaan Alam, Jacqui Shine, Sarah Miers, Maud Newton, Sarah Galo, Megan Greenwell, Kristina

Tuck, Connor Goldsmith, Steve Silberman, Jim Gabriel, Alex Heard, Colin Dickey, John Lingan, Jeb Lund, Duchess Goldblatt, and Sara Kate Wilkinson.

I must also thank @Darth. I don't know their identity, but the red panda never failed to circulate requests for sources and always championed my work.

Oftentimes, journalists who wrote extraordinary work either lent their counsel or went out of their way to be encouraging. Sometimes, as in the case of Robert Kolker (*Lost Girls*) and Matthew McGough (*The Lazarus Files*), they did both.

Bill James's *Popular Crime* was by my bedside for three years. I probably read it twenty-five times, and it informed my thinking and writing like no other book. Alexis Coe's *Alice + Freda Forever* was also a formative text.

I'm very lucky that friends agreed to read (and in many cases reread) chapters. Pamela Colloff, a saint, made the forensic stuff sing. Duncan Black and Jason Fagone did their best to ensure the Philly chapter didn't sound like the work of a literary carpetbagger. Eva Holland kept reading chapters even as she was working on her own book. Daniel Lavery and Nicole Cliffe are exceptional close readers and caught a number of crucial, avoidable errors. Gretchen Gavett, you're a beautiful human. Kristen Arnett was wise and encouraging when I really needed it. Rachel McCarthy James, Matthew Lubchansky, Morgan Jerkins, and Benjamin Dreyer were a blessing. Josh Gondelman and Catherine Nichols gave invaluable feedback on style and substance, as did John Schwartz, Karen Ho, Justin Sherin, and Rachel Corkle.

David Grann, it should be noted, is as good a friend as he is a journalist. He's done edits on most of my features ever since we met nearly a decade ago, and he line-edited much of *Last Call*, too. I don't mind saying that's a tremendous luxury. Imagine getting a dance lesson from Fred Astaire.

Sarah Weinman and Lyz Lenz (angel and devil on my shoulders, respectively) have been a part of this book since its inception. They've pushed, needled, and flattered as necessary, and I can't really imagine the last few years without them.

The same is true of Longform, where I've had a home for a decade. Thank you kindly, Max Linsky and Aaron Lammer.

Samantha Schuyler is my fact-checker, and there's none better. Any errors, however, are mine alone.

Carrie Frye is an editor who became a friend. I am doubly blessed. Carrie shepherded me through the proposal, and to a great degree conceived the structure of the book. We should all be so lucky as to have Carrie Frye in our corner.

David Patterson of Stuart Krichevsky Literary Agency has had tremendous faith in this project, and in me, which is a marvelous quality in an agent. I am grateful he took a chance on me. David's colleagues, Aemilia Phillips and Stuart Krichevsky, nurtured *Last Call* since its inception.

Henry Kaufman vetted this book, and did so with gusto.

Ryan Doherty, my editor at Celadon Books, and his assistant, Cecily van Buren-Freedman, have been all I could ask for. Macmillan Publishers' Elizabeth Catalano kept a sharp eye on production matters. Their suggestions were unfailingly smart, and made *Last Call* what it is. As it happens, "editing hell" is a term often tossed around by writers, but I'm happy to say I never experienced it. The beautiful cover is the work of Evan Gaffney.

Thank you to my wife, Ruee, and son, Elijah Marin. You are the best parts of my life.

Shortly after *Last Call* was announced in September 2018, I got a note from Lyra McKee, an investigative journalist in Derry, Northern Ireland. We had corresponded on and off for years, and I felt from the get-go that

Lyra was in another league. So I was surprised by her proposition: that we become writing partners, since we had identical due dates for our manuscripts. "It would be like we're pregnant at the same time," she said.

Lyra read only a third of this book—sharing portions of it with her partner, Sara Canning, as she went along. Her edits and suggestions, all delivered in her animated way, were unfailingly smart. Very often, after reading Lyra's drafts, I didn't have much to critique. In March 2019, she emailed: "I'm really, really stuck. My writing ends up all over the place because I'm just trying to fill space because I'm paralysed by the thought of a word count." I told Lyra to call me and informed her, as gently as I could, that she was full of shit. *The Lost Boys* would be a masterpiece.

Lyra was murdered the next month, on April 18, 2019, at the age of twenty-nine. She was shot while doing her job. I still find that hard to believe.

NOTES

1. JOHN DOE

1 *Ten minutes short of three o'clock*: John Sirriannia, court testimony, November 3, 2005. Many of the book's details come from the trial transcript, provided in its entirety by William Heisler, the former Ocean County prosecutor.

1 *moderately warm Sunday afternoon*: The Pennsylvania State Climatologist, http://www.climate.psu.edu /data/city_information/index.php?city=mdt&page=dwa&type=big7.

1 *he pulled hard on a plastic trash bag*: John Sirriannia, interview by author, August 1, 2018.

2 *AIDS could be transmitted via a toilet seat*: Sandra G. Boodman, "Public Misled, Masters and Johnson Tell Aids Panel," *Washington Post*, May 19, 1988.

2 *Eleven hundred and fifty six Pennsylvanians died*: "HIV/AIDS, Surveillance Summary Report," Pennsylvania Department of Health, December 2009, https://www.health.pa.gov/topics/Documents /Programs/HIV/HIV-AIDS%20Surveillance%20Annual%20Summary%20-%20December%20 2009.pdf.

2 *"People need to be educated"*: Editorial, "Jean White's Message," *Intelligencer Journal,* February 15, 1991.

2 *It was believed that AIDS dripped off the walls*: Nancy Helms, interview by author, June 20, 2019.

2 *the Closet, would be bombed twice*: Bill Burton, LGBT Center of Central PA History Project, Dickinson College Archives and Special Collections, January 16, 2016, www.archives.dickinson.edu/sites/all/files /files_document/LGBT_interview_Helm_Nancy_047.pdf.

2 *Jay Musser, a tall, fresh-faced officer*: Jay Musser, interview by author, September 20, 2018.

3 *The last incident that raised an eyebrow*: Associated Press, "Governor's Car Clocked at 90 mph," *Times-Leader,* January 24, 1978.

3 *a middle-aged man from Kirkwood*: Associated Press, "Amish 'Hat Bandit' Case Cracked in Lancaster," *Philadelphia Daily News,* October 1, 1988.

3 *In 1990, there were thirteen homicides*: Mary Beth Schweigert, "Homicide Statistics," *Lancaster New Era,* April 3, 2011.

3 *"This ain't like New Jersey"*: Carl Harnish, interview by author, August 31, 2018.

4 *Musser, in seven years on the criminal investigations unit*: Jay Musser, interview by author, August 2, 2018.

4 *The longtime local*: Carl Harnish, interview by author, September 20, 2018.

5 *In several areas there was lividity*: Isidore Mihalakis, court testimony, November 3, 2005.

5 *"in an eleven to five o'clock line"*: Ibid.

5 *"We have to think of jockeys"*: John M. Hoober III, "Police Wonder Whether Dead Man Was a Jockey," *Lancaster New Era*, May 7, 1991.

6 *latent fingerprint examiner was given the eight trash bags*: Dennis Loose, court testimony, November 9, 2005.

6 *Other tips were intriguing dead ends*: Carl Harnish's handwritten notes are the basis for my account of the 1991 investigation into the death of Peter Stickney Anderson.

6 *Musser, for his part, didn't often find them useful*: Jay Musser, interview by author, May 22, 2019.

7 *Among the effects were several pairs of socks*: Jay Musser, court testimony, November 3, 2005.

2. THE BANKER

8 *"like a gentlemen's lounge at a hunting lodge"*: Steven Capsuto, interview by author, August 14, 2018.

9 *A beloved, oft-remembered bit from his set*: Ibid.

9 *Peter Anderson was a regular*: Joseph Guercio, court testimony, November 1, 2005.

9 *"There were a lot of people around Michael Ogborn"*: Connie Freeman, interview by author, October 24, 2018.

9 *"a meat market"*: David Tidman, interview by author, December 6, 2018.

9 *The acquaintance didn't know Peter intimately*: William Jordan, interview by author, September 28, 2018.

9 *Musser began calling the case Banker in the Barrel*: Carl Harnish, interview by author, September 20, 2018.

9 *born on March 14, 1937, in Milwaukee*: Social Security Applications and Claims Index, 1936–2007.

9 *A sister was born in 1940*: United States Federal Census.

9 *In his yearbook photo*: *The Ivy*, 1959, 24.

10 *In May 1959, the student newspaper*: "Frosh Yachters Wind Up in Fifth Behind Harvard," *Trinity Tripod*, May 2, 1956.

10 *Two days before a football game*: "The Notorious Trinity 'Gentleman,'" *Trinity Tripod*, December 2, 1959.

10 *"Once I got into college, I just slacked off"*: Dixon Harris, interview by author, May 18, 2018.

10 *"high-living private school boys"*: Fred Gignoux, interview by author, May 18, 2018.

10 *likened the fraternity to* Animal House: W. Croft Jennings, interview by author, May 20, 2018.

10 *the Psi Upsilon bond was such*: "Ann Richmond Married to Law Student," *Democrat and Chronicle*, June 24, 1962.

11 *girlfriend of a fraternity brother remembered Peter's loneliness*: Struthers Gignoux, interview by author, May 18, 2018.

11 *He was considered an excellent candidate*: Editorial, "Good Candidates on Both Tickets," *Philadelphia Daily News,* May 7, 1991.

11 *Brooks dreamed of politics*: Jacob Seibel, "Openly Gay Councilman Shares Experience in Support of Ordinance," *Citizens' Voice,* August 10, 2016, www.citizensvoice.com/news/openly-gay-councilman -shares-experience-in-support-of-ordinance-1.2076566.

11 *he went to the gym and put muscle on*: "Brooks Offers Coming Out Story to Help Wilkes-Barre Council Vote on LGBT Law," *Times Leader,* August 9, 2016, www.timesleader.com/news/573998/coming-out -story-of-tony-brooks-offered-to-help-wilkes-barre-council-vote-on-ordinance.

12 *twenty-four-hour doorman, a health club*: *Philadelphia Inquirer,* May 8, 1988.

12 *the barons flocked*: "The Lost Mansions of Rittenhouse Square," *Curbed,* September 18, 2019, https:// philly.curbed.com/2018/1/17/16896748/rittenhouse-square-philadelphia-historic-photos.

12 *"It was equivalent to coming out"*: Marc Stein, *City of Sisterly and Brotherly Loves* (Philadelphia: Temple University Press, 2004), 88.

13 *"I'm going to make Attila the Hun look like a faggot"*: Chuck Stone, "'Rizzo Cares' All Right—for Certain People," *Philadelphia Daily News,* October 7, 1975.

13 *One of his obsessions was Humoresque Coffee Shop*: "Judge Clears Police Raids on Coffee Shops," *Philadelphia Inquirer,* December 10, 1959.

13 *a seven-acre open-air club enjoyed by hundreds*: Stein, *City of Sisterly and Brotherly Loves,* 88.

13 *"just-plain-folks"*: Rose DeWolf, "Who 'Owns' Rittenhouse Sq.?" *Philadelphia Inquirer,* September 11, 1966.

13 *"it could've used a little housekeeping"*: Kevin Dykes, interview by author, October 17, 2018.

14 *There was blood on the ceiling*: Carl Harnish, interview by author, August 31, 2018.

14 *the sale a year earlier of Geraldo Rivera's penthouse*: "Geraldo's Reel Life in Suburbia," *Daily News,* February 20, 1990.

14 *It was Browne's first fundraiser*: Robert Browne, interview by author, September 7, 2018.

14 *a gay Brigadoon*: Guy Trebay, "The Architecture of Seduction," *New York Times,* May 22, 2013.

15 *half the attendees of the fundraiser were dead*: Robert Browne, interview by author, September 7, 2018.

15 *Peter Anderson stood by the entrance*: Peter Ripley, interview by author, September 30, 2018.

15 *Hoyt remembers his own reaction*: Anthony Hoyt, interview by author, July 31, 2018.

15 *It was a doorman building*: Ibid.

16 *U.S. State Department was purged*: George Chauncey, "A Gay World, Vibrant and Forgotten," *New York Times,* June 26, 1994.

17 *The first issue, which hit the newsstands*: Alan Citron, "California, 2 Other Magazines Folding; Victims of Slump," *Los Angeles Times,* July 30, 1991.

17 *"Tony seemed to be an adequate but not extraordinary personality"*: Milton Glaser, interview by author, August 14, 2018.

17 *"he thought I was high society"*: Edith Blake, interview by author, July 31, 2018.

18 *A photo of the bride ran in the paper*: "Edith Sands Blake Married to Peter Stickney Anderson," *New York Times,* August 12, 1970.

19 *Peter and Sandy settled in Dedham*: *Trinity Reporter,* February 1973.

19 *Sandy isn't wistful*: Edith Meinfelder, interview by author, January 23, 2019.

19 *In 1979, Peter remarried*: Cynthia Anderson, court testimony, November 1, 2005.

19 *"You don't talk about who's cheating"*: Ian Fisher, "Do Threads of Five Lives Lead to One Serial Killer?" *New York Times*, August 8, 1993.

19 *Peter had been hired by Philadelphia's Girard Trust Company*: William Jordan, interview by author, September 28, 2018.

20 *the bank underwrote most of the War of 1812*: Sandy Hingston, "12 Things You Might Not Know About Stephen Girard," *Philadelphia*, March 3, 2016.

20 *elected to the board of the Philadelphia Securities Association*: Terry Bivens and Craig Stock, "She'll Design Sales Program to Revive Franklin Computer," *Philadelphia Inquirer*, April 8, 1985.

20 *Peter was notable*: David Iams, "Freely Celebrating the Fourth, and Parties Fit for the Bard," *Philadelphia Inquirer*, July 4, 1989.

20 *"He was your classic Main Line gentleman"*: Kathy Brennan, "Gay Slaying Victim Linked to N.Y. Deaths," *Philadelphia Daily News*, August 6, 1993.

20 *"That was probably good for most of the troop"*: Stockton Illoway, interview by author, January 23, 2019.

20 *The troop was still in cold war mode*: "History of the First Troop Philadelphia City Cavalry," https://www.firsttroop.com/history.

20–21 *the men trained with weapons and tanks*: a First Troop associate, interview by author, September 28, 2018.

21 *Peter traced his own lineage to Asa Stickney*: Reid Kanaley, "Slain Phila. Socialite Had Become 'A Lost Soul,'" *Philadelphia Inquirer*, June 10, 1991.

21 *In a letter to the editor*: Peter Stickney Anderson, "Mail," *People*, February 12, 1990.

21 *"he could drink like a field soldier"*: Bill Buchanan, interview by author, March 9, 2017.

21 *"a functioning alcoholic"*: Senya Isayeff, interview by author, August 30, 2018.

22 *"for sexual purposes, and it was not another woman"*: Cynthia Anderson, court testimony, November 1, 2005.

22 *the* Philadelphia Inquirer *reported that a car on Route 252*: Marlene A. Prost and Frank Langfitt, "Police Report," *Philadelphia Inquirer*, March 5, 1987.

22 *He had inherited $400,000 from an aunt*: Jay Musser, court testimony, September 22, 2005.

22 *Peter still took part in First Troop events*: David Iams, "Fetes for George Washington and Some Other Local Notables," *Philadelphia Inquirer*, February 20, 1990.

22 *He'd come to luncheons bearing a flask*: Kanaley, "Slain Phila. Socialite."

22 *on May 1, Peter showed up at the Blue Parrot*: Joseph Guercio, court testimony, November 1, 2005.

22 *May 2, Peter and Cynthia spoke*: Cynthia Anderson, court testimony, November 1, 2005.

23 *The Los Angeles Dodgers would be in town*: "1991 Philadelphia Phillies Schedule," https://www.baseball-almanac.com/teamstats/schedule.php?y=1991&t=PHI.

23 *the bartender politely but sternly*: Anthony Hoyt, court testimony, November 3, 2005.

23 *Sober enough to see where the night might proceed, Hoyt lied*: Anthony Hoyt, interview by author, July 31, 2018.

23–24 *Peter wore a bow tie, he would recall*: Frank Taormina, court testimony, November 3, 2005.

24 *A week later, a memorial service was held*: Kanaley, "Slain Phila. Socialite."

25 *Years later, a New Jersey detective was asked*: Matthew Kuehn, *Forensic Files* interview transcript, December 2009.

3. A GOOD PERSON

26 *Wayne Luker and Theodore "Pee Wee" Doyle*: Wayne Luker, court testimony, October 27, 2005.

27 *Hours later, at another rest area*: Leon Valentino, court testimony, October 27, 2005.

28 *feeding the ducks and gulls of Newton Lake*: Photo of Kuehn and his daughter by Al Schell, "Meal Time," *Courier-Post*, February 13, 1989.

28 *The first contained a head*: Lyla Perez, court testimony, October 28, 2005.

28 *mop of gray hair falling in all directions*: Photo provided by a police source.

28 *detectives found a brown plastic bag*: Matthew Kuehn, court testimony, October 25, 2005.

28 *Wondered another investigator*: Jack Repsha, interview by author, June 2, 2018.

28 *It was all a bit too familiar to Kuehn*: Matthew Kuehn, *Forensic Files* interview transcript, December 2009.

28 *Three years earlier, a woman's head was found*: "Heidi Balch Identified: Severed Head Found on Golf Course Was Serial Killer Joel Rifkin's First Victim," *HuffPost,* March 29, 2013, https://www.huffpost.com/entry/heidi-balch-head-golf-course-joel-rifkin_n_2965531.

28 *a slightly cold room*: Emily Loyd, email to author, November 12, 2018.

28 *not unlike an industrial kitchen*: Rachel Wilkinson, "The Doctors Whose Patients Are Already Dead," *Atlantic,* July 14, 2005, https://www.theatlantic.com/health/archive/2015/07/pathology-medicine-autopsy-pathologist/398288/.

29 *The medical examiner concluded*: Lyla Perez, court testimony, October 28, 2005.

30 *Kuehn noticed ligature marks*: Matthew Kuehn, *Forensic Files* interview transcript, December 2009.

30 *a pair of detectives drove to a maximum-security prison*: Thomas Macauley, *Forensic Files* interview transcript, December 2009.

30 *He dragged the corpse into the bathroom*: Matthew Kuehn, *Forensic Files* interview transcript, December 2009.

30 *"couldn't get a Dixie cup of blood out of the remains"*: John Halliday, interview by author, April 26, 2017.

30 *A senior detective was struck by the precision*: Nicholas Theodos, interview by author, June 14, 2018.

31 *The perpetrator's fastidiousness prompted another assumption*: Thomas Macauley, *Forensic Files* interview transcript, December 2009.

31 *Margaret Mulcahy was nervous*: Margaret Mulcahy, court testimony, October 26, 2005.

32 *his eighteen-year-old daughter Tracey did something*: Tracey Mulcahy, sentencing statement, January 27, 2006.

32 *Tracey learned the details from the local paper*: Ibid.

32 *He had been an employee of Bull HN Information Systems*: Bob Mura, "Police Retracing Slain Man's Steps," *Asbury Park Press,* July 15, 1992.

32 *A college newsletter noted his promotion*: "Alumni News," September 1968, https://archive.org/stream/alumninewssept1968bost/alumninewssept1968bost_djvu.txt.

32 *For the last fifteen years*: Tom Coakley and Doreen Iudica, "Sudbury Man Was Last Seen Alive in NYC," *Boston Globe,* July 14, 1992.

32 *"He had a view of life that everything was great"*: Yves Leroux, interview by author, November 17, 2018.

33 *To his kids, he wasn't physically affectionate*: Tracey Mulcahy, interview by author, October 5, 2018.

33 *He was a typical neighbor*: Fisher, "Threads."

33 *She discovered his predilection*: Margaret Mulcahy, court testimony, October 26, 2005.

33 *This became a topic of discussion*: Tracey Mulcahy, interview by author, October 5, 2018.

34 *Margaret asked that New Jersey detectives meet her*: Matthew Kuehn, *Forensic Files* interview transcript, December 2009.

34 *She flew from Logan to Philadelphia International Airport*: Thomas Macauley, *Forensic Files* interview transcript, December 2009.

34 *Tom's mother, Mary, emigrated from Ireland*: United States of America petition for naturalization, September 16, 1937.

34 *While raising Tom alone, they were perpetual guests*: Tracey Mulcahy, interview by author, October 5, 2018.

34 *Patrick Canty was thrown to his death*: "Man, 60, Killed in Toss from Speeding Auto," *Boston Globe,* January 15, 1948.

34–35 *seventeen-year-old Arthur MacGillvary stabbed Dorothy Brennan*: "Youth, Man, Held in So. End Knife Murder," *Boston Globe,* April 23, 1948.

35 *"It was an area of derelicts"*: William Burke, interview by author, October 25, 2018.

35 *In 1950, to escape the South End*: David J. Loftus, *B.C. High 1863–1983* (Boston: Addison C. Gretchell & Son, 1984), 121.

35 *"Jesuit education where there was no room"*: Jack Travers, *The Price of Love* (Otsego, MI: PageFree Publishing, 2002), 62.

35 *an unusually accomplished class*: Yvonne Abraham, "The Overachievers of the Class of '52," *Boston Globe,* April 1, 2012, https://www3.bostonglobe.com/metro/2012/03/31/overachievers-class/UZ9w8VKYs OQBfu8Kdp9dGN/story.html?arc404=true.

35 *"Jim, one of our livelier classmates"*: *Renaissance 1952.*

35 *ordained as a priest in 1959*: Linda Matchan, "Town Secret," *Boston Globe,* August 29, 1993, http:// archive.boston.com/globe/spotlight/abuse/archives/082993_porter.htm.

36 *he wrote a letter to Pope Paul VI*: "Father James Porter's 1973 Letter to Pope Seeking Laicization," BishopAccountability.org, http://www.bishop-accountability.org/news2013/05_06/2013_06_25_Fraga _FatherJames.htm.

36 *Bernard Law called the disgraced priest an "aberrant"*: "The Boston Area's First Predator Priest Case," *Boston Globe,* http://archive.boston.com/globe/spotlight/abuse/extras/porter_archive.htm.

36 *"being deluged with complaints"*: Michael Rezendes and Stephen Kurkjian, "Bishop Tells of Shielding Priests," *Boston Globe,* January 9, 2003, http://archive.boston.com/globe/spotlight/abuse/stories4/010903 _mccormack.htm.

36 *But not before seeing Margaret Mulcahy*: Bill McQueeney, interview by author, October 23, 2018.

36 *a third-floor apartment in South Boston*: Dick Lehr and Gerard O'Neill, *Whitey* (New York: Random House, 2013), 29.

36 *"always manages to come out with a quip"*: Renaissance 1952.

37 *"I think of Tom very favorably"*: William and Mary Bulger, interview by author, October 22, 2018.

37 *his brother was fatally beaten*: Katharine Q. Seelye, William K. Rashbaum, and Danielle Ivory, "Whitey Bulger's Fatal Prison Beating: 'He Was Unrecognizable,'" *New York Times,* October 31, 2018, https://www.nytimes.com/2018/10/31/us/who-killed-whitey-bulger.html.

37 *Until the mid-1960s*: History Project, *Improper Bostonians* (Boston: Beacon Press, 1999), 150.

38 *In March 1945, police raided a house party*: Ibid., 154.

38 *The* Mid-Town Journal, *a South End tabloid*: Ibid., 148.

38 *"Butch Ball Baffles Bulls" went one headline*: Lillian Faderman, *Odd Girls and Twilight Lovers* (New York: Columbia University Press, 1991), 166.

38 *the Boston Catholic Church tried, unsuccessfully*: Libby Bouvier, interview by author, December 7, 2018.

38 *nineteen-year-old George Mansour went to a party*: Michael Bronski, "Drag Lad Tells All," *Boston Phoenix,* March 6, 2003, https://www.glapn.org/sodomylaws/usa/massachusetts/manews018.htm.

38 *"rather eat dick than mashed potatoes"*: George Mansour, interview by author, December 5, 2018.

39 *he earned an occasional 80 or 90*: Tom's grades were provided to the author by Lance Hutchinson, Boston College High School's archivist, in October 2018.

39 *Tom majored in psychology*: Sub Turri (1956), 136.

39 *classified homosexuality as a "sociopathic personality disturbance"*: American Psychiatric Association, *Diagnostic and Statistical Manual of Mental Disorders* (Washington, D.C.: American Psychiatric Association Mental Hospital Service, 1952), 39, http://www.turkpsikiyatri.org/arsiv/dsm-1952.pdf.

39 *reclassified homosexuality as a "sexual deviation"*: American Psychiatric Association, *Diagnostic and Statistical Manual* (Washington, D.C.: American Psychiatric Association, 1968), 44, https://www.madinamerica.com/wp-content/uploads/2015/08/DSM-II.pdf.

39 *"new treatment for maladaptive approach behavior"*: J. R. Cautela, "Covert Sensitization," *Psychological Reports* 20, no. 2 (1967): 459–68, http://doi.org/10.2466/pr0.1967.20.2.459.

39 *"terrible stigma in those days"*: William Burke, interview by author, October 25, 2018.

39 *the city's gay men were targeted*: Alan Rogers, *The Boston Strangler* (Carlisle, MA: Commonwealth Editions, 2006), 24.

40 *paying seventy cents an hour*: Tom's salary is reported in the 1952 Library Employee list, provided to the author by Marta Crilly of Boston City Archives in October 2018.

40 *He lived a couple of blocks from campus*: The details of Tom's life in New York during graduate school (including his work at the Stork Club) were provided to the author by a lifelong friend in November 2018. The friend chooses to remain anonymous.

40 *an anti-Semitic mobbed-up former bootlegger*: Pete Hamill, "The 'In' Crowd," *New York Times,* March 7, 2000.

40 *unions attempted to organize Billingsley's staff*: "Winchell and Billingsley," *Washington Afro-American,* April 1, 1952.

41 *On October 11, 1958, after several years of dating*: Marjorie W. Sherman, "Sanders Theater Thronged by Boston Shakespeare Fans," *Boston Globe,* October 11, 1958.

41 *a hot spot for burgeoning computer companies*: Alan Earls, interview by author, January 30, 2019.

41 *On Wednesday morning, July 8, 1992*: William O'Brien, court testimony, October 27, 2005.

41 *the ninety-second floor*: Thomas J. Lueck, "Back to Work Amid Soot and Stress," *New York Times*, March 9, 1993.

42 *they got "shit-faced"*: Matthew Kuehn, court testimony, October 28, 2005.

42 *"The homosexual community wasn't very open"*: Matthew Kuehn, court testimony, November 9, 2005.

42 *blue-eyed twentysomething adorned in Brooks Brothers*: Douglas Gibson, interview by author, September 14, 2018.

42 *Tom and Gibson were introduced that night by a mutual friend*: Douglas Gibson, court testimony, October 27, 2005.

44 *She took them to the therapist*: Tracey Mulcahy, interview by author, October 5, 2018.

44 *Tom may have traveled to Atlantic City*: Bob Mura, "Police Retracing Slain Man's Steps," *Asbury Park Press*, July 15, 1992.

44 *They theorized he had been killed*: Tom Coakley, "Police Seeking Motives In Dismemberment," *Boston Globe*, July 17, 1992.

44 *A colleague remembered his attending a Boston production*: Yves Leroux, interview by author, November 17, 2018.

45 *the Mulcahys held the funeral*: Tom Coakley, "Friends, Family Gather to Mourn Sudbury Man," *Boston Globe*, July 17, 1992.

45 *"we felt that he really pissed somebody off"*: Matthew Kuehn, *Forensic Files* interview transcript, December 2009.

45 *Instead of being performed at the state crime lab*: Allen Pollard, *Forensic Files* interview transcript, December 2009.

45 *The chamber, which should have been airtight*: Thomas Macauley, *Forensic Files* interview transcript, December 2009.

46 *sold during an eight-month window*: Matthew Kuehn, court testimony, October 28, 2005.

46 *The sticker on the saw was traced to Pergament*: Paul Carpenter, court testimony, October 27, 2005.

46 *"you're looking at a potential serial killer"*: Matthew Kuehn, *Forensic Files* interview transcript, December 2009.

4. RICK

50 *he played for small crowds on Saint Martin*: Rick Unterberg, interviews by author, 2017 and 2018.

51 *the Whitney Museum paid a million dollars*: Grace Glueck, "Painting by Jasper Johns Sold for Million, a Record," *New York Times*, September 27, 1980.

51fn1 *"Louise Nevelson was on the island"*: Jasper Johns, email to author, December 3, 2019.

51 *On January 15, 1981, a man watched his lover*: Randy Shilts, *And the Band Played On* (New York: St. Martin's Griffin, 1987), 53.

52 *Nearly five months later,* Morbidity and Mortality Weekly Report: *Morbidity and Mortality Weekly Report*, June 4, 1981.

52 *the Yule concert in '74*: "Yule Concerts Sunday," *Times*, December 12, 1974.

52 *the fall production of* Arsenic and Old Lace: "Fall Play Scheduled," *Times*, November 12, 1975.

52 *vocal awards in '76*: "Thornridge Musicians Get Honors," *Times*, March 28, 1976.

53 *docked in Port Canaveral*: Amy Clark, "Starship Shines at Renaming Fete," *Florida Today*, January 9, 1989.

53 *a cozy lounge on the pool deck*: Advertisement, *Florida Today,* January 3, 1989.

53 *insurance companies could require that applicants be tested*: Bruce Lambert, "AIDS Insurance Coverage Is Increasingly Hard to Get," *New York Times,* August 7, 1989.

53 *"The awful thing is"*: Rick Unterberg, interview by author, August 1, 2018.

53 *"hunting prints, club chairs"*: Anonymous, "Memories of Extinct NYC Gay Bars," *The Data Lounge,* January 31, 2013, https://www.datalounge.com/thread/12412505-memories-of-extinct-nyc-gay-bars.

54 *Galluccio, purely out of spite*: Michael Musto, "Still Clubbing at 82," *New York Times,* October 24, 2018, https://www.nytimes.com/2018/10/24/style/paul-galluccio-townhouse-gay-piano-bar.html.

55 *He would eventually learn a thousand songs*: David Finkle, "Listings," *Village Voice,* January 29, 2002, https://www.villagevoice.com/2002/01/29/listings-115/.

55 *more than two thousand homicides*: "New York Crime Rates 1960–2018," *Disaster Center,* http://www .disastercenter.com/crime/nycrime.htm.

55 *"If you were a crime victim"*: Duncan Osborne, interview by author, February 26, 2019.

55 *The year 1992 saw 10,828 diagnoses of AIDS in New York*: HIV Epidemiology and Field Services Program, New York City HIV/AIDS Annual Surveillance Statistics 2014, https://www1.nyc.gov/assets/doh /downloads/pdf/ah/surveillance2014-trend-tables.pdf.

55 *once treated survivors of the* Titanic: Michael Daly, "St. Vincent's Hospital Leaving Legacy of Titanic Rescue, Reunion," *Daily News,* April 10, 2010, https://www.nydailynews.com/new-york/st-vincent -hospital-leaving-legacy-titanic-rescue-reunion-article-1.165554.

55 *stretchers crammed wall to wall*: Duncan Osborne, "20 Years Later, H.I.V. Center Still Has Its Doors Open," *Villager,* December 25, 2008, https://www.thevillager.com/2008/12/20-years-later-h-i-v-center -still-has-its-doors-open/.

56 *As was his wont*: Damien Cave, "As Killer Faces Sentencing, His Motive Remains Elusive," *New York Times,* January 27, 2006, https://www.nytimes.com/2006/01/27/nyregion/as-killer-faces-sentencing-his -motive-remains-elusive.html.

56 *"proper attire" bars*: John Kenrick, "Special Feature: Piano Bars," *Musicals101.com,* http://www .musicals101.com/gay11.htm.

56 *"Bermuda Triangle of showbiz aspirants"*: Michael Musto, "Musto Gusto," *Daily News,* July 9, 1993.

56 *"literally an underground bar for gay men"*: Tom Ogden, *Haunted Greenwich Village* (Guilford, CT: Globe Pequot Press, 2012), 92.

57 *"the safe, sane choice"*: Queerty Staff, "A Gay Bar Owner's Last Lament Before Closing the Doors Forever," *Queerty,* June 29, 2010, https://www.queerty.com/a-gay-bar-owners-last-lament-before-closing -the-doors-forever-20100629.

57 *its Ramble, where gay men had once been thrashed*: Doug Ireland, "Rendezvous in the Ramble," *New York,* July 24, 1978.

57 *Truman Capote and Rudolf Nureyev*: Charles Kaiser, *Gay Metropolis* (New York: Houghton Mifflin, 1997), 120.

57 *in 1977, nine men were incinerated*: Doree Shafrir, "The Gay Bathhouse Fire of 1977," *BuzzFeed News,* June 17, 2016, https://www.buzzfeednews.com/article/doree/the-gay-bathhouse-fire-of-1977# .fuz7oB3JQr.

57 *rumored to have once been a speakeasy*: Mitch Kahn, interview by author, January 18, 2019.

57 *thirteen steps between the sidewalk and the street*: Lisa Hall, interview by author, March 23, 2017.

57 *As you walked in*: Thomas Regan provided the author with a rough blueprint of the Five Oaks on August 5, 2017.

57 *she bobbed her head gently as she played*: "Marie Blake Sings 'Down in the Depths' at the Five Oaks—Feb. 1993," YouTube, https://www.youtube.com/watch?reload=9&v=wviEykwmTNs.

57 *"You have to feel the song within you"*: Richard D. Lyons, "Marie Blake, 74, Jazz Singer and Pianist in Village for 40 Years," *New York Times*, December 8, 1993.

57 *Liza Minnelli and Shirley MacLaine dropped in*: Thomas Regan, interview by author, May 26, 2017.

57–58 *Hal Prince, too*: Thomas Regan, email to author, March 20, 2019.

58 *Stephen Sondheim recalled*: Stephen Sondheim, email to author, June 15, 2017.

58 *"I stopped counting at two hundred fifty people I knew"*: Lisa Hall, interview by author, March 23, 2017.

58 *"just exactly as loathsome as the name implies"*: Sam Anderson, "The Memory Addict," *New York*, April 25, 2008, https://nymag.com/arts/books/features/46475/index1.html.

58 *locus of gay establishments*: Marcia Biederman, "Journey to an Overlooked Past," *New York Times*, June 11, 2000, https://www.nytimes.com/2000/06/11/nyregion/journey-to-an-overlooked-past.html.

58 *Mattachine Society once staged a "sip-in" there*: Jim Farber, "Before the Stonewall Uprising, There Was the 'Sip-In,'" *New York Times*, April 20, 2016, https://www.nytimes.com/2016/04/21/nyregion/before-the-stonewall-riots-there-was-the-sip-in.html.

58 *Black men who were into leather*: Fiona Anderson, *Cruising the Dead River* (Chicago: University of Chicago Press, 2019), 21.

58–59 *swaths of which had once been the estate*: Edwin G. Burrows and Mike Wallace, *Gotham* (New York: Oxford University Press, 2000), 578.

59 *very few sidewalks*: Richard Laermer, interview by author, July 17, 2017.

59 *"We did not walk on the west side of Eighth Avenue"*: Michael Shernoff, "Early Gay Activism in Chelsea: Building a Queer Neighborhood," *LGNY*, July 6, 1997, http://8th-14th.northwestern.edu/chelsea/Gay%208th%20Ave/gay_history.htm.

59 *As Sarah Jessica Parker put it*: Emily Nussbaum, "Sarah Jessica Parker Would Like a Few Words with Carrie Bradshaw," *New York*, May 12, 2008.

59 *Young people moved in first*: Marvine Howe, "Gay Businesses Follow Influx of Gay People," *New York Times*, April 10, 1994.

59 *"The older guys stayed in the Village"*: Richard Laermer, interview by author, July, 17, 2017.

59 *one could rent a studio for $900 a month*: Kirk Johnson, "Chelsea," *New York Times*, October 14, 1984.

59 *the neighborhood's first gay restaurant*: Bryan Miller, "Rogers & Barbero," *New York Times*, November 4, 1988.

60 *Applicants might wait more than a decade*: Johnson, "Chelsea."

60 *A cornerstone of Chelsea were the heavy-duty leather bars*: Much of this chapter, particularly as pertains to the ecosystem of Manhattan's queer bars and clubs, is the result of repeated interviews with Matthew Bank, the founder of *HX*.

60 *water fell over muscular pretty boys*: Rob Frydlewicz, "The Rise & Fall of Popular New York Bar, 'Splash' (1991–2013)," *ZeitGAYst*, September 2012, https://thestarryeye.typepad.com/gay/2012/09/splash-bar-celebrates-its-21st-anniversary-september-25-1990.html.

60 *"the stable of buff bartenders"*: Ibid.

60 *"muscular, nearly naked men would dance"*: Tim Murphy, "Turn the Showers Off. Splash Is Closing,"

New York Times, July 31, 2013, https://www.nytimes.com/2013/08/01/fashion/turn-the-showers-off-splash -is-closing.html.

60–61 *James Baldwin, on the cusp of publishing his novel*: "James Baldwin Residence," *NYC LGBT Historic Sites Project,* https://www.nyclgbtsites.org/site/james-baldwin-residence/.

61 *nothing gay "opened up above the 80s"*: Matthew Bank, interview by author, May 30, 2017.

61 *"you walked in, saw a few locals"*: Alan Helms, *Gay American Autobiography* (Madison: University of Wisconsin Press, 2009), 237.

61 *"obnoxiously loud and intrusive"*: "Love and Marriage," *The Gay Sixties,* http://www.nycnotkansas.com /GaySixties.htm.

61 *temporarily shuttered the bar*: Logan Hendrix, "Candle Bar Goes Dark," *New York Press,* June 23, 2015, www.nypress.com/local-news/20150623/candle-bar-goes-dark.

61 *"a fascinating hangout for trans women"*: Michael Musto, "10 Trans Nightlife Staples from New York City's Past," *Paper,* July 27, 2016, https://www.papermag.com/trans-nightlife-new-york-city-history -1946986169.html.

61 *"obvious 'fairies,' (many of them heavily made-up)"*: Kaiser, *Gay Metropolis,* 12.

62 *Samuel Delany was one of the regulars*: Carey Goldberg, "Mr. Delany's Cosmic Neighborhood," *New York Times,* February 11, 1996.

62 *on the job and penis exposed*: Samuel Delany, interview by author, July 20, 2017.

62 *"Dear sweet Jesus, was that hellhole something else"*: Anonymous, "Memories of Extinct NYC Gay Bars," *Data Lounge,* February 2, 2013, https://www.datalounge.com/thread/12412505-memories-of-extinct-nyc-gay-bars.

62 *"really, really, really gross"*: Richard Laermer, interview by author, July, 17, 2017.

5. THE TRYOUT OF EDDIE MARRERO

63 *At 7:30 in the morning*: Donald Giberson, court testimony, October 27, 2005.

63 *"Upon arrival, Mr. Giberson approached me"*: Incident report, May 10, 1993.

64 *investigated seventy-five homicide cases*: Frank Argote-Freyre, "His Work Begins When a Life Ends," *Asbury Park Press,* November 30, 1992.

64 *Growing up in Lakewood, New Jersey*: Michael Mohel, interview by author, January 7, 2019.

64 *he was unaffected by gore*: Thomas Hayes, interview by author, March 12, 2019.

64 *After a year of undercover work in Miami*: Mark Woodfield, interview by author, March 8, 2019.

64 *There was a left arm, bloodied and dirty*: Photos of the scene were provided by an investigator.

64 *torso bisected horizontally*: Geetha Ann Natarajan, court testimony, September 22, 2005.

65 *The head was contained in an Acme bag*: Mark Woodfield, court testimony, October 27, 2005.

65 *The body seemed to have been washed*: Mark Woodfield, court testimony, September 22, 2005.

65 *was inked* LINDA: George Shigo, court testimony, October 27, 2005.

65 *written in fine cursive, was* FAST EDDIE: John Way Jennings and Larry Lewis, "Could Brutal Slayings Somehow Be Linked?" *Philadelphia Inquirer,* May 13, 1993.

65 *Fingerprints in hand*: George Shigo, court testimony, October 27, 2005.

65–66 *"There may be some connection to Monmouth County"*: William K. Heine, "Police ID Body of Dis-membered Man," *Asbury Park Press,* May 12, 1993.

66 *"We know practically zilch"*: "Body Found by the Road Is Identified," Associated Press, May 12, 1993.

66 *"No one notified police Marrero was missing"*: Heine, "Police ID Body of Dismembered Man."

66 *born on May 2, 1949*: New Jersey Death Index, 1993.

66 *lived in several locations around Philadelphia*: Jennings and Lewis, "Could Brutal Slayings Somehow Be Linked?"

66 *the Social Security number is for a woman*: Kevin Mathews, interview by author, November 1, 2019.

67 *asked if he wanted a blow job*: Michael Mohel, interview by author, January 7, 2019.

67 *the place had been a hub*: Fred Loetterle, "Court Reaps & Rejects a Bumper Crop of Prosties," *Daily News*, August 27, 1967.

67 *a "hooker magnet"*: Jonathan Miller, "For Commuters, It's Not Love at First Sight," *New York Times*, December 12, 2004.

67 *known as the Minnesota Strip*: Thomas J. Lueck, "A Seedy Strip Slowly Gives Way to Assaults of the Squeaky Clean," *New York Times*, June 20, 1997.

67 *In his journals, Wojnarowicz*: David Wojnarowicz, *The Waterfront Journals* (New York: Grove Press, 1997), 29.

67 *thirty-year run as the city's tenderloin district*: Joseph Varga, *Hell's Kitchen and the Battle for Urban Space* (New York: Monthly Review Press, 2013), 101.

67 *"whenever the fleet comes into town"*: George Chauncey, *Gay New York* (New York: Basic Books, 1995), 66.

67–68 *"a pea-sized fragment of crack"*: David J. Krajicek, "Where Chicken Hawks Get Their Prey," *Daily News*, February 20, 1989.

68 *"In those days, sometimes being able to hold that over somebody"*: The Port Authority official was interviewed by the author in December 2018, and was granted anonymity for his candor.

68 *On the second floor of the bus terminal*: Thomas J. Lueck, "Possible Break in Killing of Gay Men," *New York Times*, May 30, 2001.

68 *a pal of Anthony's who lived on West Fortieth*: Carlos Santiago, court testimony, November 1, 2005.

68 *no gay bar on that corner*: Matthew Bank, interview by author, January 19, 2019.

68 *"Young entrepreneurs meet older investors"*: HX, April 7, 1993.

69 *"How are things going out on the sales floor?"*: This anecdote was relayed by a man I met at the Townhouse on January 18, 2020, as I was working on the epilogue. He asked to remain anonymous.

69 *"The guys who were for sale were on one side"*: Dale Corvino, interview by author, January 24, 2019.

69 *They had been friends for six years*: Carlos Santiago, court testimony, November 1, 2005.

69–70 *a man in Hamden, Connecticut*: Thomas Hayes, interview by author, January 15, 2019.

70 *Louis told the detectives what little he knew*: Mark Woodfield, interview by author, March 8, 2019.

71 *"Dead bodies can talk a lot"*: John Hassell, "Her Job Is to Shed Light on Death's Dark Mystery," *Asbury Park Press*, January 5, 1994.

71 *She further noted ligature marks*: Geetha Ann Natarajan, court testimony, September 22, 2005.

71 *he stripped off his suit*: Thomas Hayes, interview by author, March 12, 2019.

71 *"We gotta be dealing with the same guy"*: Mark Woodfield, interview by author, January 15, 2019.

72 *detectives briefly wondered if the men were acquainted*: Jennings and Lewis, "Could Brutal Slayings Somehow Be Linked?"

72 *The list was long*: Mark Woodfield, court testimony, October 27, 2005.

72 *may have been "recruiting" Hispanic sex workers*: Ibid.

73 *"Here I've got a serial killer, and he's never been arrested?"*: Mark Woodfield, interview by author, June 10, 2019.

73 New York Times *published a story*: Fisher, "Threads."

74fn1 *the organization has no record of Anthony's tryout*: Rob Holiday, email to author, February 21, 2017.

74 *"Their response was nothing"*: Duncan Osborne, "Too Little, Too Late," *Advocate,* September 21, 1993.

6. NO ONE HAS THE RIGHT TO BEAT THE CRAP OUT OF YOU

78 *twice in the head with a rifle*: Marlene Aig, "Arrest Made in Bizarre Slaying of Modeling Student," Associated Press, March 22, 1985, https://apnews.com/d7b4658f49590a3f55d00dddac44528e.

78 *hosted a party by Andy Warhol*: Priya Krishna, "From House of Worship to House of Sin: The History of Chelsea's Limelight Building," *Curbed,* November 30, 2016, https://ny.curbed.com/2016/11/30/13769350/limelight-building-chelsea-nyc-history.

78 *a slightly pudgy, curly-haired Manhattan art dealer*: Robert Rosamilio, "Andrew Crispo," Getty Images, May 17, 1985, https://www.gettyimages.co.uk/detail/news-photo/andrew-crispo-in-custody-after-he-surrendered-to-face-news-photo/141769944.

78 *known in the queer community as a sadist*: Rebecca Porper, interview by author, January 14, 2019.

78 *the next year he was sent to prison*: "Crispo Sentenced to 7 Years for Evasion of Income Taxes," United Press International, February 11, 1986.

78 *The jittery young man was introduced to Linda Fairstein*: Rebecca Porper, interview by author, January 14, 2019.

79 *She had run the sex crime unit*: Katherine Bouton, "Linda Fairstein vs. Rape," *New York Times Magazine,* February 25, 1990.

79 *Crispo was, again, acquitted*: Samuel Maull, "Jury Clears Art Dealer in Attack," Associated Press, October 17, 1988, https://apnews.com/e29703290a30dd40431dff3d429bccad.

79 *"success was if somebody took any of this seriously"*: Bea Hanson, interview by author, June 11, 2018.

79 *In March 1980, three men in Chelsea were attacked*: Arthur D. Kahn, *The Many Faces of Gay* (Westport, CT: Praeger, 1997), 174–75.

79 *"the defense will make a bum out of you"*: Lindsy Van Gelder, "Alarmed Gays Finding Police a Quiet Ally," *Daily News,* December 24, 1980.

80 *Pete Hamill, writing the year before about protests*: Pete Hamill, "It's Rough When You're 'Cruising' on a Censorship," *Daily News,* August 1, 1979.

80 *Between 1985 and 1989, the number of anti-queer incidents*: Gregory M. Herek and Kevin T. Berrill, *Hate Crimes* (Newbury Park, CA: Sage Publications, 1991), 36.

80 *"A striking feature of most murders"*: B. Miller and L. Humphreys, "Lifestyles and Violence: Homosexual Victims of Assault and Murder," *Qualitative Sociology* 3, no. 3 (1980): 169–85, https://doi.org/10.1007/bf00987134.

81 *The precinct commanding officer refused*: Kahn, *Many Faces,* 175.

81 *"YOUR NEIGHBORS ARE ORGANIZING"*: Chelsea Gay Association flyer found in the files of the Lesbian, Gay, Bisexual, and Transgender Community Center library.

81 *activists secured meetings*: Kahn, *Many Faces,* 175.

81 *"devoted to each other"*: Patricia Klees, interview by author, March 16, 2019.

81 *"As time went on," a CGA board member wrote*: Thomas von Foerster, *The Antiviolence Hotline, Now Project: 1982*, November 16, 1989.

82 the Native *reported the hotline was overtaxed*: "Entrapment Reported Widespread in Riis Park: Hotline Looking for New Volunteers," *New York Native*, September 13, 1982.

82 *That year, with the help of Duane*: Alex Michelini, "Safety for Gays," *Daily News*, April 10, 1983.

82 *A press release announced a new name*: Press release found in the files of the Lesbian, Gay, Bisexual, and Transgender Community Center library, November 15, 1982.

82 *reports of more than a dozen anti-queer crimes*: Alex Michelini, "Safety."

82 *"They didn't know how to go about it except to scream at them"*: Rebecca Porper, interview by author, January 14, 2019.

82 *Outreach to the police began at the precinct level*: Shernoff, "Early Gay Activism."

83 *an officer sitting in the front row*: David Wertheimer was interviewed repeatedly by the author in 2019.

83 *"They didn't want to know from gay guys"*: This and all subsequent quotations are from a January 14, 2019, interview with Rebecca Porper.

83 *the cops referred to Greenwich Village's Sixth Precinct*: Jack Engelhard, *The Days of the Bitter End* (British Columbia, Canada: DayRay Literary Press, 2013), 20.

83 *"a tongue-in-cheek reference to the gay community"*: Carl Zittell, interview by author, March 18, 2019.

84 *many of its officers accused of taking payoffs*: Leonard Buder, "Change Pledged in Precinct Cited in Investigation," *New York Times*, January 22, 1983.

84 *as an alternative to an arrest*: Steven C. Arvanette, "Police and Gays Talk It Out," *New York Native*, May 23, 1983.

84 *Edward Koch's office founded the Police Council*: Transcript, "Anti-Gay Violence: Hearing Before the Subcommittee on Criminal Justice," October 9, 1986, https://www.ncjrs.gov/pdffiles1/Digitization /120033NCJRS.pdf.

84 *arrest seventeen members of ACT UP*: "ACTUP Capsule History 1987," ACT UP Historical Archive, https://actupny.org/documents/cron-87.html.

84 *Sometimes they did*: David Wertheimer, interview by author, January 9, 2019.

85 *The young woman, Jacqueline Schafer, was tasked*: I granted anonymity to a longtime staff member at the Manhattan District Attorney's Office, who talked to me about the various councils and liaisons. We spoke on February 1, 2019.

85 *sex crimes unit oversaw more than five hundred cases*: Bouton, "Linda Fairstein."

85 *"There had been so many times when"*: Linda Fairstein, interview by author, March 7, 2019.

85 *"The truth is, in fact, exactly the opposite"*: Ann Northrop, interview by author, March 7, 2019.

86 *three variants of defense theory*: Jordan Blair Woods, Brad Sears, and Christy Mallory, "Model Legislation for Eliminating the Gay and Trans Panic Defense," *Williams Institute*, September 2016, https:// williamsinstitute.law.ucla.edu/wp-content/uploads/2016-Model-GayTransPanic-Ban-Laws-final.pdf.

86 *"that bullshit excuse"*: Robert Morgenthau, interview by author, January 31, 2019.

86 *"You don't understand, I want to get these men before they get me"*: Joe Mozingo, "Man Who Killed 5 L.A. Gays in 1980s Gets Life Sentence," *Los Angeles Times*, June 22, 1999, https://www.latimes.com /archives/la-xpm-1999-jun-22-me-48900-story.html.

87 *"A courtly figure in his mid-sixties"*: David France, *How to Survive a Plague* (New York: Vintage Books, 2016), 69.

88 *Kennedy obtained a conviction*: David Wertheimer, interview by author, March 1, 2019.

88 *a lecturer in pastoral theology*: "Anti-Violence Project Hires New Executive Director," *New York Native*, October 28, 1985.

88 *a same-sex domestic violence program*: "Gay Domestic Violence Program Announced," *New York Native*, November 1, 1986.

88 *the first seven months of 1986*: Transcript, "Anti-Gay Violence."

88 *"Young people growing up gay all over America"*: "Sodomy Ruling Spurs New York Rally," Associated Press, July 5, 1986.

89 *"I don't think [Conyers] was an activist"*: Kevin Berrill, interview by author, March 21, 2019.

89 *Among them was Robert*: Transcript, "Anti-Gay Violence."

90 *"Attacks on homosexuals appear to have increased sharply"*: William Greer, "Violence Against Homosexuals Rising, Groups Seeking Wider Protection Say," *New York Times*, November 23, 1986.

91 *the American Bar Association's official condemnation*: "American Bar Association Condemns Anti-Gay Violence," *New York Native*, September 7, 1987.

91 *"We're against homosexuals . . . working with homosexual officers"*: Larry Celona and Ruth Landa, "Cop Units Hit Gay Recruitment," *Daily News*, May 19, 1987.

91 *"outrageous verbal acts of bias violence"*: Ruben Rosario, "Gays Hit Recruitment Critics," *Daily News*, May 20, 1987.

91 *"filthy AIDS carrier" and a "faggot"*: "Anti-Gay Violence Escalates," United Press International, September 26, 1987.

91 *credited with a dramatic spike in violence*: Gary David Comstock, *Violence Against Lesbians and Gay Men* (New York: Columbia University Press, 1991), 218.

91 *A Black man named Michael Griffith*: Joseph P. Fried, "Howard Beach Defendant Given Maximum Term of 10 to 30 Years," *New York Times*, June 23, 1988.

92 *"a tacit condoning of anti-gay violence"*: Adam Nagourney, "Crime Bill Stalls," *Daily News*, July 1, 1987.

92 *a Vietnam War veteran stabbed in the chest*: Jim Smith, "Killed for Being Gay: Jimmy Zappalorti's Death, Nearly 25 Years Later," *Staten Island Advance*, December 8, 2014, https://www.silive.com /gaylesbianlife/2014/12/killed_for_being_gay_jimmy_zap.html.

92 *"a good gay, not a pervert"*: Mary Engels and David J. Krajicek, "Rage over S.I. Slaying," *Daily News*, January 26, 1990.

92 *Foreman, hired in January 1990*: "Anti-Violence Project Announces New Director," *New York Native*, January 15, 1990.

92 *That July, Julio Rivera, a twenty-nine-year-old gay Puerto Rican*: James Barron, "2 Charged in Slaying of Gay Man," *New York Times*, November 14, 1990.

93 *"cocksucking fag"*: Eric Pooley, "With Extreme Prejudice," *New York*, April 8, 1991.

93 *"could not have had a more classic gay-bashing case"*: Andrew Maykuth, "Rising Tide of Anti-Gay Violence," *Philadelphia Inquirer*, November 30, 1991.

93 *"We felt we had a responsibility to the community"*: Bea Hanson, interview by author, May 20, 2019.

93 *After the murder of Thomas Mulcahy*: Osborne, "Too Little."

94 *"If you had a pie, and it had eight slices"*: Stephen Colantonio, interview by author, November 19, 2018.

94 *thick-necked predator*: Arthur S. Leonard, "AVP Wins a Round with Bowen," *Gay City News,* April 28, 2004, https://www.gaycitynews.com/avp-wins-a-round-with-bowen/.

94 *"They were an easy target"*: Matt Foreman, interview by author, February 25, 2017.

94 *"There was an internalized hatred"*: Bea Hanson, interview by author, June 11, 2018.

7. I'LL BE SEEING YOU

95 *At 10:30, regulars filed in*: An account of this evening and the next morning is taken from a police department assignment sheet, dated August 11, 1993.

95 *"It was boisterous and loud"*: Gregory Fienhold, interview by author, February 22, 2019.

95 *"true gustatory delight"*: Al Salerno, "Night Life," *Brooklyn Daily Eagle,* May 23, 1952.

95 *Nina Simone, it was rumored*: Alton Slagle, "$uburbia Slowly Erodes All Those Savings," *Daily News,* November 9, 1976.

96 *In 1976, Normand sold the Five Oaks*: The history of the Five Oaks was provided to the author by Thomas Regan, interviewed on May 26, 2017.

96 *At 11:30 P.M., Hall belted out a few songs*: Lisa Hall, interview by author, April 7, 2019.

97 *Every night except Mondays*: Police department assignment sheet, August 11, 1993.

97 *"I spent more time with him than anybody else"*: Lisa Hall, court testimony, September 21, 2005.

98 *"brown glassy eyes"*: Police department assignment sheet, August 11, 1993.

98 *patrons had seen the man around the bar*: Thomas O'Brien, court testimony, November 3, 2005.

98 *Sitting nearby was an editor*: Donald Parsons, court testimony, September 21, 2005.

99 *Hall and Marie Blake left*: Lisa Hall, court testimony, September 21, 2005.

99 *Barely a day later, at 7:00 A.M.*: Stephen Colantonio, court testimony, November 2, 2005.

99 *The man considered keeping the bounty*: Stephen Colantonio, court testimony, September 21, 2005.

99–100 *That morning, he stopped for coffee*: Task force interview with Ronald Colandrea, October 7, 1993.

100 *Colandrea's family had sold hot dogs*: John Dalmas, "Frankly Speaking, He's a Hot Dog Man," *Rockland Journal-News,* August 27, 1972.

100 *he was inclined to dump garbage*: Nicholas Theodos, interview by author, June 14, 2018.

100 *They, too, were double-bagged*: Matthew Kuehn, *Forensic Files* interview transcript, December 2009.

100 *"cut nice and even, like butchering a cow"*: Henry Frederick, "Body Parts Found in Haverstraw," *Rockland Journal-News,* August 1, 1993.

100 *It wasn't their case by statute*: Stephen Colantonio, interview by author, February 27, 2019. Colantonio was interviewed dozens of times by the author, on the phone and in person, during 2018 and 2019. His recollections help form the basis of chapters 7 and 8.

100 *He lived eight miles away*: "Engagements/Weddings," *Journal-News,* April 14, 1988.

101 *he'd earned a bachelor's degree*: "Long Island University: Candidates for Graduation," *Journal-News,* June 15, 1989.

101 *He'd been studying karate*: Henry Frederick, "Karate Expert a Champ with Students, Too," *Journal-News,* May 9, 1990.

101 *"He had to be dumped overnight"*: Frederick, "Body Parts."

101 *This was soon confirmed by the medical examiner*: Frederick Zugibe, court testimony, September 21, 2005.

101 *"I couldn't eat hot dogs now"*: Frederick, "Body Parts."

101 *It was sent out late that night*: Stephen Colantonio, court testimony, September 21, 2005.

102 *Until seven months ago, he told them*: Frederick, "Body Parts."

102 *"You work backwards," Colantonio said*: Stephen Colantonio, interview by author, March 28, 2019.

102 *born in Youngstown, Ohio, on September 19, 1937*: Ohio Department of Health, Index to Annual Births, 1968–1998; Ohio Department of Health, State Vital Statistics Unit.

102 *bought a few years after Michael was born*: According to records supplied by the Mahoning County Recorder, the Sakaras purchased the home on May 26, 1940.

102 *He was a machinist*: "Michael Sakara, 87," *Youngstown Vindicator,* June 30, 1994.

103 *He had been incarcerated*: "Reformatory Arrivals Boost Population," *Mansfield News,* December 8, 1927.

103 *She quit school*: Marilyn Sakara, interview by author, May 10, 2019.

103 *"participated in domestic violence"*: Marilyn Sakara was interviewed, repeatedly, by the author between 2017 and 2019. All quotes by Marilyn in this chapter are from those interviews.

103 *"grumpy, tightwad son of a bitch"*: Richard Jonesco, interview by author, February 22, 2019.

103 *In Youngstown, Black neighborhoods were bulldozed*: Sean Posey, "America's Fastest Shrinking City: The Story of Youngstown, Ohio," *Hampton Institute,* June 18, 2013, https://www.hamptoninstitution.org /youngstown.html#.XmajdZNKjOR.

104 *"He had these huge, long legs"*: Marilyn Sakara, August 8, 2017.

104 *He was, said his mother, a "handsome cuss"*: Mark Mueller, "Five Slayings, a Suspect, and a Long Search for Proof," *Star-Ledger,* June 2, 2002.

104 *He was in South High's a cappella choir*: *South High 1954,* 77–79, 87.

104 *"He had a lot of poise"*: Mark Zigoris, interview by author, June 19, 2019.

105 *"I knew Michael wasn't a regular guy"*: Roger Danchise, interview by author, March 29, 2019.

105 Saturday Evening Post *famously dubbed it*: David Grann, "Crimetown USA," *New Republic,* January 10, 2000, https://newrepublic.com/article/68973/crimetown-usa.

105 *"Black Youngstown"*: Posey, "America's Fastest Shrinking City."

105 *no room for any population other than heterosexuals*: Sean Posey, interview by author, May 1, 2019.

105 *"thriving little metropolis"*: Dharl Chintan, interview by author, April 15, 2019.

106 *"Dayton Population of Homosexuals Reported Rising"*: Jessie Donahue, "Dayton Population of Homosexuals Reported Rising," *Journal Herald,* May 31, 1965.

107 *probably the city's first licensed gay bar*: Dharl Chintan, interview by author, May 24, 2019.

107 *"It was a typical, low-grade bar"*: Mike Lipski, interview by author, May 24, 2019.

107 *Two patrolmen were shot*: Patricia Meade, "Remembering the Rage," *Vindicator,* April 6, 2008, https:// www.vindy.com/news/2008/apr/06/remembering-the-rage/.

107 *There were riots the next year, too*: Josh Medore, "Flashback: Remembering Jim Crow in Youngstown," *Business Journal,* March 7, 2016, https://businessjournaldaily.com/flashback-remembering-jim-crow-in -youngstown/.

108 *"The violence spread across the city"*: Ibid.

108 *Hillman residents fled and businesses closed*: Sean Posey, interview by author, May 24, 2019.

108 *a dam completed in 1917*: "The Flood of 1913," *Mahoning Valley Historical Society,* March 14, 2013, https://mahoninghistory.org/2013/03/14/the-great-flood-of-1913/.

109 *"He was too big for Youngstown"*: Roger Danchise, interview by author, March 29, 2019.

109 *Michael was terminated by "undesirable discharge"*: Certification of Military Service for Michael Sakara, provided to the author by the National Archives and Records Administration on January 3, 2019.

109 *gay men were considered susceptible*: G. Dean Sinclair, "Homosexuality and the Military: A Review of the Literature," *Journal of Homosexuality* 56, no. 6 (2009): 701–18, https://doi.org/10.1080/00918360903054137.

109 *"undesirable" was often code for queer*: Chris Johnson, "91-Year-Old Gay Veteran Sues to Update Discharge to 'Honorable,'" *Washington Blade,* November 19, 2016, https://www.washingtonblade.com/2016 /11/19/91-year-old-gay-veteran-sue-to-update-discharge-to-honorable/.

109 *arrested for an unspecified "lewd act"*: Confidential document provided by an investigator on March 28, 2019.

109 *converted to co-op in 1980*: Brent Cox, email to author, April 12, 2019.

110 *"The circumstances of our meeting were awkward"*: Ann Murray, "Michael J. Sakara, One of an Endangered Species," *Hagfish Chronicles,* December 13, 2006, http://hagfishchronicles.blogspot.com/2006 /12/michael-j-sakara-one-of-endangered.html. Murray's blogs were posted over a period of more than eight years, from September 9, 2004, to May 14, 2013.

111 *In 2016, Ann died in hospice*: "Obituary: Ann Murray," *Shippensburg News-Chronicle,* September 2, 2016, http://www.shipnc.com/obituaries/article_f9558d10-705b-11e6-9d49-af227aa05d44.html.

111 *"Whenever Michael showed up, the party began"*: Roger Danchise, interview by author, March 29, 2019.

112 *Midway through 1984*: "N.Y. Victim of AIDS Treated at Hospital," *Vindicator,* July 17, 1984.

112 *There were heroes, too*: Sean Posey, interview by author, May 1, 2019.

113 *Baffin talked to the* Daily News: Linda Yglesias, "Slain Gay's Ex a Suspect," *Daily News,* August 6, 1993.

113 *Eva Pryor told them*: Notes provided by retired detective Stephen Colantonio.

114 *"pain in the ass . . . talk to anybody"*: John Gorman, interview by author, April 7, 2017.

114 *he worked at a device*: Frank Romano, interview by author, April 3, 2019.

115 *"A thinker, discussed philosophy"*: The impressions of Michael's colleagues are quoted from undated detectives' notes.

115 *Marilyn watched the garbage pile up*: Jennifer Latson, "Why the 1977 Blackout Was One of New York's Darkest Hours," *Time,* July 13, 2015, https://time.com/3949986/1977-blackout-new-york-history/.

115 *"Our encounter was probably no longer than two hours"*: Karen Gaylord, interview by author, August 8, 2017.

116 *She couldn't stick with it*: Lisa Hall, interview by author, April 7, 2019.

117 *A local boy*: "Frederick T. Zugibe Ph.D., M.D.," *Journal News,* https://obits.lohud.com/obituaries /lohud/obituary.aspx?n=frederick-t-zugibe&pid=166840542&fhid=17075.

117 *Zugibe likened this to cracks on an egg*: Frederick Zugibe, court testimony, September 21, 2005.

118 *the medical examiner talked to the* Journal News: Stephen Britton, "Man Beaten Before Butchering," *Journal News*, August 3, 1993.

8. THE LAST CALL KILLER

119 *three days had passed*: During 2018 and 2019, the author conducted more than a dozen interviews with Stephen Colantonio, who helped flesh out the contours of the Sakara investigation.

119 *He could have been killed anywhere*: Russell Ben-Ali and William K. Rashbaum, "Grisly Slayings Linked? Body Parts Found in Trash," *Newsday*, August 3, 1993.

119 *1981's Trooper of the Year*: New Jersey State Police, https://www.njsp.org/trooper-of-year/1980s.shtml.

119 High Times *named him*: Nicholas Theodos was interviewed by the author on four separate occasions during 2018 and 2019.

120 *the apprehension of a serial rapist*: Charles Strum, "Paroled Rapist Charged with Killing 5 Women in New Jersey," *New York Times*, April 14, 1992.

120 *Haverstraw's detective, for example*: Frank Alessio, LinkedIn, https://www.linkedin.com/in/frank-alessio-6a123245/.

120 *One faction saw Mulcahy and Sakara as the connective thread*: Stephen Colantonio, interview by author, May 31, 2019.

121 *"In my mind, there was no doubt about it"*: Mark Woodfield, interview by author, June 10, 2019.

121 *the phantom sighting in Philadelphia*: Nicholas Theodos, interview by author, June 14, 2018.

121 *The task force was up and running*: The details in this chapter are largely taken from dozens of daily Task Force Updates, written each morning by Nicholas Theodos.

121 *push-button phones, half-eaten food*: James Walsh, "Tracking a Killer," *Journal News*, October 24, 1993.

121 *"We thought we would have this guy in custody"*: Nicholas Theodos, interview by author, May 20, 2019.

121 *The perpetrator seemed to have slipped up*: Mark Woodfield, interview by author, June 10, 2019.

122 *He had seen Michael*: Task force interview with Eugene Williams, August 5, 1993.

122 *He was, Hall said, a nurse*: Lisa Hall, court testimony, September 21, 2005.

122 An interesting and credible statement, *thought Repsha*: Jack Repsha, interview by author, June 18, 2019.

122 *Early that morning, Smith said*: Task force interview with Robert Smith, August 7, 1993.

123 *"You want to get the son of a bitch"*: Donna Malkentzos, interview by author, May 14, 2019.

123 *Sex workers made the best witnesses*: Donna Malkentzos, interview by author, June 11, 2019.

123–124 *smelled something "foul"*: James Beninson, court testimony, November 2, 2005.

124 *the most high-profile story on the case*: Fisher, "Threads."

124 *The young reporter*: Ian Fisher, interview by author, June 13, 2019.

124 *"Gay men and lesbians have been killed for a long time"*: Terence Samuel, "Threat of Serial Killer Stirs Anger in Gay Community," *Philadelphia Inquirer*, August 7, 1993.

125 "LOOKING FOR A GOOD TIME?": Mike McAlary, "He's the 'Last Call Killer,'" *Daily News,* August 9, 1993.

126 *hanging effigies dipped in red paint*: Matt Foreman, email to author, September 13, 2019.

126 *Foreman, Commissioner Kelly, and Mayor Dinkins*: Karen Matthews, "Gay Community Concerned, Not Panicked, by Serial Murder Reports with AM-Gay Stalker-List," Associated Press, August 10, 1993, https://apnews.com/badd8f2c997a012d569c9f0874c99ec8.

126 *"We do not know if a gay serial killer"*: William K. Rashbaum, "2 Recall Man in Gay Bars' Killer Hunt," *Newsday,* August 9, 1993.

126 *"Your name is the Last Call Killer"*: McAlary, "'Last Call Killer.'"

127 *Lisa Hall was on the subway*: *Mark of the Killer,* season 1, episode 2, "The Last Call Killer," aired January 27, 2019.

127 *"a vague and ominous threat"*: Matt Colagiuri, interview by author, October 5, 2019.

127 *"Everyone's frightened"*: Greg B. Smith, "N.Y. Gays Help Cops Track Serial Killer," *San Francisco Examiner,* August 10, 1993.

127 *"Nothing like this has ever happened"*: Lisa Anderson, "Grisly Deaths of Gays Raise Fear of Stalker," *Chicago Tribune,* August 11, 1993.

127 *"we usually use double bags"*: Frederick Zugibe, court testimony, September 21, 2005.

128 *used to the open door of Doctor Nat*: Jack Repsha, interview by author, June 18, 2019.

129 *"Why should I share the information?"*: Nicholas Theodos, interview by author, May 20, 2019.

129 *Theodos turned to Peter Modafferi*: Steve Lieberman, "Rockland's Chief Detective Retiring After 45 Years Investigating Murders, Corruption," *Journal News,* June 9, 2017, https://www.lohud.com/story/news /local/rockland/2017/06/09/rocklands-chief-detective-retiring-after-45-years-investigating-murders -corruption/373344001/.

129 *Modafferi didn't laugh, but it took some effort*: Peter Modafferi, interview by author, June 5, 2019.

129 *Zugibe found a copy of* The New York Times: Frederick Zugibe, court testimony, September 21, 2005.

130 *The newspaper painted a picture*: William K. Rashbaum, "Serial Slayer's Profile Killer Preying on Gays Called Smart, Cunning," *Newsday,* August 21, 1993.

131 *"A squirrelly character"*: Jack Repsha, interview by author, June 18, 2019.

132 *He and the kids stuffed envelopes*: Matthew Kuehn, *Forensic Files* interview transcript, December 2009.

132 *"I remember having songs sung about me"*: Mark Woodfield, interview by author, June 10, 2019.

132 *"They were like technical advisors"*: Jack Repsha, interview by author, June 2, 2018.

133 *visited the Townhouse and the Five Oaks*: Matthew Kuehn, *Forensic Files* interview transcript, December 2009.

133 *It was Pierce's opinion*: Raymond Pierce, interview by author, July 30, 2018.

133 *"limited amount of psychological stress"*: Raymond Pierce, interview by author, June 21, 2019.

134 *"Well, people do strange things"*: Ibid.

134 *A detective observing the interview*: Jack Repsha, interview by author, June 18, 2019.

135 *It was never far from anyone's mind*: Lily Rothman, "How the Son of Sam Serial Killer Was Finally Caught," *Time,* August 10, 2015, https://time.com/3979004/son-of-sam-caught/.

135 *"We did everything we could to eliminate [Holland]"*: Matthew Kuehn, *Forensic Files* interview transcript, December 2009.

135 *"It was a weird time in my life"*: Tony Plaza, interview by author, June 24, 2019.

137 *"his hair is similar"*: Lisa Hall, court testimony, November 2, 2005.

137 *he knew something about the mysterious perpetrator*: Mark Woodfield, interview by author, June 10, 2019.

138 *"You never want to start drawing conclusions"*: Jack Repsha, interview by author, June 18, 2019.

138 *"If I had drawn it myself"*: Lisa Hall, court testimony, September 21, 2005.

138 *He was alternating nights with Marie Blake*: Kevin Fox, interview by author, February 23, 2019.

140 *"The thing with this particular killer"*: Matthew Kuehn, *Forensic Files* interview transcript, December 2009.

9. THE NURSE

144 *"You should be careful who you are with"*: Matthew Kuehn, court testimony, October 28, 2005.

144 *The Brit thought the man was quite nice*: The British nurse was interviewed by the author in July 2019 and was granted anonymity to tell his story.

145 *halfway through a recruitment drive*: Marjorie Gulla Lewis and Sylvia Barker, *The Sinai Nurse* (West Kennebunk, ME: Phoenix Publishing, 2001), 134.

145 *During his first year, he took a sick day in May*: Many details regarding the life of Richard Rogers are taken from a document investigators assembled in preparation for trial. The document is based on Rogers's personal calendar, work calendar, credit card records, and vacation slides.

145 *It was his ten-year college reunion*: Letter from the Office of the Ocean County Prosecutor to Hon. James Citta, January 20, 2004.

145 *born in Plymouth, Massachusetts, on June 16, 1950*: Department of Public Health, Registry of Vital Records and Statistics, *Massachusetts Vital Records Index to Births [1916–1970]*.

145 *His father was a lobsterman*: Richard Weir and Alice McQuillan, "Putting Together Puzzle of Polite Nurse as Slayer," *Daily News*, June 3, 2001, https://www.nydailynews.com/archives/news/putting-puzzle-polite-nurse-slayer-article-1.901577.

146 *"normal—normal as could be"*: John Fillebrown, interview by author, May 5, 2017.

146 *tossed him into a shower stall*: Steve Hays, interview by author, August 17, 2017.

146 *would have been "persecuted"*: Joan Legue, interview by author, April 26, 2017.

146 *one of the few boys in French Club*: Palm Echo 1968, 126.

147 *when Richard moved into Wofford Hall*: Dowling Watford, email to author, January 30, 2020.

147 *"He was somewhat of a loner"*: Richard Brelsford, interview by author, July 3, 2019.

147 *"goddamn independents"*: Dowling Watford, interview by author, August 14, 2019.

147 *United Methodist Church held its annual conference*: "Methodists, Both Black and White, Join Hands," *St. Petersburg Times*, June 4, 1969.

147 *Richard wasn't harried by fellow students*: Diane Baum, interview by author, August 13, 2019.

147 *"I know about being lonely, but* wow*"*: Jeffrey Kline, interview by author, February 17, 2017.

147 *The first, Donald Cubberley, was from New Jersey*: Donald Cubberley, interview by author, January 28, 2019.

148 *Richard graduated in 1972*: Interlachen 1972, 286.

148 *"where you begin to become yourself"*: "Mapping the Future," *Southern News*, Fall 2018.

148 *serving as a host for homecoming events*: Jonathan Casiano and Mark Mueller, "The Friendly Man and the Frightening Crimes," *Star-Ledger*, June 3, 2001.

148 *"he was very engaging"*: Lynn Dennis, interview by author, August 19, 2019.

148 *last seen in a Daytona Beach*: "Police Seek Help to Identify Body," *Orlando Sentinel*, April 21, 1982.

149 *on his way to visit his ex-wife*: Ibid.

149 *scooped up for sleeping on a park bench*: Leslie Kemp, "Murder Victim Identified as Man Who Helped Start Center for Teens," *Orlando Sentinel*, December 2, 1982.

149 *The case has not been solved*: Sergeant Matthew Schaefer, email to author, November 22, 2019.

149 *Richard was one of a half-dozen nurses*: Randall Griepp, interview by author, August 22, 2019.

150 *never-ending hum of the vacuum*: Weir and McQuillan, "Putting Together Puzzle."

150 *It served an older crowd*: *HX*, December 26, 1991.

150 *precisely what Richard looked for in a bar*: Thomas O'Brien, court testimony, November 3, 2005.

151 *which were on the upswing*: Alexandra Twin, "Dow Ends Best July in 20 Years," *CNNMoney.com*, July 31, 2009, https://money.cnn.com/2009/07/31/markets/markets_newyork/index.htm.

152 *"He was always very pleasant"*: Rick Unterberg, court testimony, November 3, 2005.

153 *investment banking was a second career*: Sandy Harrow spoke to the author occasionally in early 2020. At the time, he was in a rehabilitation facility on the Upper East Side. Then in his late seventies, Harrow told the author about his prebanking career as a priest.

153 *"It was the hottest day of the year"*: The account of this evening and the subsequent trial are taken from the transcript of docket 8R005036.

156 *"It was like Mayberry"*: John Murphy, interview by author, September 12, 2019.

162 *the judge rendered her verdict*: In September 2019, the judge, Rose McBrien, told the author she did not recall the trial.

162–163 *he could lift an adult patient onto a gurney*: Michael Mohel, interview by author, September 17, 2018.

164 *"It was grim"*: Tony Plaza, interview by author, June 24, 2019.

164 *Marie Blake died at Mount Sinai*: Lyons, "Marie Blake."

164 *"People tell me I'm a legend"*: Wayman Wong, "She's the Village's Long-Playing Pianist," *Daily News*, June 16, 1993.

164 *When a New Jersey schoolteacher disappeared*: John Way Jennings, Stephanie Grace, and Larry Lewis, "Teacher's Disappearance Stirs Attention of Police Investigators," *Philadelphia Inquirer*, March 9, 1994.

164 *James Rutenberg, twenty-four*: James Rutenberg, interview by author, July 25, 2019.

165 *around the Loop, a five- or six-block radius*: Bruce Lambert, "Gay Bar Shut in 'Loop,'" *New York Times*, September 4, 1994.

166 *over which were the words "THE STALKER"*: James Rutenberg, "Will the Gay Slayer Strike Again?" *Manhattan Spirit*, March 10, 1994.

167 *Meanwhile, the Five Oaks closed*: Andrew Jacobs, "Five Oaks Faces Swan Song," *New York Times,* May 12, 1996.

167 *She showed up to find padlocks*: Lisa Hall, interview by author, March 23, 2017.

167 *servers and bartenders pretended to be strippers*: Lisa Hall, text to author, August 26, 2019.

167 *In early May 1997*: Somini Sengupta, "Receipts Offer Hints of a Manhattan Visit," *New York Times,* July 25, 1997.

167 *he'd gained some weight*: Helen Kennedy, "Double Life of the Party Boy a Dark Side Foretold Years Ago," *Daily News,* May 15, 1997.

167 *He seemed to have a job*: Michael Ferreri, interview by author, August 24, 2019.

168 *a piano bar on East Fifty-third*: David Masello, "Time, Gentlemen," *New York Times,* September 26, 2004, https://www.nytimes.com/2004/09/26/nyregion/thecity/time-gentlemen.html.

168 *legal proofreader with a pinkish complexion*: Rick Unterberg, interview by author, August 23, 2019.

168 *Richard and Gallagher had been friendly*: Joe Gallagher, interview by author, August 21, 2018.

169 *the PI was reinvestigating the murder*: Matthew Kuehn, *Forensic Files* interview transcript, December 2009.

169 *Mrs. Mulcahy contacted Kuehn herself*: Matthew Kuehn, court testimony, October 28, 2005.

170 *particularly useful for lifting old fingerprints*: Stephanie Howard, email to author, December 19, 2018.

170 *the print had been left by one person only*: Jeffrey Scozzafava, interview by author, July 3, 2019.

170 *Theodos wrote himself a note*: Nicholas Theodos provided the author with the note on July 3, 2019.

10. GOLD DUST

171 *Kuehn called Allen Pollard*: Matthew Kuehn, court testimony, October 27, 2005.

171 *assisted in solving more than a dozen cases*: Sherri Davis-Barron, "RCMP Team Helps Solve World's Most Baffling Murders," *Vancouver Sun,* August 31, 1996.

171 *TPS would process evidence*: Allen Pollard, court testimony, November 2, 2005.

172 *In July 2000*: Stephen Colantonio, court testimony, September 21, 2005.

172 *upward of forty bags*: Allen Pollard, court testimony, November 2, 2005.

172 *carefully sealed in clear plastic*: Stephen Colantonio, interview by author, September 16, 2019.

172 *a few pairs of state-police-branded sweatshirts*: Matthew Kuehn, *Forensic Files* interview transcript, December 2009.

172 *"advances in forensic testing"*: Matthew Kuehn task force proposal, March 1, 2000.

172 *Headed by Kuehn*: "Probe Resumes into Killings Involving Gay Men," Associated Press, April 17, 2000.

172 *"There is new technology out there"*: Duncan Osborne, "Police Renew Focus on Murders of Gay Men Last Seen in Manhattan," *Lesbian & Gay New York,* April 6, 2000.

173 *he also was a trained cinematographer*: Allen Pollard, interview by author, October 17, 2019.

173 *purchased recently for 100,000 Canadian dollars*: Barry Brown, "Toronto Police Find Prints in N.Y. City Killings," *Buffalo News,* June 3, 2001, https://buffalonews.com/2001/06/03/toronto-police-find-prints-in-n-y-city-killings/.

173 *treat the evidence as if it had been untouched*: Allen Pollard, *Forensic Files* interview transcript, December 2009.

173 *four feet high, four feet in depth*: Allen Pollard, court testimony, November 2, 2005.

174 *"like in outer space"*: Allen Pollard, *Forensic Files* interview transcript, December 2009.

175 *Then he called Matthew Kuehn*: Matthew Kuehn, *Forensic Files* interview transcript, December 2009.

175 *Pollard sent Kuehn copies of fifteen prints*: Matthew Kuehn, court testimony, November 9, 2005.

175 *seventy-five copies*: Matthew Kuehn, court testimony, October 28, 2005.

175 *contacted each state crime lab*: Stephen Colantonio, interview by author, September 19, 2019.

176 *Kimberly Stevens, a forensic scientist*: Kimberly Stevens, *Forensic Files* interview transcript, December 2009.

176 *To Whom It May Concern*: This letter, signed by Captain Frank M. Simonetta, was sent on May 2, 2001. It is included in the crime laboratory's case file.

176 *Stevens, twenty-nine*: Kimberly James, née Stevens, interview by author, September 26, 2019.

177 *perform many searches for outside agencies*: Kimberly James, interview by author, April 4, 2017.

177 *"The patrolman or the sheriff"*: Richard Arnold, interview by author, October 1, 2019.

180 *"His name," she said, "is Richard Rogers"*: Kimberly James, interview by author, October 3, 2019.

11. THE EDGE OF THE WOODS

181 *On Monday, Jason Manchester did his laundry*: Jason Manchester, interview by author, September 8, 2019.

181 *They'd hung out together the previous Friday*: Manchester kept a ledger during those years and provided the author with notes on events described in this chapter.

182 *Students had to sit at desks*: Jason Manchester, interview by author, October 25, 2019.

182 *He thought Richard was a strange guy*: James Herlan, interview by author, October 25, 2019.

184 *A reporter from the* Bangor Daily News: Paul Macaulay, interview by author, July 16, 2019.

184 *the worst flooding seen in a half century*: "Area Hit by Worst Flood in 50 Years," *Penobscot Times,* May 3, 1973.

185 *That afternoon, two cyclists*: "Bicycles Come upon Bloody Body," *Bangor Daily News,* May 1, 1973.

185 *wrapped in green canvaslike material*: W. Lawrence Hall, "Affidavit and Request for Search Warrant," May 2, 1973.

185 *traced to a post office box in Orono*: Paul Macaulay, "Key Leads Police to Suspect," *Bangor Daily News,* May 2, 1973.

185 *met at the University of Michigan*: "Obituary: Louise Spencer," *Evening Sun,* https://www.evesun.com /obituary/4402.

185 *After a move to Boston in 1946*: "Obituary: Claude F. Spencer," *Evening Sun,* https://www.evesun.com /obituary/20221.

185 *born on May 13, 1950*: Jim Wright, "Service Is Saturday for Slain Collegian," *Press and Sun-Bulletin,* May 3, 1973.

185 *It was insulated from current events*: Jim Harris, interview by author, November 5, 2019.

185 *To the extent there was a divide*: The author interviewed Patricia E. Evans, the Chenango County historian, on October 30, 2019, and that discussion helped with the portrait of Norwich and the surrounding county.

186 *the Pharmacy employed thousands*: Brian Golden, "Historical Society Unveils Norwich Pharmacal Exhibit," *Evening Sun,* September 17, 2010, https://www.evesun.com/news/stories/2010-09-17/10487 /Historical-Society-unveils-Norwich-Pharmacal-exhibit.

186 *"well-mannered, well-behaved, very bright"*: Joseph Stewart, interview by author, October 29, 2019.

186 *In his senior year, he won an award*: *Archive* (1968).

186 *They met in homeroom junior year*: Jenny Riley, who has been given a pseudonym, spoke to the author in October 2019.

187 *In a large clamshell*: Jim Harris, interview by author, November 5, 2019.

187 *to the University of Michigan*: University of Michigan, "Proceedings of the Board of Regents (1969– 1972)," https://quod.lib.umich.edu/u/umregproc/ACW7513.1969.001/1621.

188 *On Tuesday morning, May 1*: Hall, "Affidavit and Request for Search Warrant."

188 *They pounded on the front and rear doors*: William Mazerolle was interviewed extensively by the author on April 24, 2017, and November 1, 2019.

189 *sang in the Newman Center church folk group*: Roxanne Saucier, interview by author, March 9, 2017.

189 *covered his eyes*: Jason Manchester, interview by author, September 8, 2019.

189 *"based on his outstanding academic record"*: David E. Leonard, "Spencer Remembered," *Bangor Daily News,* June 22, 2001, https://archive.bangordailynews.com/2001/06/22/spencer-remembered/.

190 *found some spongy material in the hallway*: Hall, "Affidavit and Request for Search Warrant."

190 *confessed to killing Fred*: "Murder Suspect Fights Extradition," Associated Press, May 31, 2001.

190 *Fred's body was flown home*: Wright, "Service Is Saturday for Slain Collegian."

190 *Richard was arraigned*: "Arraigned in Murder of Norwich Youth," Associated Press, May 3, 1973.

191 *"It was very awkward"*: Roxanne Saucier, interview by author, March 9, 2017.

191 *On Monday October 29*: "9 Jurors Picked in Murder Case," *Bangor Daily News,* October 30, 1973.

191 *who gravitated toward controversial cases*: "Tractor Accident Kills Bangor Lawyer Paine," *Bangor Daily News,* October 15, 1979.

191 *He didn't, as a rule, do much pretrial preparation*: Peter Weatherbee, interview by author, April 26, 2017.

191 *"without a note in his hand"*: William Cohen, interview by author, November 13, 2019.

191 *"Littering"*: Donald Thompson, interview by author, May 1, 2017. All information related to Thompson, including what he witnessed during trial proceedings, is taken from this interview.

191 *"massive head injuries"*: "Court Told Student Died of Head Injuries," *Bangor Daily News,* November 1, 1973.

192 *Richard claimed Fred hadn't seemed dead—just unconscious*: Ibid.

192 *He found the questions "inane"*: David E. Leonard, "Spencer Remembered," *Bangor Daily News,* June 22, 2001, https://archive.bangordailynews.com/2001/06/22/spencer-remembered/.

192 *Paine made a motion to reduce the charges*: Lionel Rosenblatt, "Jury Finds Student Not Guilty," *Bangor Daily News,* November 2, 1973.

192 *"Rogers said that he wrestled the hammer"*: Ibid.

193 *"in passion under sudden provocation"*: Jim Wright, "Verdict of Innocent Returned in Slaying of Norwich Man," *Press and Sun-Bulletin,* May 3, 1973.

193 *"Putting the plastic bag over his head"*: Peter Weatherbee, interview by author, April 26, 2017.

193 *In a "daze," he said*: Rosenblatt, "Jury Finds Student Not Guilty."

193 *put Fred's body into his 1968 Dodge Dart*: Hall, "Affidavit and Request for Search Warrant."

193 *like the middle of nowhere*: Bob Norman, interview by author, September 25, 2019.

193 *But at least one spectator remembers something to that effect*: Paul Pierson, interview by author, October 31, 2019.

194 *"It was in the rumor mill"*: Theresa Morrow, interview by author, July 9, 2019.

194 *"I can't thank you enough"*: Rosenblatt, "Jury Finds Student Not Guilty."

12. INDISPUTABLE EVIDENCE

196 *Kuehn was celebrating his twenty-fifth wedding anniversary*: Matthew Kuehn, *Forensic Files* interview transcript, December 2009.

196 *was encouraged not to interrupt the man*: Stephen Colantonio, interview by author, November 11, 2019.

197 *"That's the way it's gotta be"*: Thomas Hayes, interview by author, November 14, 2019.

197 *"You wanted to be low-key"*: Jack Repsha, interview by author, November 14, 2019.

198 *Three days earlier, they'd released a suspect*: Laura Italiano, "Bronx Cops: We Were Conned by Body-Part Killer," *New York Post,* May 30, 2001, https://nypost.com/2001/05/30/bronx-cops-we-were-conned-by-body-part-killer/.

198 *"This is all bullshit"*: Michael Mohel, interview by author, November 15, 2019.

199 *had been a patient at Mount Sinai*: Elisabeth Bumiller, "Judge Orders Mayor's Friend Barred from Gracie Mansion," *New York Times,* May 22, 2001, https://www.nytimes.com/2001/05/22/nyregion/judge-orders-mayor-s-friend-barred-from-gracie-mansion.html.

199 *"This really doesn't make any sense"*: Bernard Kerik, interview by author, October 10, 2019.

199 *"Members of the task force"*: John Marzulli, "Cops Slam Gay-Slay Arrest," *Daily News,* June 6, 2001.

200 *calm, methodical interrogator*: Jack Repsha, interview by author, November 14, 2019.

200 *"He's a serial killer, but he's not stupid"*: Michael Mohel, interview by author, November 15, 2019.

200 *small table, a few chairs*: The account of the questioning of Rogers is based largely on the court testimony of David Dalrymple on October 28, 2005, and Thomas Hayes on November 9.

200 *pink Oxford shirt, khaki pants*: Thomas Hayes, interview by author, November 14, 2019.

201 *A man named Sandy or Fred*: David Dalrymple, court testimony, October 28, 2005.

201 *Richard did not mention*: Thomas Hayes, court testimony, November 9, 2005.

204 *In the application for the search warrant*: Matthew Kuehn, court testimony, November 9, 2005.

204 *Before the search began*: John Halliday, interview by author, November 20, 2019.

204 *remote controls, evenly spaced*: Photos taken during the search were provided to the author by John Halliday.

205 *On a nightstand was a copy*: Matthew Kuehn, court testimony, October 28, 2005.

205 *which was under the couch*: John Halliday, interview by author, November 20, 2019.

206 *An NYPD detective flipped through it*: Michael Mohel, interview by author, November 15, 2019.

206 *"carted out 15 large cardboard boxes"*: Richard Weir, Joe Williams, and Alice McQuillan, "Gay-Slayer Suspect on Suicide Row," *Daily News*, June 1, 2001.

206 *Richard was held under suicide watch*: Ibid.

206 *while he fought extradition to New Jersey*: "Suspect in Dismemberments Fighting Extradition from N.Y.," Associated Press, May 31, 2001.

206 *Several months later, he lost*: "Suspect in Slayings of Dismembered Men Will Be Extradited to N.J.," Associated Press, September 11, 2001.

206 *"This just renews the pain"*: "Mounties Help ID Prints in Gay Killings," *Bangor Daily News*, June 1, 2001, https://archive.bangordailynews.com/2001/06/01/mounties-help-id-prints-in-gay-killings/.

206 *"We're glad there appears to be an answer"*: April Adamson, "Break in Gruesome Death of Local Banker," *Philadelphia Daily News*, June 1, 2001.

207 *"We're pleased an arrest has been made"*: John Ellement, "Links Sought to Other Grisly Murders," *Boston Globe*, May 31, 2001.

207 *"I'm not out for blood"*: Mark Mueller, "Five Slayings, a Suspect, and a Long Search for Proof," *Star-Ledger*, June 2, 2002.

13. GET HIM OUT OF HERE

210 *interviewed "scores" of people*: MaryAnn Spoto, "New York Man Indicted in Grisly Killings," *Star-Ledger*, January 22, 2003.

210 *"it wasn't unusual"*: William Heisler, interview by author, January 2020.

210 *He wasn't facing the death penalty*: Carol Gorga Williams, "Death Penalty Ruled Out," *Asbury Park Press*, February 15, 2003.

210 *In October 2005, Richard was offered a plea*: Honorable James N. Citta, plea discussion, October 18, 2005.

211 *"They found DNA on the victims"*: Richard Rogers, letter to Diane Baum, February 13, 2005.

211 *"I'm hoping there will be a pre-trial hearing"*: Richard Rogers, letter to Diane Baum, December 27, 2003.

211 *"We want to know if you have any biases"*: Honorable James N. Citta, voir dire, October 19, 2005.

211 *"Thomas Mulcahy, sixteen fingerprints"*: William Heisler, opening statement, October 26, 2005.

212 *"Meek like a mouse"*: Susan Kelly, interview by author, August 28, 2017.

212 *"It seemed kind of weak on his part"*: Donna Maerz, interview by author, November 18, 2019.

212 *Another juror held her hand*: Kathleen Hopkins, "Ex-Nurse Convicted in 2 Decapitation Murders," *Asbury Park Press*, November 11, 2005.

212 *"On the first count of the indictment"*: Honorable James N. Citta, verdict, November 10, 2005.

212–213 *a presentencing statement by Tracey Mulcahy*: Tracey Mulcahy, sentencing statement, January 27, 2006.

14. EPILOGUE

215 *"inquire into the secret lives of those five persons"*: Thornton Wilder, *The Bridge of San Luis Rey* (Harmondsworth, United Kingdom: Penguin Books, 1941), 9.

216 *eligible for parole on September 18, 2066*: State of New Jersey Department of Corrections.

216 *"almost looks like a funeral home"*: Michael Musto, interview by author, March 2, 2017.

216 *"It's mostly unchanged"*: Mitch Kahn, interview by author, January 18, 2020.

218 *"Somebody called me daddy last night"*: Rick Unterberg, interview by author, January 18, 2020.

About the Author

Elon Green has written for *The New York Times Magazine, The Atlantic, The New Yorker,* and *The Columbia Journalism Review,* and appears in the true-crime anthology *Unspeakable Acts*. He has been an editor at Longform for nearly a decade.

CELADON
BOOKS

NEW YORK

Founded in 2017, Celadon Books, a division of Macmillan
Publishers, publishes a highly curated list of twenty to
twenty-five new titles a year. The list of both fiction
and nonfiction is eclectic and focuses on publishing
commercial and literary books and discovering and
nurturing talent.